EPPING

CRIME SCENE
CHEMISTRY
FOR THE
ARMCHAIR SLEUTH

CRIME SCENE
CHEMISTRY
FOR THE
ARMCHAIR SLEUTH

Cathy Cobb
Monty L. Fetterolf
Jack Goldsmith

Prometheus Books

59 John Glenn Drive
Amherst, New York 14228-2197

Published 2007 by Prometheus Books

Inquiries should be addressed to
Prometheus Books
59 John Glenn Drive
Amherst, New York 14228–2197
VOICE: 716–691–0133, ext. 210
FAX: 716–691–0137
WWW.PROMETHEUSBOOKS.COM

11 10 09 08 07   5 4 3 2 1

Library of Congress Cataloging-in-Publication Data

Cobb, Cathy.
    Crime scene chemistry for the armchair sleuth / by Cathy Cobb, Monty L. Fetterolf, and Jack G. Goldsmith.
        p. cm.
    Includes bibliographical references and index.
    ISBN 978–1–59102–505–4 (alk. paper)
    1. Chemistry, Forensic. 2. Crime scene searches. 3. Criminal investigation.
I. Fetterolf, Monty L. II. Goldsmith, Jack (Jack G.) III. Title.

HV8073.C584 2007
363.25'6—dc22

2007008263

Printed in the United States on acid-free paper

CONTENTS

Part II. Felonious Interactions

Part III. Interrogation Lights

Part IV. Corpus Delicti

Acknowledgments

We again extend our heartfelt thanks to Dr. and Mrs. Cobb and Judy Dailey for suffering through typo-riddled drafts to provide excellent, perceptive commentary. We thank Captain Earl Wells, South Carolina Law Enforcement Division Department of Forensics, for his generous gift of time. You agreed to read a few chapters and ended up reading the entire book, and for this you have our deepest gratitude. The errors that remain are our own.

We thank Linda Regan, as always, for her guidance, and we thank Chris Kramer and the entire Prometheus production staff, models of excellence, patience, and diplomacy.

Drs. Cobb and Fetterolf would like to extend a special thanks to their children, Mathew, Benjamin, and Daniel Fetterolf. Although it was a little unsettling how quickly you got into the crime, you were a huge help with demonstrations, story ideas, and by keeping your sense of humor when your parents lost theirs. We love you very much.

Dr. Jack Goldsmith would like to thank his wife, Edie, for her encouragement and comments during the writing and revising process.

We would like to thank our colleagues and the staff of Aiken Preparatory School and the University of South Carolina Aiken, for their help and encouragement.

We would like to thank the Lexington, South Carolina, police department for their generous and tolerant instruction and assistance.

And last, but by no means least, we are very grateful to Linda Muse, whose wonderful artwork graces these pages.

Oh, Mortimer, don't be so inquisitive. The gentleman died because he drank some wine with poison in it.

. . . how did the poison get in the wine?
Well, we put it in wine because it's less noticeable. When it's in tea it has a distinct odor.

Joseph O. Kesselring, *Arsenic and Old Lace*, 1944

APOLOGIA

Drama is life with the dull bits cut out.

Alfred Hitchcock, ca. 1950

All right. We confess. Of the three authors, only Jack Goldsmith is connected with crime (in a positive manner, of course), so we will spend as many words on chemistry as we do on crime. But we feel no remorse. Much of forensic chemistry evolves from the basic principles of chemistry, so it is an appropriate framework for a logical development of chemistry—with a little entertaining intrigue thrown in for good measure.

But given the prevalence of explications of the forensic sciences,[1] does forensic chemistry really warrant another treatment? We believe so. In our research we found that works focusing on forensic chemistry fall essentially into two categories: elementary- or secondary-school educational materials and technical treatises for the professional chemist. In fact, Suzanne Bell, in the preface to her excellent textbook *Forensic Chemistry*, advises, "If this is your first course in chemistry, get out while you still can!"[2] Our book does not fit into this second category because it does not assume any specific technical background on the part of the reader. Rather, we integrate and develop the necessary chemical principles as part of the narrative. Our book does not fit into the first category because its demonstrations are for an adult audience, designed around household materials, and do not require access to an academic laboratory. We have also stepped away from the textbook format by choosing to enliven each of our presentations with a fictional relevant vignette. The situations we describe may not all be murders, but none are mundane. It is a maxim of criminology that many big crimes start with small crimes, so all crimes are taken seriously. Whether the case involves cruelty to animals or the abduction of a child, it is forensic chemistry that contributes to its closure.

In writing this book, we have another motive to which we must admit. We would like, as best we can, to help set the record straight concerning the realities of forensic chemistry. Forensic chemists have been depicted as heroes and villains when, in fact, they are neither: they are just part of a team that works to solve crime. Technology has been a wonderful boon to law enforcement—but it has been a bit of a bane, too. Juries now expect, even demand, state-of-the-art evidence (an observation known as "the *CSI* effect"), and the public anticipates overnight results. In reality, results are never immediate and rarely definitive. There is no such thing as a "perfect" match; each test has an associated margin of error. There is no such thing as an instant result; narrowing this margin of error takes time. Tests have to be confirmed, quality controlled, and certified, and there isn't a crime lab in the country that doesn't have a backlog. It is hard to imagine a police investigation that is not an emergency, so it's also tough to move to the front of the line. Forensic chemistry and the other forensic sciences are marvelous, but not miracles. In the real world, DNA evidence doesn't help if you don't have someone to match it to, and fingerprints are more often smudged than not. Forensic chemistry provides facts, but it takes the excellent chemistry of the human mind to put these facts together.

But without the fast-paced action, isn't forensic chemistry a little, shall we say, deadly? We think not. Chemistry has always been about finding clues and fitting them together; so the application of chemistry to forensic science is just sauce for the goose—the cooked goose, that is. After all, one could claim that chemistry is basic to all aspects of forensic science, from pathology to psychology to toxicology. Therefore, an attempt to consider crime solving without chemistry would be, well, . . . criminal.

And so, please: do the demos, ponder the puzzles, forgive the puns, and, above all, enjoy—as we take our armchair tour of forensic chemistry.

Introduction

The Chemistry of Crime

Holmes was seated at his side-table clad in his dressing-gown and working hard over a chemical investigation. A large curved retort was boiling furiously in the bluish flame of a Bunsen burner, and the distilled drops were condensing into a two-litre measure. . . . He dipped into this bottle or that, drawing out a few drops of each with his glass pipette, and finally brought the test-tube containing a solution over to the table. In his right hand he held a slip of litmus-paper.

"You come at a crisis Watson," said he. "If this paper remains blue, all is well. If it turns red, it means a man's life."

Sir Arthur Conan Doyle, *Naval Treaty*, ca. 1900

As chemistry books go, we believe this work to be a bit unusual in that we will be introducing each crime-scene chemistry topic with a crime-scene-setting minute mystery. As such, we thought it appropriate to commence our introduction with just such a narrative: "The Case of the Innovative Introduction."

THE CASE OF THE INNOVATIVE INTRODUCTION

Officers Vince Veteran and Rick Rookie were on routine patrol when the call came to check out a complaint of excessive noise from a party in progress. On their way to respond, they finished their conversation concerning innovations in law-enforcement equipment.

"Yep, it's amazing what the chemists are coming up with nowadays," said Officer Veteran. "All kinds of new field tests for alcohol, drugs, saliva, semen . . . handheld detectors that look like penlights . . . multipurpose . . . real James Bond stuff—but they do the job. Pick out the bad guys and protect the vics."

Officer Rookie nodded in appreciation.

When the officers arrived at the scene, they heard loud music emanating from the house and saw revelers spilling out onto the lawn. As they pulled into the driveway they noticed a young man standing by a car. He was attempting to open the rear door while supporting a young woman who was very unsteady on her feet. The officers approached the young man and asked him if he had a problem.

"No, sir. I'm just taking her home. Some friends of mine introduced her to me at the party and, well, as you can see, we were having such a good time that she went a little overboard." He grinned sheepishly as he finally managed the door and eased his groggy passenger into the backseat. "Luckily she gave me her phone number and address before she was too far gone."

"So you think you're okay to drive?" asked Officer Veteran.

"Oh, yes, sir," the young man stated with assurance. "I don't drink at parties when I know I'm going to have to drive. I don't want to smash up my new car!" He smiled winningly at the two officers and gestured at a soda can sitting on a low brick wall that framed the driveway. He shut the back door of the car and started to open the driver's side door.

"One moment, son," said Officer Veteran. "I'd like to have a look in that backseat."

As the young man reopened the rear door, Officer Veteran pulled a flashlight from his utility belt. He turned on the light and brought it momentarily close to the girl's face. He pulled back out of the car, replaced the flashlight in his belt, and turned grimly to the young man.

"All right, son. Turn around and put your hands on the car . . ."

Officer Rookie, recognizing the preliminaries of detainment, gestured toward the girl in the back seat and asked, "Too much alcohol?"

"Nope," responded his partner. "Not enough."

The Chemistry of the Case

After we have introduced each chapter's topic via vignette, as above—and before we resolve it at the chapter's end with a final "Case Closed"—we will proceed to a discussion of the pertinent chemistry in sections we have titled "The Chemistry of the Case." Here, to prepare for explanations of Officer Veteran's "James Bond stuff" and the instruments with the many flashing lights and glowing monitors we see on television crime dramas, we commence with a briefing on the chemistry and crime to come.

In parts I and II, we begin with a background in chemical principles, using examples from forensic chemistry. We can use forensic chemistry to illustrate basic chemical principles because forensic chemistry began when chemistry was basic. When we consulted a fellow chemist concerning one of the reactions we will be using for a demonstration, she commented that the chemistry seemed "rather nineteenth century," and she was right. In the 1840s, Mathiew Orfila set a precedent for forensic chemistry when he analyzed for arsenic in the body tissue of Marie LaFarge's late husband and found enough to convince a court that Madame LaFarge had served it to her husband on a plate. Although modern analysis for arsenic uses more elaborate methods than were available to the prosecutors of Marie LaFarge, there are forensic techniques in use today that employ chemistry that would have been familiar to Orfila. For instance, the presumptive field tests—tests that indicate the presence of substances such as cocaine or heroin—involve fairly elementary procedures, as we will learn in chapter 1. However, to be of evidentiary value, these presumptive tests must be backed up by confirmatory tests, which will introduce a discussion about the uncertainty in chemical analysis.

In chapter 2, we explore atomic structure and show how knowledge of atomic structure and isotopes can be key in forensic chemistry. In chapter 3, we introduce the elements, the chemical building blocks, and show how straightforward elemental analysis can sometimes provide the pivotal clue. In chapter 4, we examine compounds built from the elements as well as screening tests based on fundamental chemical principles. We will learn that these screening tests not only help determine if more expensive, time-consuming testing is needed, but they also can provide quick results. Law enforcement needs these preliminary results to focus their investigative efforts and to move swiftly to detain suspects who might otherwise flee. In chapters 5 through 8, the pieces come together as we investigate intermolecular forces and how these forces influence the different phases of substances—gas, liquid, and solid—and how knowledge of the properties of these phases is essential to the forensic chemist. For instance, in chapter 6, we will explain the functioning of the workhorse of the forensic lab: the mass spectrometer.

Part II focuses on interactions of the compounds described in part I and the laws that govern these interactions. Chapter 9 examines the difference between physical and chemical changes and how recognizing the difference can provide a missing link. In chapter 10, we will demonstrate how chemical reaction behaviors help track human social behaviors. In chapters 11 through 13, we look at acid-base, oxidation-reduction, gas-producing, and, of course, combustion reactions, and how they factor into law enforcement. In chapters 14 and 15, we discuss the role of energy in chemical reactions and how reaction rates can determine both a chemical and a criminal time line. In chapters 16 and 17, we show how physical equilibrium and chemical equilibrium help to sort out the identity of unknown materials, even in matrices as complicated as dirt and grease, various bodily wastes and discharges, plant and animal residue, or a mixture of all of the above.

In part III, we begin our consideration of the interaction of light with matter, a topic so crucial to forensic chemistry that it deserves a division unto itself. In chapter 18, we look at infrared spectroscopy as an analytical technique, and in chapter 19, we explore two important types of microscopy: light and electron. In chapter 20, the use of lasers and other specialized techniques will be considered, and in chapter 21, we examine light produced by chemical reactions, such as the fluorescence of luminol in contact with blood.

In part IV, we round up all our chemical principles, reactions, and techniques and line them up to show how biological materials are analyzed forensically: fingerprints to DNA. In our last chapter, we extend our investigation of bodily materials to bodily gases, and explain how these and other gases are related to the future of forensic chemistry—just as they resolve "The Case of the Innovative Introduction."

Case Closed

Officer Rookie peered inquiringly at his partner as the older man started a pat-down search of the detainee. Rookie now realized that the flashlight Officer Veteran had pulled from his utility belt was a PAS—Passive Alcohol Sensor—the type of device Officer Veteran had been describing to him in the patrol car. Officer Veteran recited in a monotone, "Do you have any weapons? Needles? Anything I need to know about before I check your pockets?"

"Hey!" the young man objected. "What did I do? You can't go through my pockets!" He started to remove his hands from the car roof, but Officer Veteran's no-nonsense command stopped him.

"Get your hands on the car. You are in investigative detention on suspicion of attempted kidnapping. Now is there anything in your pockets I need to know about?"

"Attempted kidnapping! That's crazy! She's drunk and I'm trying to get her home!"

Officer Veteran began methodically patting the boy's pockets and legs. "She's not drunk, son. There's no alcohol on her breath. But she is under the influence. When we test the contents of that soda," he pointed to the abandoned can sitting on the brick wall, "what are we going to find?"

A look of concern passed over the boy's face. Officer Veteran extracted a bag of pills from the boy's front jeans pocket. He looked at the pills carefully and then intoned, "You have the right to remain silent . . ."

After the boy had been booked, the pills had been cataloged, and the paperwork had been completed, Officer Rookie asked Veteran to see his handheld Passive Alcohol Sensor.

"This thing can tell if there is alcohol on someone's breath from six inches away? They don't have to blow into it? Pretty impressive. Darn good flashlight, too. But what tipped you off to test the girl?"

"I got suspicious when the guy said he didn't drink at parties because he didn't want to mess up his new car, but he was willing to put an inebriated young lady in his backseat. It's pretty common knowledge what a drunk can do to the upholstery of a backseat. I figured it was worth a quick check."

"It's a good thing you found those pills in his pocket, otherwise it might have been hard to make the charges stick."

"Maybe," agreed Veteran. "But I'll bet a GC mass spec will find traces of the drug in that soda can we confiscated and cyanoacrylate fuming will produce some prints . . ."

Officer Rookie nodded his approval. "Sounds like you know a lot about this stuff."

Officer Veteran shrugged. "I've made it a habit to try to keep up. I figure it's important to know how things work, when they work—and when they won't."

Officer Rookie smiled. "I wouldn't mind knowing some of what you know."

"Sure," said Veteran. "We can talk. Anytime." He reached for the squawking radio on his belt. "But right now we have to roll . . ."

PUBLIC SAFETY—
AND PERSONAL, TOO

The sad duty of politics is to establish justice in a sinful world.

Jimmy Carter, ca. 1980

Let's review the basics.

If you don't own a pair of safety glasses, go to the hardware store and buy a pair. Wear them while doing the demonstrations in this book.

Read the safety precautions included in the demonstrations and take them to heart.

Resist the urge to get creative. Random mixtures of household chemicals can create some pretty nasty brews that can have deadly consequences. *Never mix ammonia with bleach!*

Be aware of sources of sparks, which can include batteries, cell phones, or electric appliances. Some of these demonstrations require batteries, so please be aware that even low-voltage, low-current batteries can generate significant amounts of heat if the leads are connected directly, even for a short period of time.

Pour waste into the toilet, not the kitchen sink or bathroom sink.

Keep amounts to a minimum. The difference between a bang and a pop is a matter of magnitude. As we will discuss, virtually any substance is harmful if there is enough of it. Water is an essential nutrient, but drowning is also a cause of death. Any pure chemical poses some sort of risk, so it must be handled with respect. If skin is exposed to pure or concentrated chemicals, rinsing the exposed area with large amounts of water is the best idea.

Know the location of the nearest working shower, fire extinguisher, and phone.

Keep everything away from children and pets.

You will be directed to use kitchen utensils in many of the demonstrations. Don't assume this means that the chemicals are nontoxic. Use plasticware and paper plates whenever possible and throw away the paper and plastic after use. Because you will probably do most of the demonstrations in the basement, garage, or bathroom, be sure to keep the chemicals well separated from toothbrushes and foodstuffs, as well as any surfaces that might come in contact with food or toothbrushes. You should cover your counters with newspaper for added protection.

Never leave a demonstration unattended unless directed to do so and then only when the materials are secured and protected from chance encounter by other people or pets.

Do not use a microwave for warming chemicals and solutions. Some solutions contain volatile components. You do not want to coat the inside of a microwave oven that will be used later for food. For warming solutions, a workable double boiler arrangement will do, as described in the following section, "Crime Lab and Crime Solutions."

Be careful that you don't expose open wounds or unprotected body parts to any of the chemicals used in the demonstrations. Do not, under any circumstances, eat, drink, or splash them in your eyes. Do not expose them to flames or sparks (unless it's part of the demonstration). Protect your clothes or wear old clothes. Protect your hands. Wear examination gloves (flexible, close-fitting gloves, usually latex) when handling chemicals and wear yardwork gloves when handling steel wool. Treat all chemicals used in these demonstrations as you would chlorine bleach, gasoline, insecticides, and other things you know to be hazardous.

Whether dealing with chemicals or criminals, a little bit of safety goes a long way.

CRIME LAB AND CRIME SOLUTIONS

The demonstrations selected for *Crime Scene Chemistry* are designed around readily available household materials or materials that can be obtained from retail outlets. Nowadays, of course, these "retail outlets" include those found on the Internet, which greatly broadens the definition of "readily available." Because it makes sense to have what you need on hand (and ordering over the Internet takes time), we provide here a list of supplies. After this list, we will give directions for a setup with celery that requires time to develop and a separate section devoted to copper sulfate. Copper sulfate, an ingredient used in several of the demonstrations, has its own heading because it may be obtained from a variety of suppliers and because it warrants special precautions.

The list may look rather formidable, but it is arranged alphabetically by outlet, so that after securing the "Absolute Essentials," you have the option of waiting for your next trip to the grocery store or drugstore to collect the remaining items. Entries under the heading "Internet" will most certainly have to be ordered ahead of time. You should also scan for items marked with a double asterisk, since these may not be locally available but are possible to acquire on the Internet, too.

ABSOLUTE ESSENTIALS

Safety glasses

It is extremely important to conscientiously wear a pair of safety glasses. These glasses can be purchased at a hardware store, a scientific supply house, or an educational supplies outlet. They should be plastic and have side shields or be goggles that fit flush to the face and offer complete coverage.

Examination gloves (latex gloves) and apron

These close-fitting, flexible, disposable gloves are available in drugstores and grocery stores that sell pharmaceuticals. Some are latex and may contain a powder on the inside of the glove. Some people have a sensitivity to the latex and may have a sensitivity to the powder, so gloves made of alternative materials (hypoallergenic gloves) are also available. Find the kind that works well for you. You may also want to invest in a waterproof or water-resistant apron. *Some of the materials you will be using can stain clothing. So beware!* Wearing old clothes is an option, too.

SUPPLIES LISTED BY OUTLET

Culinary supply outlet: measuring cups, a small paring knife, canned cooking fuel, a small double boiler, tongs, disposable chopsticks, a mortar and pestle, a plastic funnel, and a food scale

You will not be able to reuse any of this equipment with food, so be sure to buy inexpensive versions that you don't mind discarding.

You will need a set of see-through measuring cups, preferably marked in metric units. We have provided measurements in both English and metric units; however, a set of measuring cups marked in milliliters (500-, 200-, and 100-milliliter) is required for one of the demonstrations. If possible, choose a set that is marked in 10- or 50-milliliter increments.

Look for the kind of canned cooking fuel that might be used on a camping trip or on a buffet steam table to warm food. It is the kind that you take the lid off to light and that burns in the can. To extinguish the flame, replace the lid.

You will need tweezers or tongs for handling glass without leaving fingerprints. And you will need disposable chopsticks (or other flat wooden sticks) to stir with.

The type of mortar and pestle used to grind spices will do nicely. You can usually find these in grocery stores that have an extensive spice selection, but if not, a gourmet shop is sure to have a set.

Your food scale needs to measure only a couple of ounces, so an 8-ounce (240-gram) scale will suffice. Make sure the scale measures in grams and ounces.

Backyard or the park: two samples of dirt

The dirt samples should be chosen to be visually different from each other and should be taken from just the top of the soil, not more than an inch down. You'll need about a tablespoon (15 milliliters) of each.

Dentist's office: dental casting material, also called "dental stone"**

If you aren't on good enough terms with a dentist to request a free sample, you can purchase this item over the Internet. You'll need about a cup (240 milliliters or so).

> Drugstore: aspirin, ibuprofen, acetaminophen, caffeine, and iron tablets; eyedroppers**; boric acid; mineral oil; glucose tablets; hydrogen peroxide; cotton swabs; cotton balls; and a small bottle of tincture of iodine

The aspirin, ibuprofen, acetaminophen, caffeine, and iron should all be in pill form, and if white pills can be found, that would be best. If the pills have a colored coating they are still usable, but the coating has to be removed. Generic store brands are often the best choice because they are less likely to have coatings and colorings.

You will need at least six plastic or glass eyedroppers.** These droppers, also called disposable transfer pipettes, are available in educational supplies stores or over the Internet, too.

Boric acid is sold as a disinfectant in full-service pharmacies, and mineral oil is sold as a laxative. Glucose tablets are carried by many diabetics as an emergency treatment for hypoglycemia and are a standard item at pharmacy counters.

> Educational supplies store: a bar magnet, preferably 6 or more inches (15 centimeters) long; a thermometer; a prism; different-colored see-through plastic disks or squares; and microscope slides (a nice addition, but not necessary)**

You will need an old-fashioned liquid thermometer (not a digital thermometer) that reads in the range of room temperature (not a fever-measuring thermometer). A red-alcohol thermometer would be better than a mercury thermometer. Such a thermometer could be purchased over the Internet, too. *This thermometer cannot be reused for any application that involves contact with food or with the mouth.*

The colored disks are sometimes carried by hobby shops.

Electronics supply store: a voltmeter, 20-gauge and 30-gauge copper wire, at least five 9-volt batteries, snap-on wire leads for each 9-volt battery, at least ten alligator clips, etchant, electrician's tape, and a small light-emitting diode (LED)**

An inexpensive voltmeter will do. You will only need to measure direct-current voltages on the order of 50 volts, maximum. You will need to hook up 9-volt batteries one to another, so you will require the type of snap-on cap connector that provides hook-up wires. To make the connections, you will need alligator clips, which get their name from the teeth on the clamplike connector that terminates each end. If you are in doubt about any of these items, the sales staff at an electronics supply store will be able to help. You may also look on the Internet.

Copper wire is described by the "gauge," which is a measure of the diameter of the wire. The smaller the gauge number, the thicker the wire: 20-gauge wire corresponds to a diameter of 0.032 inch (0.81 millimeter); 30-gauge wire corresponds to a diameter of 0.01 inch (0.254 millimeter). You will need a spool of insulated 30-gauge copper wire, which is sometimes called magnet wire. You will also need a spool of 20-gauge or lower copper wire. Noninsulated 20-gauge wire will work for some experiments, but we will need insulated for others, so it will be easier to buy insulated wire and strip off the ends with wire strippers when needed. Sometimes the insulation is painted on, in which case it must be sanded off rather than stripped off.

Etchant solution is used to remove unwanted copper from custom-configured circuit boards. The mechanism for removing the copper is a redox reaction, which we will discuss later. Etchant solution can be purchased from electronics supply stores or online. *You will want to make certain you wear old clothes or an apron when working with etchant.* The active ingredient is an iron compound (ferric chloride) that makes a nice rust-colored stain. Etchant can be disposed of down the toilet, but please be sure to flush immediately and several times so the nice rust-colored stain doesn't attach itself to your toilet bowl.

The LED should have the lowest voltage requirement you can find: a 3-volt or less LED would be best; more than 4 volts will not work.

Stationery or office supply store: a notebook, a laser pointer, a permanent marker, a couple of magnifying glasses, a calculator, a green felt-tip water-soluble color marker, a permanent marker, and cyanoacrylate instant adhesive (superglue)

A bound notebook, such as a composition notebook, will be required for at least one demonstration, but you may want to take notes for the other demonstrations, too. You will also need a pen. It is best to write with a pen because pencil can be too easily rubbed away. If you like, number the pages and leave room in front for an index. If an error is made, put one line through it. Do not erase or obliterate it. Good data are reproducible, but it is a shame to have to repeat work because you thought you didn't need it. The permanent marker is for labeling.

You will need an electronic calculator, but just for one of the demonstrations, so the calculator does not have to be a scientific calculator or anything fancy. In fact, many cell phones or computers come equipped with calculators that are adequate for our purposes.

You will need a green washable colored marker. Water-insoluble permanent markers or dry-erase markers will not work. The type of instant adhesive you will need is liquid, not gel, and the label should state that it contains cyanoacrylate. This adhesive is sold under brand names such as Super Glue and Krazy Glue, but any liquid instant adhesive with cyanoacrylate will do. Because the term *superglue* has become genericized to mean cyanoacrylate-containing instant adhesives in general (as the word *kleenex* has come to mean facial tissue in general), we will follow the forensic chemist's tradition of referring to cyanoacrylate instant adhesives as superglue.

General store: a hair dryer, sunglasses,** and a thin-stemmed margarita glass

Although the demonstrations that use a laser pointer require a regular pair of sunglasses, you will also need a pair with polarized lenses. Polarized lenses, however, are not as easy to find as they once were. Antiglare sunglasses are now made with other materials. Check the label to see if you are getting sunglasses with polarized lenses. You might be able to find polarizing lenses in an educational supplies store, or, once again, you might check the Internet.

Grocery store, baking supplies: water soluble food colorings, including red food coloring; a small birthday candle; corn-starch; plain, unflavored gelatin; salt; sugar; and baking soda

Grocery store, liquids: distilled water, vinegar, ammonia, red wine, rubbing alcohol (70 percent isopropyl alcohol, also called isopropanol), liquid vegetable oil (canola oil works well), liquid bleach, milky white dishwashing liquid, and a small bottle of tonic water that contains quinine (check the label)

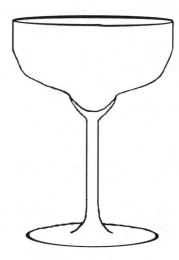

Figure 0.1. For our purposes, the best glass will have a thin stem, a broad base, and a broad squat bowl, such as a margarita glass.

You will need about a gallon (four liters) of distilled water and one small bottle of each of the other liquids. If you cannot locate water that is explicitly labeled as distilled, buy the least expensive store brand of bottled drinking water, since it is most likely to be pure water and nothing else. You'll need distilled, that is, clear vinegar, because we will be observing color changes and colored vinegar could interfere with the result. You will want unscented, uncolored, additive-free household cleaning ammonia. In general, the less expensive versions of these items, including the red wine, work best. Expensive red wine should be reserved for other purposes.

Grocery store, laundry supplies: dry laundry bleach with brighteners

Grocery store, perishables: fresh spinach or other fresh green leafy vegetables, an uncooked hotdog, eight fresh lemons, a dark red apple, purple cabbage, a large pickle slice, milk, a jar of jelly, and fresh red meat

The subject of this book is forensic chemistry, so there are a couple of demonstrations that require a blood sample. Blood from the butcher's paper of packaged red meat works well.

Buy the pickles in a glass jar with a twist-on lid because you will need the empty, washed-out jar. You will also need a small glass vessel (sufficient to hold about 8 ounces or about 240 milliliters) for another demonstration, so if you don't have such a vessel already, buy a jar of jelly while you are at it.

Grocery store, picnic supplies: paper plates, paper bowls, disposable pie pans, plastic spoons, plastic forks, clear plastic tall glasses, and a pack of lotion-free tissues

The best paper plates are the least expensive paper plates because they are real paper with only a thin moisture-resistant coating. Plastic spoons and forks are best because they are relatively inert and will not react with the chemicals in the demonstrations and confound the results. We also suggest using disposable plastic glasses, plastic flatware, and paper plates because these articles cannot be reused with food items.

Grocery store, plastics: plastic cups, plastic containers with snap-on lids, and any food item packaged in a cylindrical container with a thin metal bottom and a plastic, see-through lid

Throughout the demonstrations we will be using small plastic cups, so you should get at least a couple dozen. By "small plastic cups" we mean small drinking cups, such as purchased for a bathroom dispenser, but plastic, *not* plastic-coated paper. These cups generally hold about 50 milliliters or a quarter cup of liquid. Plain white or clear plastic cups are required because we will be observing the color of several solutions, and this is most easily accomplished against a white background. You will also need a half dozen tall, clear plastic drinking glasses.

You will need a cylindrical container that you can make into a pinhole viewer, so the container needs a plastic see-through lid. In the United States, there are potato chip cans and coffee cans that fit these specifications quite nicely.

You will need a half dozen or so plastic disposable storage containers about 3 inches by 5 inches (about 8 centimeters by 15 centimeters). You will also need cylindrical plastic containers that are about 6 inches in diameter and perhaps 8 inches tall (about 15 centimeters in diameter by 20 centimeters tall), and these must have snap-on lids. A small disposable food-storage container will do just fine.

> Grocery store, spices: "lite" salt (potassium chloride) and sour salt (citric acid)**

"Lite" salt is a salt substitute for people on sodium-restricted diets. Sour salt (citric acid) might be a bit hard to find. It can be found in some specialty food stores or ordered over the Internet. If your store has a food-canning section, you may find citric acid there.

> Hardware store: very fine steel wool, at least ten 3- to 5-inch zinc-coated galvanized nails, and aluminum wire

Aluminum wire used to be common in electrical wiring, but it may be harder to find because it is being phased out. The Internet, again, may be your best recourse.

> Internet: luminol and fluorescent fingerprint powder with a fine-haired applicator brush

You will almost certainly have to purchase these three items over the Internet. There are several grades of luminol available. We had the best results with the better grade, although it was a bit more expensive. The best grade—the professional grade that is designed not to destroy DNA—is the most expensive, but this level of quality is not necessary.

We hope you will find a fluorescent powder that comes with a brush, but if you have to buy the brush separately, please be sure the bristles are as fine as possible.

> Kitchen drawer: plastic wrap, aluminum foil, plastic sandwich bags (self-sealing), rubber bands, paper clips, adhesive tape, safety matches, eight fairly clean pennies, a needle or straight pin, white coffee filters, toothpicks and a couple of rolls of white paper towels

We group these as "kitchen drawer items" because we hope you already have them in your kitchen drawers. However, if you plan to put them back in the kitchen drawer, please take what you need before you start work on the demonstration and be certain to keep unused items well away from the demonstration area to avoid contamination.

Novelty shop: a black light, a cap gun, some caps, and glow sticks

We will be using a black light as our "alternative light source." A true alternative light source provides several selectable frequencies of light, but for our demonstrations, a less expensive black light works well. The type of black light needed can usually be purchased in novelty stores or in stores that sell music targeted to a teenage audience. There are some filament lightbulbs that are sold as "black light," but these will not work for our demonstrations. For our demonstrations you need a fluorescent-tube-type black light.

The cap gun we found looks like a small revolver (starter's pistol) and the caps come on a plastic ring.

Glow sticks are sometimes sold at fairs or may be purchased at novelty shops. They are thin plastic tubes of chemicals that start to glow when an internal membrane is broken by bending the stick. Glow sticks are sometimes found with camping supplies.

Plant nursery: a soil test kit that includes tests for nitrogen, phosphorus, and potassium

Pet store: a total-salt aquarium test kit, an aquarium pH test kit with indicator, and pH adjusting solutions

The aquarium pH indicator should list bromothymol blue as the active ingredient. There should be two solutions in the pH adjusting kit, one to raise the pH (containing sodium hydroxide) and one to lower the pH (containing sulfuric acid).

Recycle bin: enough newspaper to spread on counters for twenty-five demonstrations with one sheet left over

PREDEMONSTRATION CELERY PREP

You will need a bunch of celery that has young stalks with leaves attached in the center. Separate these young stalks and cut off the bottoms. Fill three tall plastic cups two-thirds full with water and add enough drops of red food coloring so that the water is deeply colored. Put a couple of the prepared celery stalks into each cup. Put a couple of stalks in a cup of plain water.

In one of the food-coloring cups, wrap one leaf of one stalk gently but thoroughly in adhesive tape. Cut the leaves off of another stalk in this cup. Put the cup with the unaltered celery in food-colored water in the refrigerator and leave the other cups on the counter. Allow them to sit at least overnight. We will discuss the results of this demonstration in chapter 2.

COPPER SULFATE

High-purity copper sulfate is sold as a sewer root killer, cattle foot bath, algae killer, weed killer, and freshwater snail killer. If you have ever purchased copper sulfate for any of these purposes, you are familiar with the beautiful, deep-blue crystals. However, in the United States, it is against federal law to use pesticides in a manner inconsistent with the labeling, so you may need to investigate other available preparations. For instance, copper sulfate, also known as blue vitriol or blue stone, may be found as a ceramic glaze colorant at an art-supply outlet. Alternative sources may be located on the Internet.

Crystals obtained from some sources may be the size of sand, while others may be as large as raisins. The only difference the size makes is in measurement and dissolving. If the demonstration calls for a teaspoon (5 milliliters), for instance, then this could mean several crystals or one big crystal, depending on the type of sample you've obtained. The larger crystals also take more time to dissolve.

Whatever the source, copper sulfate needs to be treated with respect. *It can cause damage if it should get into the eyes. Some people may experience an allergic reaction to copper sulfate. Directly breathing in the dust and exposure to skin should be avoided. Heated solutions may generate irritating fumes, so work with copper sulfate and copper sulfate solutions in an open area as you would if you were working with solvents, varnish, or paint thinner. Any utensil or container that comes in contact with copper sulfate or copper sulfate solutions cannot be reused for drinking or storage for any consumable.*

Use gloves and a funnel when handling copper sulfate and copper sulfate solutions. If you do get some on your hands, rinse your hands with water.

Because copper sulfate can take twenty minutes or longer to completely dissolve, you may want to prepare a solution of a teaspoon (5 milliliters) of copper sulfate in a cup of water (240 milliliters) and have it on hand for the demonstrations. Label any solutions with the date, your name, and "copper sulfate." Add in large letters, "CAUTION: TOXIC!" Store the solution in a secure location, well away from children and pets. Alert any adults to its presence.

And now, fully equipped, let us proceed—to chemistry and crime.

PART I
BARE-BONES
CHEMISTRY

Like all other arts, the Science of Deduction and Analysis is one which can only be acquired by long and patient study. . . . Before turning to those moral and mental aspects of the matter which present the greatest difficulties, let the inquirer begin by mastering more elementary problems.

Sir Arthur Conan Doyle, *Study in Scarlet*, ca. 1887

As we said, technology has been a wonderful aid to law enforcement. Cold cases have been closed. Cases that could not have been solved twenty years ago are now being quickly cleared. Clues that were not even clues before are now routinely assessed. But there have been some drawbacks, too. Technology, it seems, makes good theater.

While a well-executed crime drama is certainly enjoyable, it has to be acknowledged that these productions exercise poetic license when portraying forensic science. Unfortunately, the distinction between fact and fiction can become blurred. Even docudramas can be misleading for the simple reason that uncleared or slowly proceeding cases don't make good TV. A program that portrayed detectives struggling with smudged fingerprints, waiting for DNA screenings that come back with no definitive match, and combing for hours, days, or weeks through a trampled, compromised crime scene would not stay on the air too long. But this description is usually much closer to the truth. So it is appropriate to take a few minutes to elaborate on some misconceptions before we proceed.

Perhaps the greatest misperception is that forensic analysis can be turned around quickly. In fact, most results qualified for use in court or as the basis for a warrant can take days or weeks. There are several reasons for these delays. First, tests must be done by licensed, certified labs or questions will arise concerning their reliability. A *chain of custody* must also be clearly established or the question of evidence tampering can be raised. Most municipalities have to share lab facilities with other municipalities. The question "Why aren't the police doing anything?" is many times justifiably answered by "They are waiting on laboratory results." And wait they must. Improper arrests waste time, money, and resources—and result in acquittals.

Even if lab facilities are readily available, local labs often only have basic instrumentation and techniques. When requested, in cases of violent crime, the FBI may process the evidence using their more extensive repertoire of techniques, but requesting tests from the FBI, and getting results, again, takes time.

There is also the perception that forensic tests "prove" guilt or innocence. Not so. Only a jury can decide guilt or innocence, and they do this by evaluating the evidence. Evidence must be evaluated because there is no such thing as a perfect match or a perfect result— each test has an associated margin of error, and narrowing this margin of error takes time. Instruments have to be calibrated, technicians have to be trained, and tests have to be confirmed, quality controlled, and certified. "These truths are self-evident" applies to political law, not science. In the end, the only thing an expert witness can really say is that the findings "are consistent with" poison, a knife wound, a bullet's origin, and so on, because of the uncertainty involved. "Consistent with" is not the same as "proves."

In chapter 1, we will get a feel for the amount of effort necessary to secure *evidentiary data*, that is, data certified to be correct to within a determined confidence level and that can stand up to the rigors of a court of law. We will then proceed, in chapter 2, to discuss atomic structure and how a knowledge of isotopes and atoms can lead to incriminating evidence. In chapter 3, we will examine the classification of atoms into elements, and in chapter 4, we look into the coalescence of atoms into compounds. In chapter 5, we will examine the intermolecular forces that cause gases to condense to liquids and solids. In chapters 6, 7, and 8, we investigate the properties of these phases and show the relevance of these properties to forensic investigations.

So, with no further delay, let's get down to cases.

DEMONSTRATION 1
A SIGNIFICANT DIFFERENCE

The devil is in the details.

Attribution unknown

First responders must routinely make quick decisions concerning the extent of danger and/or the nature of a crime. The following is a demonstration of what is called a *presumptive drug test*: an on-the-scene assessment that tests for the presence of certain illegal substances.

You will need a notebook, a pen, paper plates, white plastic cups, and samples of these four over-the-counter pharmaceuticals: aspirin, ibuprofen, acetaminophen, and caffeine. The pills should have a white coating, not a colored coating. If it is difficult to find pills without a colored coating, try to gently crack the pills and remove the colored coating before proceeding. The demonstration requires two pills of each variety, so if you have to remove a colored coating, do it for two pills.

After donning your safety glasses and protective gloves, label four paper plates with the name of each medication and then place two white plastic cups on each paper plate. Label a fifth paper plate "null response," and put two empty white plastic cups on this plate, too. We use "null response" to indicate no response in the test rather than another term, such as "negative response," because the lack of a response does not necessarily mean the material being tested for is not present. It might be present, but in levels too low to be detected by the test. The term *null response* conveys that "the test is showing no response" rather than "the test shows the absence of the substance." These last two samples will serve as our control samples. A control sample is a sample that should *not* show a positive result and can be used to demonstrate that a positive result, when it is achieved, is an actual positive and not just a coincidence.

Take an aspirin tablet and place it in the mortar (suggested for purchase in "Crime Lab and Crime Solutions") and grind it with the pestle until it is a fairly fine powder. Remember, this is a sacrificial mortar and pestle. Do not reuse this equipment for anything intended for consumption.

Dump the aspirin powder into one of the cups on the aspirin paper plate. Take a second aspirin tablet, grind it as before, and dump that powder into the second aspirin cup on the aspirin paper plate. Rinse the mortar and pestle with water and dry them thoroughly.

Take a second medication and repeat the grinding procedure given for aspirin and transfer the results for each tablet into its separate cup. Clean the mortar and pestle as before and repeat the grinding procedure for the third and fourth medications, placing each one into its own cup after it is ground. Make sure to clean the mortar and pestle between each use.

You should now have eight cups with a ground medication tablet (two samples of each kind of medication) all resting on labeled paper plates. The fifth plate labeled "null response" should still have two empty plastic cups.

Add a tablespoon (about 15 milliliters) of distilled water to each cup. Swirl the cups so that more medication will dissolve. In the medicine cups there will probably be insoluble material left over—the starch carrier for the medicine—but it will not interfere with the tests.

On each of the plates, choose one of the cups, label it with the letter "I" (for "indicator"), and add 3 or 4 drops of the indicator from the aquarium pH adjustment kit. Swirl these cups. The cups on the plate labeled "null response"—with no medication, just water and indicator—will serve as a comparison. Note any color change in your notebook.

On each of the plates, chose the remaining cup, and label it "E" (for "etchant"). Add 2 or 3 drops of etchant solution to the "E" cups, and swirl. Note any color change that occurs. Do not add etchant to a cup with aquarium indicator and vice versa.

Make a table with four columns headed with the name of each medication and two rows headed with the name of the additive, either aquarium indicator or etchant solution, and transfer your observations for each test onto this table.

Your table should look like the table shown below. You can see that there is a pattern of responses unique to each medication. If there is no interaction, then the powder remains the color of the test solution, which is yellow for both the etchant and the indicator.

	Aspirin	**Ibuprofen**	**Acetaminophen**	**Caffeine**
Indicator	Yellow (null response)	Yellow (null response)	Dark Blue/ Green	Green
Etchant	Purple	Yellow (null response)	Purple	Yellow (null response)

Based on our results, we might feel fairly confident that we have a test that could distinguish aspirin from ibuprofen because aspirin would turn purple in the presence of etchant and ibuprofen would not. On the other hand, a powder that turns purple in the presence of etchant could also be acetaminophen. The second test, run with indicator, could distinguish between aspirin and acetaminophen: aspirin would not react with the indicator, but acetaminophen would turn dark blue or green. When two or more tests are positive for a substance, then you gain confidence in your conclusion. But after tests such as these, would you be confident enough in the identity of a white powder to take it for a headache? Being confident in your results is not the same as being certain. Being sure is different from being dead sure. Uncertainty certainly plays a part in "The Case of the Presumptive Perp."

CHAPTER 1

CONFIDENCE IN CHEMISTRY AND CONFIDENCE IN CLUES: THE SIGNIFICANCE OF DIGITS

After all, facts are facts, and although we may quote one to another with a chuckle the words of the Wise Statesman, "Lies—damn lies—and statistics," still there are some easy figures the simplest must understand, and the astutest cannot wriggle out of.

Leonard Henry Courtney, ca. 1895

THE CASE OF THE PRESUMPTIVE PERP

The car with two passengers was going a fairly modest 55 mph when it passed Officers Juan Luke and Hanna Cuffs. But the speed limit on this stretch of highway was 35. The officers pulled out to follow the car and clock it. They gave it a flash of lights and a quick chirp of the siren to pull it over. The car obligingly eased onto the side of the road. Officer Luke stepped out to request the driver's license while Officer Cuffs walked to the passenger side of the car to give the interior a quick once-over for any immediate threats, open containers, or contraband. After securing the driver's license, Officer Luke returned to the cruiser to check for wants and warrants. He found that the driver had prior drug-related arrests and currently had an outstanding bench warrant for a no-show on a traffic violation. Officer Luke returned to the car and asked the driver to step out and put his hands on the car. The driver complied with a sheepish shrug. Luke told the driver he was under arrest for the traffic warrant, informed the driver of his rights, placed him in handcuffs, and frisked him.

The driver was cooperative during the arrest and pat-down search of his person. A quick look around the car revealed that the floor was clear and the console between the two front seats contained only a fast-food soda cup, a pile of used tissues, and a box of headache powder packets.

"Do you mind if I test some of those powders?" Luke asked.

"Naw," answered the driver, leaning against the car. "I've got an open one in my pocket."

Officer Cuffs retrieved the open packet of headache powder from the driver's pocket and tested it with field test kits for cocaine and heroin. Both tests were negative. Officer Cuffs asked the passenger if she was okay to drive the car back to the detainee's home, and she said she was.

"Do you have any drugs in there or anything else we should know about?" Luke asked the driver.

"No, sir. I've been in rehab."

Officer Luke led the driver back to the patrol car, and Officer Cuffs began packing up the test set to place back in the trunk. Cuffs turned to her partner and asked, "I'm going to let her take the car now. Okay?"

Officer Luke shook his head. "No. Not quite yet."

The Chemistry of the Case

Even on routine traffic duty, officers have to make quick decisions about reasonable suspicion of criminal activity. One way they do this is to use *presumptive tests*: tests involving chemical reactions that give quick color responses in the presence of substances such as methamphetamine, cocaine, or heroin.

These tests produce wonderfully colorful results, but it goes without saying that illicit drugs should never be procured for experimentation—chemical or otherwise. And even though test kits for illegal drugs are accessible in our Internet age, some contain chemicals that require professional handling. In addition, some states consider possession of these kits drug paraphernalia, so the temptation to investigate these tests should be resisted. But luckily, illegal drugs are not necessary to demonstrate how presumptive tests work. The demonstration preceding this chapter is a presumptive test for the drug aspirin. And the test acts basically the same way a presumptive test would for an illicit drug, including the realistic possibility of obtaining a false positive and the need for a *confirmatory test*.

A confirmatory test is necessary because the goal of a presumptive test is tentative, not definitive, identification. These tests let the officers know when the substance they are testing is probably *not* the substance of interest, but even if the test seems to indicate the substance is present, a positive, confirmatory test will be required to stand up to the rigors of court.

For instance, it has been found that several over-the-counter medicines can give false positives in amphetamine and heroin presumptive tests and that combinations of drugs can mask a color-based result.[1] Because of these complications, courts insist on more precise testing when it comes to evidentiary data. But if this is the case, then a couple of questions immediately spring to mind. If the presumptive tests are not decisive, then should they be used at all? And if the confirmatory tests are so much better, then why not subject all suspect powders to these tests in the first place?

The answer to both questions is the same: time and money. The presumptive tests allow law enforcement to make quick and relatively inexpensive determinations as to *possible* criminal activity. If police officers had to run the samples to the lab to do a test while the suspects were detained on a curb or in the back of a patrol car, the cost in time and personnel would be prohibitive. In addition, there is the constitutional issue of how long a person can be detained without being charged.

Any notion that tests can be run in a matter of hours is a misconception. The test itself might not take long, but the equipment needed to run the tests is expensive and many labs have only a single setup, so the waiting list for tests is predictably long. In forensic chemistry, it is hard to imagine a test request that is *not* an emergency, so getting a particular test bumped to the head of the line probably happens about as often as criminals voluntarily turn themselves in.

Even when a particular case reaches the top of the pile, the time that the actual test takes still may not be the limiting factor. The instruments have to be calibrated for each test and the results have to be certified and peer reviewed. Trained personnel must do the testing and they must follow an approved procedure. Why all this peer review and certification? Because we like our science certain. We like to believe that we can trust our science to send rockets to the moon and they will not end up on Mars.

When building the space shuttle, each bolt had to be checked to make sure it was torqued to the proper specification, and after it was checked, it was marked by two stripes of tape, one from a military and one from a government inspector. This careful procedure is why space shuttles take years to build. In forensic science, lives may be at stake, too, and equal care is taken.

So in the forensic chemistry lab, with all the instruments with their flashing lights and the highly trained operators and all the results torqued and striped, we should have a dead-certain result, right? Wrong. Even with all this effort, scientists always admit to a certain degree of uncertainty. Science is a series of estimations. Scientists have no problem accepting that a currently established scientific theory might someday be proven flawed or in need of revision. In science, this is called progress. But criminal law tolerates much less uncertainty. In criminal law, the yardstick is "beyond a reasonable doubt," and to meet this measure, a great deal of effort is required. While there can be no doubt that technology has improved the science of criminology, there is a bit of a downside, too, called "the *CSI* effect." One aspect of this effect is that juries now often expect their reasonable doubts to be completely eliminated through technology. While uncertainty can never be eliminated, the forensic chemist must keep the degree of uncertainty regarding the scientific evidence to a minimum so that the focus is on solving the crime. The process used— *uncertainty analysis*—is nearly a science unto itself.

To understand how uncertainty analysis might work, take out the set of metric measuring cups suggested for purchase in "Crime Lab and Crime Solutions." Measure out an amount of tap water that is between two increments on your measuring cup and that is less than half the capacity of the cup. For instance, if your cup is marked off in 10-milliliter increments and has a capacity of 50 milliliters, measure out 5 or 15 milliliters, halfway between the smallest marking and less than half of the capacity. If your cup is marked off in 50-milliliter increments and has a capacity of 1 liter, measure out something like 125 milliliters or 225 milliliters. (If your measuring cup is marked off in 25-milliliter increments, measure out 37 milliliters as closely as you can.) To aid your measurements and make them as accurate as possible, place the measuring cup on a flat surface and bring your eyes down to the level of the liquid. If you look straight at the water at eye level, you will see that the surface of the water curves slightly downward. This curvature, caused by the adherence of the water to the sides of the measuring device, is called the *meniscus*. The bottom of the meniscus is normally taken to be the level of the liquid. If necessary, adjust the level using your eyedropper.

Write down the measured amount in your notebook. After you have recorded the amount, pour the water into a separate container, being careful to transfer it all. In the first cup, measure out the same amount again as closely as you can, record the amount, and pour the new water into the receiving container. Now pour the combined amount back into the original measuring cup. Do you have *exactly* twice the original amount? Even if the amount appears to be very close, honest reflection will help you admit that the amount can only be an estimate because the amounts that went into the receiving container were estimates.

Another aspect of uncertainty can be illustrated with an experiment designed to measure the density of sugar. Density is defined as the mass of a given volume. It can be understood in terms of marbles. Blindfolded, you can distinguish a steel marble from a glass marble because of a difference in heft. Same-sized steel and glass marbles will have a different mass, a different density.

Take your smallest measuring cup and weigh it on the food scale we suggested for purchase in "Crime Lab and Crime Solutions." You may have to calibrate your food scale. In this instance, when we say "calibrate," we mean set the initial reading to zero. When using a precision laboratory instrument, calibration might mean setting the initial reading to zero and also setting several other points to their expected values. For instance, a thermometer might be calibrated by checking and adjusting its measurement for the freezing point of water *and* the boiling point of water. Why does calibration matter? Ask anyone who has ever been on a diet and watched his or her progress using a bathroom scale. The dial lands back on zero about half of the time, and every time the scale is moved recalibration is necessary.

Record the weight in your notebook. Then pour in sugar, measuring it out to one decimal point, estimating the last digit. For example, if you've measured out about 10.0 milliliters, use 10.0 or 10.1 milliliters as your best estimate. The thing to remember about measurements is that they can be very personal. Forensic chemistry is basically a branch of analytical chemistry and analytical chemistry can be just that—anal. So it is nice to have something personal. The measure is *your* best estimate.

Now weigh the cup with the sugar and again estimate the last digit.

To get the weight of the sugar, subtract the weight of the empty cup from the total weight of the cup with sugar. (When we did this measurement, we measured 25.0 grams for 10.1 milliliters of sugar.) Now calculate the density of sugar as the number of grams in a milliliter by taking your calculator and dividing the number of grams by the number of milliliters.

When we did this, an interesting thing happened: the calculator displayed 2.4752475.

Wow. That appears to be a pretty precise number. But does that number make sense? If we did the experiment again, we would probably get something around 2.45 or 2.51, but it is highly unlikely that we'd get exactly 2.4752475. We can really only say that we measured the density of sugar to be 2.48 grams per milliliter, using only three numbers, because we only used measurements that had three numbers. In fact, the last digit in 2.48 grams per milliliter, the 8, is itself an estimate because it is based on estimates.

The fact that the last number is an estimate does not have to be as troubling as it sounds. There are rules for determining the percentage error in instrument measurements, just as there are rules for reporting the results in opinion polls. For example, although newscasters may give the additional information hurriedly at the end of a report, the results of all opinion surveys have an accompanying uncertainty, such as, "Our survey found the approval rating for the senator is riding at 33 percent, plus or minus 3 percentage points."

For this type of situation, this margin of error is acceptable. But now consider such estimates when legal issues are involved. What if the current law dictates that someone can be sent to jail if they have in their possession a sweetener with a density of 2.47 or greater? If you were the lawyer defending the person accused of carrying our sample with a reported density of 2.48 plus or minus 0.03 grams per milliliter, you would be ethically obligated to challenge this measurement, especially if you knew that the last digit was an estimate. For this reason, the evidence would probably not even be submitted because the prosecutor would know that it was not sufficient.

By now it has become apparent that the measuring device we used was far too crude for our liberal state that allows people to walk around with sweetener in their pockets as long as it does not exceed a density of 2.47 grams per milliliter. New instrumentation is, of course, a possibility, but the more sophisticated the machinery, the more expensive and the more training required for the personnel who use it. A more cost-effective method for reducing the margin of error might be to repeat the test several times. Statistically, if the measurement is made many times, the results may be averaged and the degree of uncertainty in the result reduced.

We will not go through the mathematics that justifies this state-ment, but it makes intuitive sense: if you make the measurement more times, you have more faith in its validity. This approach has its own difficulties in practice. It is time-intensive because each one of the tests has to adhere to established standards and be quality checked. And if statistical analysis is to be applied, then the sample size has to be large enough to warrant a statistical treatment. A memorable (and hypothetical) example of a nonvalid statistical analysis was once offered for a study done with rats: a third of the rats died, a third of the rats recovered, and the last one got away.[2] So the bigger the sample size the better. Flipping a coin ten times and having it come up heads nine of those ten times does not shake our faith that pennies are two-sided, but it certainly would not prove this fact in a court of law.

The drawback of the requirement for a large enough sample size to be statistically valid is, again, that each test costs time and money—and there has to be enough sample for repetitions. In addition, it is always best to have a *control sample*, and this sample has to be accu-rately tested, too. For instance, if blue paint found on a red car is being tested to see if it came from a collision, a control sample from another spot on the car would have to be tested, too. Finding blue paint on the right fender doesn't prove anything unless it is established that the rest of the car had *no* blue paint. When news reports about a case of poi-soning say that the toxicology results are not back yet, there is a reason: certifiable results take time.

But time was not on the side of the officers in "The Case of the Presumptive Perp." A presumably innocent passenger was being detained when no particular suspicion of wrongdoing had been established. But Officer Luke had one more question.

Case Closed

After placing the handcuffed driver into the back of the squad car, Officer Luke returned to where Officer Cuffs stood talking with the female passenger. He leaned down to speak to the passenger through the window of the car.

"Could you please step out of the car?"

When she complied, he leaned in the driver's seat and lifted out the box of headache powder on the console. "Do we have any test materials left?"

"Sure do. But didn't we just test that stuff?" asked Officer Cuffs.

"We tested one sample. The sample he wanted us to test. Let's test some more."

A few minutes later Officer Luke confirmed. "One of the open packets tests positive for cocaine. Heck of a headache powder."

Officer Cuffs shook her head. "I guess he thought if we found one package that tested negative we'd assume the rest were negative, too."

Officer Luke concurred, "Pretty presumptive."

DEMONSTRATION 2
CASHING IT IN

It is no secret that organized crime in America takes in over forty billion dollars a year. This is quite a profitable sum, especially when one considers that the Mafia spends very little for office supplies.

Woody Allen, ca. 1970

In the United States justice system, guilt must be established "beyond a reasonable doubt." The verdict must be guilty or not guilty; there can be no in-between. In the sciences, however, the question as to whether or not something exists can be answered only after another question is answered: How closely do you want us to look? Just because something is detectable does not necessarily mean it is present in a significant amount. Significance is not a question of chemistry, it is a question of law. As the next demonstration shows, in chemical analysis, there can always be a reasonable doubt. Sometimes things show up where you don't expect them, and sometimes the things that show up aren't quite what you expected.

After donning your safety glasses and protective gloves, crush an acetaminophen tablet into a fine powder, as was done in demonstration 1. Dump the powder into a sandwich bag with a sealable flap and take a dollar bill (or some other denomination paper bill) and place it in the bag. Shake the bag vigorously to expose all areas of the bill to the powder. Remove the bill from the bag and shake the bill off until any visible powder has been removed. Lay the bill on a countertop, remove your gloves, and wash your hands thoroughly. Change into a new pair of gloves, taking care to avoid cross-contamination from the old pair.

Swab the bill several times with a damp cotton swab. Use distilled water to dampen the swab so as not to introduce any external contamination. Add two small drops of etchant reagent to the test end of the swab. You should see dark blue color develop, indicating a positive test for our drug of interest, acetaminophen. Although the bill appeared clean, a positive result means it still had a detectable amount of the drug.

As a control, dampen the other end of the swab with distilled water and add two drops of etchant reagent to this end. This end of the swab should remain dark yellow, which is a null response.

But how much of the drug remained on the bill? Our test does not tell. This test is a *qualitative test*, meaning that it indicates the probable presence of the drug but does not give a *quantitative* result, which would tell us how much. Before reporting the presence of the drug, however, a confirmatory test would be required: another drug, such as aspirin, could also react with the etchant, yielding a false positive.

Powders tend to stick well to money because bills are printed with a process known as intaglio printing. In this process, the printing plates are covered with ink and then wiped so that the only ink left is in the grooves that make up the design. The paper is pressed onto the plate at such a high pressure that the paper is forced into the grooves and picks up the ink. The result is a three-dimensional surface that can trap powder—such as the trapped powder that figures significantly in "The Case of the Significant Other."

CHAPTER 2

IMPROBABLE PROFILING: FINDING MASSIVE CLUES

Crime is terribly revealing.

Agatha Christie, *The ABC Murders*, ca. 1936

THE CASE OF THE SIGNIFICANT OTHER

District Attorney Sue Case stepped forward and shook hands warmly with Detective Detain. "Thank you so much for coming."

Detective Detain returned her smile. "No problem. I'm as anxious as you are to get this guy off the streets."

Prosecutor Case motioned toward two chairs with a low table between them, and then seated herself in one of the chairs. "What do you have?"

Detective Detain sat down and placed his briefcase on the table. He opened the case, extracted a legal pad, and began to read.

"The arresting officers observed the suspect with a female companion, jaywalking—"

"Jaywalking?" interrupted Ms. Case. "A lot of people jaywalk. . . ."

"They usually don't stagger and bump into other people at the same time. There has been pickpocket activity in the area. The officers thought it was worth a check."

Case nodded.

"As the officers approached the couple, they observed the suspect reach into his pocket and hand something to his companion. At this point, the first officer ordered the couple to stop and put their hands in the air. The suspect complied, but the female companion continued walking."

Detain turned over a page on his pad. "Believing this to be an indication of possible criminal activity, the second officer pursued the girl, who then claimed she had not heard the order to stop."

Case asked, "Did an officer frisk her?"

Detain nodded. "Officer Juana Break patted her down and retrieved a packet of powder from her pocket. They called in for backup and found the outside of the packet tested positive for cocaine."

Case frowned. "The suspect hands his stash to the girl—"

"Because the girl has no priors," Detain finished for her. "Even given the amount, the courts will probably go a lot easier on her than they would have on him."

"Did the companion admit he had passed the packet to her?"

"Nope. She went along with it. Claims the dope was hers all along."

"Did you test the bag for prints?"

"Yes, but we couldn't come up with anything usable."

Sue Case let her shoulders slump.

"So we don't have this guy after all!"

"Well, there's more," the detective continued. "During the frisk we found a sizable roll of bills in his pocket, and a wipe of the top bill tested positive for cocaine."

Sue Case looked down at her folded hands for a long moment and then turned her eyes sadly to the detective. "I'm sorry, but that's not a significant finding. Nearly half of all the bills in circulation in this country show trace contamination with cocaine. Saying you found cocaine on a dollar is like saying you found fleas on a dog. The probability is about the same."

"Yes," admitted Detective Detain. "But fortunately not all fleas are the same."

The Chemistry of the Case

In chapter 1 and demonstration 2, we used a presumptive test to determine if a particular material could possibly be acetaminophen. The key word here is *possibly* because the presumptive tests only confirm or exclude possibilities. They do not provide definite proof of any material. Other *confirmatory* tests provide more definitive answers. For our first discussion of a confirmatory test, we zoom in on the chemistry—into the chemicals that make up the reactions, into the atoms that make up the chemicals, and right down to the protons, neutrons, and electrons that make up the atoms.

All the elements on the periodic table—carbon, hydrogen, oxygen, copper, and so on—are collections of like atoms. The atoms of the elements are very small (one hundred billion billion average-sized atoms could dance on the head of a pin), and all atoms are composed of even smaller protons, neutrons, and electrons. The first two of these particles—the protons and the neutrons—make up the nucleus of the atom.

The nucleus is extraordinarily tiny. If an atom were the size of a normal living room, then the nucleus would be the size of the period at the end of this sentence. For this reason, the traditional diagram of an atom—the prominent nucleus surrounded by electrons in satellite-like orbits—is inherently flawed. An atom could not be drawn to scale on any reasonably sized page, so we are forced to show the nucleus disproportionably large in order to convey any information concerning its structure and composition. If we were concerned with accuracy of scale, pictures of atoms would consist of only the negatively charged electron *orbitals*—the fuzzy regions of space where the probability of finding an electron is high—around a nucleus too tiny to be seen. In fact, in future discussions of atoms and compounds, we will concentrate mainly on the electron orbitals, and not worry much about the nucleus, because the electron orbitals not only take up the most space, but they are also at the heart of chemical reactivity. At first, however, let us focus on the protons and neutrons of the nucleus.

There are three important considerations for the protons and neutrons that make up the nucleus. First, for our purposes, all protons are identical, all neutrons are identical, and all electrons are identical. Second, virtually all the mass of the atom is found in the protons and neutrons. (The mass of an electron is approximately two thousand times less than the mass of a proton or a neutron.) Third, the number of protons dictates the identity of the atom: electrons and neutrons may come and go, but for an atom to be a certain element, the number of protons has to stay the same.

To understand how important this last consideration is, look at the periodic table in the appendix. Each element, starting with hydrogen, H, reading from left to right, is identified by a number, called the atomic number, given above the symbol for the element. Hydrogen's atomic number is 1, and the atomic number for helium, He, is 2. The elements on the periodic table are, in fact, listed by atomic number. The significance of the atomic number is that it stands for the number of protons in the nucleus of an atom of that element. Hydrogen's atomic number of 1 means that it has one proton in its nucleus. Helium's atomic number of 2 means that an atom of helium has two protons in its nucleus. An atom of lithium (Li) has three protons in its nucleus and so forth.

To reiterate, the number of protons in an element can be thought of as its defining feature. Just as "roundness" is the defining feature of a sphere and "squareness" is the defining feature of a cube, the number of protons in its nucleus is the defining feature of an atom. Neutrons, however, are a different story. The nucleus of an atom of hydrogen has to have one proton (in order to be classified as hydrogen), but it can have none, one, or even two neutrons. In other words, atoms of hydrogen come in different varieties. One type has no neutrons, one type has one neutron, and one type has two neutrons. The different varieties of atoms of an element are called *isotopes*.

Oxygen, O, is an atom that has eight protons (as evidenced by the atomic number 8 for oxygen on the periodic table) and has three isotopes: oxygen with eight neutrons, oxygen with nine neutrons, and oxygen with ten neutrons. Chlorine has two isotopes, while sulfur has four.

Elements occur as specific isotopes because there are limits on the number of neutrons that stable, nonradioactive atoms may have. For instance, oxygen atoms are not naturally found that have five, fifteen, or twenty-five neutrons—just eight, nine, or ten. The reason for this consistency is that some proportions of protons and neutrons (for reasons beyond the scope of this book) are just too unstable. Other arrangements, such as eight protons and ten neutrons for oxygen, are stable enough to be found in any naturally occurring sample of oxygen atoms: wherever oxygen atoms are found, there will be some oxygen atoms with eight neutrons, some with nine, and some with ten—and in a consistent ratio. This naturally occurring distribution of isotopes is called the *natural abundance* of isotopes, and the natural abundance is amazingly consistent all over the Earth. For instance, magnesium with twelve neutrons, magnesium with thirteen neutrons, and magnesium with fourteen neutrons are found with the natural abundance of 78.70, 10.13, and 11.17 percent, respectively, whether you are harvesting magnesium from the ocean or mining magnesium in Australia. There are, however, ways to sort the isotopes artificially and (as we will see shortly) some surprising natural processes that can change the ratio, too.

One reason the natural abundance is so consistent is that isotopes of the same element may have slightly different masses, but the chemistry of the atoms stays mainly the same. A chemical reaction happens when a new material is formed. For instance, when a fizzing antacid tablet is dropped into water, the citric acid and the sodium bicarbonate combine to form carbon dioxide—the fizz—a new material. The antacid would be just as fizzy with different isotopes of oxygen. Physical processes, however, are changes that do not change the identity of the material. A melting ice cube changes shape, but it is still water. As it turns out, the mass differences of isotopes can have some interesting consequences in the physical behavior of materials.

Let's use bowling balls as an analogy. All bowling balls are spheres, just as all magnesium atoms have twelve protons, and bowling balls come in different weights, just as magnesium comes in different isotopes. The real difference, however, comes when the ball rolls down the lane. The same person, throwing with the same amount of strength, will throw a lighter ball faster and a heavier ball more slowly. The same type of mass consideration can come into play with atoms of different isotopes. In normal situations, the mass difference in the isotopes is much too small to be of any concern, but in situations where a force is being applied to the atoms, the difference can be significant. Surprisingly, under special circumstances, one of the forces that can make a difference is the force of gravity. One of the special circumstances under which gravity can have a measurable effect in the behavior of isotopes is in plants, such as the plants that produce drugs.

Many drugs are natural products. It is much less expensive to harvest morphine and cocaine from the opium poppy and coca plant, respectively, than to manufacture these drugs synthetically. But different growing conditions can leave a natural marker on the product. Remember the celery you were asked to put in the food-colored water in "Crime Lab and Crime Solutions"? With the batch that sat on the counter, you should have seen the food coloring appear in the celery top within a couple of hours and appear on the leaves within twenty-four hours. But in this same amount of time, the celery that was in the refrigerator should not show any food coloring rising up the stem, or perhaps only a very little. The leaf that was wrapped in tape in the counter sample should also show very little color or color developing much more slowly.

Why were you asked to put celery in clear water without food coloring? That was our control. The control samples show that the red color could only reasonably come from the food coloring.

The food-colored water rises up the celery stem by *capillary action* (which we will explore more fully later), and this pull is aided by the water leaving the stem via the leaf. Wrapping the leaf in tape impedes evaporation from the leaf. Capillary action is also limited by the force of gravity, which pulls water down, and the force of gravity depends on the mass. The exact daily conditions of rain, wind, and sunlight that a particular crop experiences will determine the distribution of isotopes of hydrogen and oxygen, the two constituents of water, H_2O.[1] The water molecules made from the lighter isotopes of hydrogen and oxygen will travel higher up the stalk of the plant, which will result in an unnatural abundance at the top or in the leaves. This new ratio of isotopes in a plant material is unique to the history of the plant and can be an impressive clue, as it was in "The Case of the Significant Other."

Case Closed

Sue Case made an attempt not to sound disappointed. Detective Detain was trying to prove the possession of the cocaine, but his declaration that he had found traces on bills in the perp's pocket was not encouraging. She knew that cocaine on money is much too common an occurrence. As Detective Detain explained that he had requested further tests, Ms. Case interrupted, "If you're talking about drug profiling—finding out how much starch or sugar they used to cut it—that really isn't going to help. Dilutants don't narrow the field by much at all. A lot of dealers use the same approximate cut because they don't want to get the reputation of being a cheat. If finding cocaine on money is like finding fleas on a dog, then finding two batches with the same dilutants is as common as two beagles with long ears."

"Well, you're right about that. The match for the materials used to cut the cocaine was good, but like you said, it won't hold up on its own."

There was a pause while Detain flipped over a page in his notes, and Ms. Case sat looking grim.

"But," he said slowly, "dilutant profiling wasn't the only type of profiling we requested."

Ms. Case now looked at Detective Detain with new interest. "The other profiling you requested was . . ."

Detain smiled. "Isotope profiling."

"What did you find?"

"A near perfect match with the cocaine in his girlfriend's possession."

The prosecutor's face admitted a grin. "You found a match with the dilutant profile *and* the isotope profile?"

"Yep."

"So you're certain!"

Detain shrugged. "Well, within reasonable error."

Case frowned. "What are the odds that the two samples aren't from the same batch?"

"About the same as finding a two-headed flea on a dog—in December."

Prosecutor Case shrugged. "I can live with that."

Canned Cooking Fuel

DEMONSTRATION 3
THE COLOR OF CRIME

The Laws of Nature are just, but terrible. . . . The elements have no forbearance. The fire burns, the water drowns, the air consumes, the earth buries.

Henry Wadsworth Longfellow, ca. 1850

C hemistry is a curious science in that it is based on something too small to be seen: an atom. It would require 3.4 million hydrogen atoms to span the diameter of the period at the end of this sentence. An atom is so tiny that a ray of visible light can knock it for a loop, which is the reason for its invisibility. However, as we will see when we begin part III, light interacts with atoms, and atoms, in mirrored processes, can give off light. Light emitting from atoms was one of the principle tools originally used to study atomic structure. In part III we will discuss further the origins of this light, but here we will see that when it comes to identifying materials, light can produce colorful clues.

This demonstration requires the canned cooking fuel recommended for purchase in "Crime Lab and Crime Solutions." It also requires a location such as a patio or a large flat grassless area in your backyard where the flame from the cooking fuel won't be a fire hazard or set off smoke detectors. Because we will be observing flame colors, the demonstration works best in shadow, dim light, or even at night. This demonstration also requires safety glasses and protective gloves, so please put them on now.

In this demonstration we will be making *aqueous solutions*, that is, solutions made with water. Our aqueous solutions will also be saturated: *saturated solutions* are solutions that have so much solid added that no more will go into the solution. You will be able to tell when your solution is saturated because some solid will remain undissolved in the bottom of the container.

Prepare a saturated aqueous solution of each of these compounds in a small white plastic cup: copper sulfate, boric acid, and copper sulfate with an equal volume of potassium chloride (lite salt). Stir each with a toothpick. Keep adding small amounts of each solid until no more solid will dissolve. These solutions could be poisonous if ingested, so observe the normal precautions of keeping them away from children, pets, and food. You might notice that as the potassium chloride and boric acid (which isn't very soluble) dissolve in water, the cup becomes cool to the touch. This type of process is called an *endothermic process*, which means "heat into," and will be discussed in more detail in chapter 14.

Cover each cup with plastic wrap and use a rubber band to secure the wrap in place.

When you are outside and ready to start the demonstration, get three large metal paper clips, one for each solution, and bend them so that one end is a loop and the other end is straight (see the illustration at the beginning of this demonstration). Ignite the cooking fuel carefully (to extinguish the flame, just replace the lid on the can). Uncover the solutions and, one by one, hold each paper clip in the fire to clean the test surface. Contaminants on the paper clip should color the flame, so keep the paper clip in the flame until the flame color returns to normal. Place the cleaned end of each clip into its assigned solution and let it stand for a minute or so before use.

When you are ready, grasp one of the paper clips by the straight end and hold the looped end into the canned fuel flame. (You may use a pair of pliers to hold the clip in the flame if you wish.) The fire may sputter and jump a little as the solution boils away. As it boils, the vapor from the boiled solution will get into the flame and turn the flame the characteristic color of the compound of interest. Copper sulfate is green, boric acid is a more pastel green, and copper sulfate with potassium chloride should be a mix of blue and green.

You can repeat the performance by placing the paper clips back into their respective test solutions (but be careful not to mix them up). If the solution cups are tightly covered with plastic wrap so the solution does not evaporate, the solutions can be stored (away from children, pets, and food) and reused. Don't leave the paper clips in the solutions because they may react with the solution over time.

The changing colors—as the various chemicals were put into the flame—show that different materials produce different colors of light. Sometimes this light can be used to identify both a material and its environment, as we saw with the different flame color for copper sulfate and copper sulfate mixed with potassium chloride. As it turns out, an atom can also absorb the same type of light that it emits. An analytical instrument called an atomic absorption spectrometer exploits this property of elements for elemental analyses, such as the analysis performed in "The Case of the Mystifying Metal."

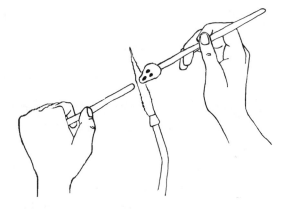

CHAPTER 3

My Dear Watson: Elements and the Evidence They Contain

"Excellent!" I cried.
"Elementary," said he.

Sir Arthur Conan Doyle, *The Crooked Man*, ca. 1893

The Case of the Mystifying Metal

Detective D. Flagration spoke quietly over the phone to Inspector Ashley Remains of the state fire marshal's office. "If we don't find something pretty soon, we're going to have to put this one down as accidental. But that old guy was sharp. He'd been blowing glass in that warehouse for the last forty-seven years. I just can't see him catching his place on fire—and then not getting out in time. It just doesn't make sense."

Inspector Remains matched the seriousness in the detective's tone. "You knew him personally?"

"Sure. He was a local landmark. The kids from the elementary school take—took—a field trip to his glassblowing shop every year. I went myself when I was a kid. He was sixty-seven years old, bragged that he still had his own teeth, worked out every day."

"There's really that much call for glassblowing?"

Detective Flagration consulted the tablet on his desk. "Not really. The guy that's been sharing the warehouse with him for the last couple of years said that he thought the glassblower was going to retire. Not that much work anymore, and the fire regs kept changing on him. And some of the young punks in the neighborhood had started coming in and harassing him about this and that, trying to figure out if he kept anything of value on the premises."

"Did he?"

"Naw. Not unless you're another glassblower. It would be hard to unload anything they might have stolen."

"So you think they just came in to trash the place and accidentally set it on fire?"

"Don't know. I doubt the old guy would've let anybody touch his stuff without a fight."

"Were there signs of a fight?"

"Nothing obvious. The body and the scene were pretty badly burned. It looks like some papers caught and then some wood."

"Did the lab turn up any accelerants?"

"No. But he used a propane-oxygen torch, so accelerants wouldn't be necessary to start a pretty good fire."

"Did you find anything else?"

"Nothing that couldn't be explained, except this little metal nugget that looked like it had been melted in the fire. I had the lab run an AA analysis, and they found gold, copper, silver, and palladium, but they don't have the exact percentages yet."

"Gold, silver, and palladium? Sounds like something worth stealing to me. Do you think it was some material he worked with?"

"Don't know, but it didn't seem likely. Sometimes glassblowers use metals when they do fancy decorative work, but he did strictly specialty industrial glass. I looked up gold alloys in general and found they are used in jewelry, tooth caps, medallions, and coins, and for some scientific and electronic instruments. So maybe he was working on something that required an unusual glass-to-metal seal."

"Hmm," the inspector's voice came back, questioningly. "But if it was contract work, if it was an item on someone else's budget, why wouldn't he just let an intruder have it and then call the police?"

There was a pause and then Flagration answered with a sigh. "I don't know. The torch was lying near the body. Maybe he was trying to get out. Maybe he was trying to defend himself."

"Did you check the hospitals to see if anyone showed up seeking burn treatment?"

"Not yet." There was another long pause and then the detective's voice came back with quiet assurance. "You know, I think you're right. We need to check for emergencies. But not at the hospital . . ."

The Chemistry of the Case

Detective D. Flagration's analysis of the metallic sample was performed on an atomic absorption (AA) spectrometer. An AA works on the principle that elements absorb light of specific frequencies and emit light of these same frequencies. To understand why, we need to zoom back in on the atom, but this time we will be looking at the electrons as well as the protons in the atom.

Our first observation is that every electrically neutral atom—that is, an atom that has as many negatively charged electrons as it has positively charged protons—has at least one electron in an orbital around its nucleus. The heaviest atoms have more than one hundred electrons. To accommodate these electrons, nature stacks them in concentric *shells* or *energy levels* around the nucleus, as artistically interpreted in figure 3.1.

Figure 3.1. A neutral atom consists of a central nucleus and anywhere from one to more than one hundred electrons. These electrons are accommodated in concentric energy levels around the nucleus.

Living in the irregular world that we do, with cats of many colors, no two snowflakes alike, and clouds in formations from castles to Winnie-the-Pooh, it is fascinating to see such regularity in the atom. The number of electrons that each level can contain increases in a neat mathematical progression. The first level, the smallest level, can hold two electrons; the second level, a larger level, can hold eight electrons; the third level can hold eighteen; and the fourth level can hold thirty-two— the number of the level squared, times two. The first level holds 2×1^2 = 2 electrons, the second level holds $2 \times 2^2 = 8$ electrons, the third level holds $2 \times 3^2 = 18$ electrons, and the fourth level holds $2 \times 4^2 = 32$ electrons. There are higher-order levels, and theoretically the number of levels can increase infinitely, but this is enough for our purposes.

We said that the lightest atom (hydrogen) has one electron and that the heaviest elements have more than one hundred electrons, but how do you tell who has what? As it turns out, the number of electrons in a neutral atom of an element is the same as the number of protons. In a neutral atom, each negative electron in the orbitals is balanced by a positive proton in the nucleus. (If the number of electrons does not match the number of protons, then the particle has a net positive or negative charge and is called an *ion*, not a neutral atom.) The number of protons, as previously stated, is the atomic number for the element, which can be read from the periodic table. So by looking at the periodic table you can determine the number of protons—and electrons— in a neutral atom of an element.

As you can see on the periodic table in the appendix, carbon has an atomic number of 6, which means it has six protons. If it has six positively charged protons, then it needs to have six negatively charged electrons to be neutral. For carbon, the six electrons fit into the first two levels of the carbon atom. The first level, closest to the nucleus, holds two electrons, and the second level holds the remaining four. In fact, the shape of the periodic table reflects the filling of the levels. As you can see in figure 3.2, hydrogen sits up at the top of the periodic table with its one electron, beginning the first row. Helium, which has two electrons, sits at the far side. Because its first level is filled with its two electrons, helium completes a row. Lithium, Li, starts the next row with three electrons: two stay in the first level and one new electron begins filling the second level. Neon, Ne, on the far right, completes this row. Neon has ten electrons: two in the first level and eight more to complete the second level. The rest of the periodic table reflects the same type of patterning. By referring to figure 3.2, we can see that every filled row completes a level.

Life becomes a little complicated after this because the energy levels start overlapping like the layers of an onion, so we will limit our

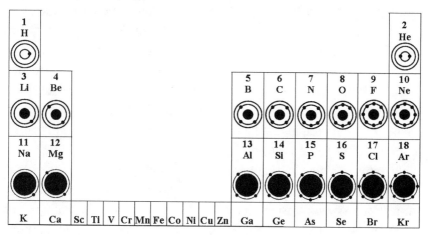

Figure 3.2. The number of electrons around a neutral atom is the same as its atomic number, which is the integer number over the symbol for the element on our periodic table. This number also represents the number of protons in the nucleus.

present discussion to the first two rows. But be assured that the more complex order is reflected by the shape of the periodic table and can be discerned by the practiced eye. For our present discussion, however, it is sufficient to know that the electrons around an atom exist in energy levels, and that with the input of energy, they can go level hopping. Where could this energy come from? From light.

Light, as we currently understand it, can be modeled as a particle or a wave. This statement may seem a bit confusing at first, but in fact there are several phenomena that can be modeled as particles or waves, including one we experience every day: sound. Sound acts like a particle when it shatters glass. When intense enough sound hits exactly the right frequency, the glass shatters as if it has been hit by a bullet. But sound acts as a wave when it bends around corners and allows us to hear conversations from separate rooms. A particle-like bullet shot though an open barn door will not bend around the corner to hit a cow.

The movement of water in the ocean can also be treated as a particle or a wave. When watching the ocean gradually wash a sandcastle out to sea, the model of choice would be a wave: an oscillating energy field that imparts a forward and a backward movement to the sand as the wave moves forward and backward. But for anyone who has ever stood in the path of a crashing wave when the surf is up, the effect on the body is more like a particle: a cannonball. Light has these two aspects, too. When the oscillating field of a light wave interacts with the electric field of the separated electron and proton of an atom, it can cause an oscillation in that field. When a light wave of the right energy comes crashing into an electron in an orbital, light can act like a particle, bumping the electron up to the next higher energy level.

Now here is where water waves and light waves diverge. When a water wave comes crashing in, it will move anything in its path: big or small; good, bad, or ugly. But when light comes crashing along, it has to be just the right energy to move an electron. In other words, the levels the electrons occupy are more like bookshelves. Books can be moved from the bottom shelf to the next higher shelf if just the right amount of energy is applied. If too much energy is applied, the book might overshoot and end up midway between two shelves. If too little energy is applied, the book might fall back into its original position. So it goes with electrons and light. Just exactly the right-sized light-energy packet, called a *photon*, is needed to cause an electron transition from one level to another.

Why can electrons be on only certain levels, like shelves of a bookcase? Why can't they be anywhere they want to be outside the nucleus? To answer these questions, we must first acknowledge that electrons, too, can be modeled as either particles or waves.

To understand why this might be, consider the waves on the circle in figure 3.3. As you can see, only one of the waves "fits" on the circle. For the other wave, the crest at the beginning of the wave coincides with the trough of the tail. When this happens with waves—when a crest meets a trough—you have a calm. The wave dies. But for the first wave, the head of the wave meets up with the tail exactly. This type of wave is a self-reinforcing wave—a *standing wave*.

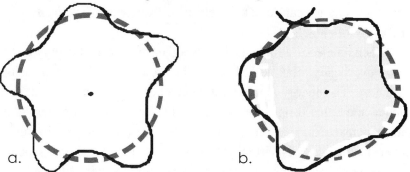

Figure 3.3. Standing waves result when waves are synchronized, when the crest of one wave meets up with, and reinforces, the crest of another. In the simplified picture, our electron wave is traveling around a two-dimensional circle. In (a) our wave is of just the right frequency to meet up with itself after traveling around the circle and thus forms a standing wave. In (b) the wave is not the right frequency to fit around the circle; thus, the wave clashes with and cancels its own effect.

A standing wave is familiar to anyone who has observed a cup of coffee on an airplane flight. On its surface, the coffee will have a pleasing formation of waves from the vibrations of the engines. But these waves are not at random locations. They form a specific pattern of concentric circles that remains impressively constant. Standing waves can also be demonstrated on terra firma with the thin-stemmed margarita glass suggested for purchase in "Crime Lab and Crime Solutions." Place an inch or so of water in the glass and then wet the tip of your index finder by dipping it in the water. Run the flat of this finger around the rim of the glass while holding the base of the glass (not the stem!) steady with the other hand. If you use just the right pressure and speed, you should elicit an excellent tone (or irritating hum, depending on your sensibilities) from the glass. It's a bit tricky to do, but once you have figured out how to get a tone, watch the surface of the water while the tone is sounding. You should observe standing waves.

Modeling electrons as waves helps to explain why electrons exist only in certain levels. Modeling light as a particle helps to visualize how light energy can knock an electron from one level to the next higher energy level.

When an electron finds itself in a higher than normal energy level, it will eventually relax back down to the ground state by the emission of energy. The energy that is emitted can be in the form of light, too, such as the colored light we saw given off by the heated materials in the demonstration that preceded this chapter. The energy difference between the levels is virtually the same whether the light is being absorbed or given off, so if a material gives off a certain color of light, it also absorbs that color. In other words, if red light contains the right energy to cause an electron to move up an energy level, red light will be absorbed by the material. When the electron relaxes back to its ground state, the material can give off the same amount of energy as light: red light.

This principle is at work in the atomic absorption spectrometer. The materials to be analyzed are dissolved in an aqueous (water) solution, and then the material is broken down into atoms using the combination of a *nebulizer* and a flame. The nebulizer acts somewhat like the atomizer of a fine perfume bottle, but *atomizer* is a misnomer because it doesn't separate materials into atoms, it just creates a fine mist. In the spectrometer, a gas flow is used to suck liquid into a nozzle, which creates an aerosol. This fine mist is drawn up into the flame, and it is in the flame that the true atomization takes place.

A lamp that emits the same frequency of light as is absorbed by the element of interest—the analyte—is positioned so that it shines on the sample in the flame. If the analyte is present, it will absorb some of the light. The instrument measures the amount of light going into the flame and compares it to the amount of light that comes out. The light will be diminished by an amount proportional to the amount of element in the flame. The procedure works especially well for metals, which is how it was used in "The Case of the Mystifying Metal."

Case Closed

Inspector Remains shook his head and looked down at the AA analysis of the metal that had been found at the site of the glassblower's fire. He read the analysis again—gold, copper, silver, and palladium—but he still didn't understand what the detective was saying.

"You agree that we ought to look to see if someone sought emergency care, but you don't think we should check with the hospitals?"

Detective Flagration nodded gravely, "That's right. I don't think we should check the hospitals. I think we should check the dentists. The AA analysis matches the composition of an alloy used for gold teeth. The glassblower must have been able to strike out before he accidentally started the fire with his torch. In the process, he may have knocked the decorative gold cap from the tooth of his assailant."

Inspector Remains nodded, now comprehending. "The glassblower got in the last blow."

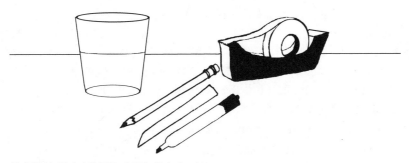

DEMONSTRATION 4
CHROMATOGRAPHY AND CRIME

Chemists employed by the police can do remark-able things with blood. They can weave it into a rope to hang a man.

Margery Allingham, *The Tiger in the Smoke*, ca. 2000

The ability to identify drugs, toxins, dyes, and other molecular materials is critical to forensic chemistry. Many times, however, the molecules must be separated one from another to be analyzed accurately. This demonstration illustrates a separations technique that is a standard in analytical labs: chromatography.

For this demonstration, you will need the green felt-tip water-soluble color marker and four water-soluble food colorings suggested for pur-chase in "Crime Lab and Crime Solutions." You will also need white coffee filters, though a white paper towel can be substituted with only slightly less satisfactory results. You will also need a tall clear glass or a plastic cup, a pencil or pen, sticky tape, and water.

Cut a strip of coffee filter (or paper towel) about a half inch (1 cm) wide and about 8 inches (20 cm) long, and trim one end into a point. Wrap the other end of the strip around the pencil and secure it with tape. Roll up the paper strip onto the pencil until the length is about 1 inch (2.5 cm) shorter than the depth of the cup (see figure 4.1). Use the felt-tip marker to draw a horizontal line onto the paper, about an inch from the tip of the point. Using the pencil as a support, dangle the paper into the cup. Being careful not to splash the paper strip, pour water down the side of the cup until the pointed tip of the paper just breaks the surface of the water. We have found that the tip doesn't have to go in more than an eighth of an inch (3 mm). Within fifteen minutes, the water should have traveled far enough up the paper strip to have come in contact with the marker ink. As the ink is carried upward by the water, it should separate into two bands—one yellow and one blue—though these bands may be overlapping. It may be difficult to see the yellow band clearly until the paper is removed and allowed to dry.

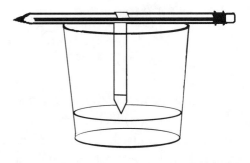

Figure 4.1. Wrap one end of the strip of coffee filter around the pencil and secure it with tape. When water is added, the strip should just touch the surface.

The dye separates into two colors because two different dyes are used to make green: yellow dye and blue dye. To prove that these two dyes make a green dye, put a drop of yellow food coloring and a drop of blue food coloring into a cup of water, swirl, and observe the color. For a more colorful demonstration, repeat the experiment, but this time take a shallow bowl or plate and make a small puddle of all the food colorings mixed together. Dip in the tip of the felt-tip pen and draw the line with all the colors. This time you should see several bands of color separating out over the length of the coffee filter.

The principle that accounts for the separation of the dyes on the coffee filter is that different molecules have different solubilities in water and different attractions for the paper. The idea of different materials having different solubilities becomes plausible when one considers the solubility of alcohol in water versus oil in water. Alcohol and water are so mutually soluble that it is very difficult to obtain alcohol with no dissolved water. Even if you went through the trouble to obtain pure alcohol; it would, once exposed to a normal atmosphere, absorb moisture from the air and become a water-alcohol mixture again. Oil, on the other hand, is virtually insoluble in water. Between these two extremes is a gradation of solubilities, the differences sometimes being so subtle that it requires a technique such as our coffee-filter setup to cause a separation.

Differences in solubilities can be traced to differences in *molecular structure*—the type and arrangement of atoms in a molecule. Both dyes in the water-soluble ink of the marker are attracted to water, but to have exactly the same attraction they would have to have identical structures, which they do not because they are different colors (see chapter 21). Both dyes are also attracted to the fiber of the coffee filter or paper towel, so it becomes a molecular tug-of-war between the moving water and the stationary fiber. Although results may vary with the brand of marker used, usually the blue dye has a slightly stronger attraction for the fiber of the filter, which means it spends less time in the water and does not move up as far as the yellow dye. The opposite is true for the yellow dye, which spends more time in the water and thus moves farther up the filter than the blue dye. Because the dyes travel different distances up the fiber, they are now physically separated. Once you are done, you can allow the filter with the separated colors to dry and save it by taping it in your notebook.

A method that separates molecular compounds based on their relative solubility in a mobile solvent is generally classified as a *chromatographic technique*. One reason the term *chromatography* was chosen was that the original technique separated botanical materials into different-colored bands. The word *chroma* means "color" in Greek. The second reason for the choice was that the Russian botanist who perfected the technique in the early 1900s was named Mikhail Tsvet—and *tsvet* is the Russian word for "color." Throughout the history of science, many advances have been named for their champions, but this may be the only instance where the name is also a pun. We believe Mikhail still smiles.

Several techniques have evolved that use different mobile phases and different supports. A technique called thin-layer chromatography (TLC) works in essentially the same way as our coffee-filter chromatography and it is used routinely by forensic chemists to separate the components of mixtures such as ink, stomach contents, and blood. Although TLC is generally too crude of an appraisal to give certifiable identification and rarely can be used for quantitative results, it has the virtue of being inexpensive and relatively quick, which makes it useful for determining if further, more expensive and more time-consuming tests are needed. In addition, TLC can be used to screen for the presence of legal, illegal, and over-the-counter drugs, which can help investigators construct reasonable scenarios surrounding events that may or may not be criminal in nature. As with other aspects of forensic investigations, sometimes chemical clues must be separated and individually investigated before the puzzle fits together, as we will see in "The Case of the Dueling Drugs."

CHAPTER 4

ISOLATING THE WITNESS: SCREENING TESTS TELL

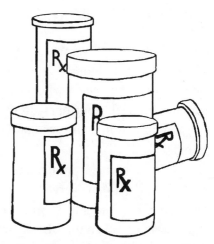

Separation penetrates the disappearing person like a pigment and steeps him in gentle radiance.

Boy George, ca. 1980

THE CASE OF THE DUELING DRUGS

D r. Y. Incision leaned forward on the podium as he addressed a civic group on the state of AIDS prevention and treatment.

"Currently," he informed the assemblage, "there are a number of treatment options, including chemotherapy 'cocktails,' which contain synergistic drugs; that is, drugs that work in concert to achieve their beneficial effect."

He was explaining how chemical mixtures could have either a cooperative or an adversarial interaction in the body when the cell phone in his left jacket pocket began to vibrate. His cell phone number was known only to the police, so Dr. Incision made his apologies and graciously but quickly closed the discussion. It was time to assume his duties as county coroner.

The house to which the coroner was directed was the scene of a death of undetermined cause. The deceased, a woman, had been discovered by a neighbor who had come to feed the woman's pet bird. The neighbor explained that the woman had been suffering from the flu, and her husband, who could not handle the bird, had been leaving the back door open so that the neighbor could enter. When the neighbor found the woman collapsed on the kitchen floor, she called 911.

After the coroner pronounced the woman dead, he questioned the neighbor, Ms. Lotta Nerve, and learned that the deceased woman's husband was a pharmacist and that the woman had suffered no medical problems other than being treated for chronic depression. The depression, the neighbor reported, was well controlled by medication, and the medication had not been changed in years.

"She had the flu, of course, and was taking the cold medicine her husband brought her," reported Ms. Nerve.

The coroner, on returning to his office, packaged the blood samples collected from the deceased for shipment to the state crime lab. Knowing that the official drug and toxicology report would take several weeks, he asked to be faxed the results of the preliminary screening on the blood sample. He signed the order for an autopsy and then settled back to arrange his notes.

At the state forensics lab, the chemist separated the liquid, serum, portion of the blood from the solid cells by centrifugation and filtration, then subjected a sample to TLC to obtain a quick, preliminary assessment of the blood. She faxed the results to the coroner.

When Dr. Incision received the report sent by the forensic chemist, he saw nothing remarkable. The chemist found an antidepressant in the victim's blood, but Dr. Incision had expected that. There was also an over-the-counter antihistamine and an analgesic, which also was not surprising given the neighbor's report that the woman had the flu. The autopsy report was not official, but a telephone conversation with the pathologist suggested that the woman appeared to have suffered a stroke, although she had no history of high blood pressure. When the coroner asked the pathologist if the flu could have been an aggravating factor, the pathologist expressed doubt but added that the symptoms of a hypertensive crisis might initially resemble the flu. As the coroner pondered this, he received a phone call from the lead detective in the case. The detective related a communication the department had received from the same neighbor: the deceased's parrot was screeching inside the house, and she was concerned that the animal was not being cared for. When asked why she did not contact the husband about the bird, she said that she had not seen him since he had been informed of his wife's death.

At this news, Dr. Incision frowned, staring at the TLC report. The chemicals in the blood had been separated by TLC, but . . .

"I believe," said Dr. Incision, "we have some work to do."

The Chemistry of the Case

Properties of materials are a consequence of their structure. When you combine two hydrogen atoms and one oxygen atom, you have H_2O, water, something you bathe in. When you combine two hydrogen atoms and *two* oxygen atoms, you have H_2O_2, hydrogen peroxide, something you would definitely not take a bath in. Structure is a consequence of *chemical bonds*, the balanced forces that bring atoms together. Although a chemical bond is the result of a complex trade-off between shifting electrical attractions and repulsions, one factor remains constant: electrons like to be in pairs. A bond is formed when electrons pair up between atoms. How they accomplish this pairing, however, can vary. Chemical bonds fall roughly into three categories: *ionic*, *metallic*, and *covalent*.

Perhaps the most straightforward type of bonding is ionic bonding. *Ions* are charged particles. Sometimes ions are formed from single atoms, such as the ion from sodium, Na^+, and the ion formed from chlorine, Cl^-. Ions can also be groups of elements that carry a charge, such as OH^-, the hydroxide ion, or the ammonium ion, NH_4^+. A negative ion acquires its charge because it has more electrons than protons, and a positive ion acquires its charge because it has fewer electrons than protons. Charge is always based on changes in the number of electrons. As was discussed in chapter 2, changing the number of protons would change the identity of the element.

Opposites attract in chemistry, and positive ions are attracted to negative ions. When they come together to form a unit, called a *formula unit*, the force that holds the ions together is called an *ionic bond*. Table salt, NaCl, is the compound created when the sodium ion and the chlorine ion form an ionic bond. NaCl is termed the formula unit of sodium chloride because this formula—one part sodium to one part chlorine—is the ratio in which sodium ions, with a +1 charge, and chlorine ions, with a –1 charge, combine.

Metallic bonds are visualized differently. In a metallic bond, outer electrons are not confined to a particular nucleus, but are shared over the billions on billions of atoms that make up a metallic sample. This sea of electrons, as metallic bonding has been described, lends special properties to metals, such as the ability to conduct heat and electricity.

Between the extremes of ionic and metallic bonding is covalent bonding. *Covalent bonds*, or molecular bonds, also involve the sharing of electrons, but form in a slightly different way. We have said that electrons in an atom arrange themselves in energy levels, and after a certain number of electrons, these energy levels are filled. Additional electrons outside the filled energy levels are called the *valence electrons*, and it is these electrons that are most engaged in covalent bonding. Valence electron clouds around two atomic nuclei can blend, like two merging bubbles, distributing electrons so that each nucleus ends up with a filled level. This sharing of electrons for mutual fulfillment is the basis of covalent bonding.

Sharing electrons makes for an exceptionally rugged arrangement. Water, H_2O, is held together by covalent bonds, and although there are other considerations that we will address shortly, when table salt is placed in water, it is the NaCl that separates, not the water.

A covalently bonded compound is called a *molecule*. A molecule is described by its *molecular formula*, which lists the elements in the compound and uses subscripts to show how many atoms of each element there are. Strictly speaking, there are no individual atoms in molecules because the "atom" ceases to exist when it blends its electron cloud with that of other nuclei. However, for ease of communication, we will use common parlance and speak of atoms in molecules. For instance, H_2O is the molecular formula for a molecule of water, and the subscript "2" tells us that there are two hydrogen atoms in one molecule of water. Oxygen has the understood subscript of "1," which means water has one oxygen atom in its molecule.

Organic molecules—molecules made primarily from carbon and hydrogen, which form the basis for organic life, in other words, us— are covalently bonded. Carbon is the basis of life because it not only can form covalent bonds but it can also form long chains of covalent bonds, a property called *concatenation*. When covalent bonds form, electrons that were located on the atoms are now spread over the entire molecule, and orbitals that were atomic orbitals become molecular orbitals.

Two electrons are shared in a covalent bond, usually one from each entity in the bond. The rationing of two electrons per bond means that there are normally many electrons left over that do not participate in bonding. These unshared electrons can't be crowded too closely together because electrons not involved in bonding repel each other. The result is that molecules have a three-dimensional structure. This structure—in addition to the identity of the atoms that went into making the molecule—makes each type of molecule unique and there- fore able to be separated one from another by techniques such as TLC. Just as a coin counter uses the unique properties of each coin type to sift coins into appropriate bins, so TLC sorts molecules based on their properties, and these properties are based on structure.

In thin-layer chromatography (TLC), the thin layer is an absorbent material (such as the cellulose fiber used to make paper) that is painted onto a flat plate. The sample is spotted onto one end of the plate, and then the end of the plate nearest the spot is lowered into a reservoir of solvent. When the solvent contacts the absorbent, it travels up the absorbent. When it reaches the sample, the solvent begins to carry material from the sample up the plate, too. Different dissolved components will travel at different rates up the plate, depending on their structure.

Visualization of the components as they separate can be tricky. Drugs are rarely as conveniently colored as Mikhail Tsvet's botanical compounds, and the quantities may be very slight. To deal with this limitation, the plate can be dipped in or sprayed with various dyes, including fluorescent dyes, visualized with UV light (as we will discuss in part III), or exposed to iodine vapor. Once they can be seen, the distance between each of the separated spots and the solvent front can be measured. The ratio of the distance the component traveled to the distance the solvent traveled can be used for preliminary compound identification.

As we mentioned, however, TLC provides only one indication of a compound's identity, and this identification must be confirmed and quantified by other, more sensitive, more exacting (and more expensive) techniques before it is of forensic value. However, by doing a preliminary screening with TLC, a more informed choice can be made for the secondary separation and identification method. For instance, some methods are better for water-soluble compounds and some are better for oil-soluble compounds. Gas-liquid chromatography, in which the material to be separated is dissolved in a liquid, vaporized, and then separated by the action of a mobile gas, is useful to separate many oil-soluble materials, but it requires that the material be heated, which might destroy certain substances. Ion-exchange chromatography, which uses an ion-exchange resin similar to that used in water softeners, can separate charged molecules such as proteins. Immobilized metal-ion affinity chromatography is, as the name implies, a technique based on the relative attraction of the target molecules to stationary metal ions and is useful for separating charged materials.

When you performed the demonstration preceding this chapter, you probably noticed that the blue and yellow bands, while visible, were overlapping and rather indistinct. This possible limitation of TLC led to the development of a powerful chromatographic technique called high-performance liquid chromatography (HPLC). In this technique, liquid is forced over a solid absorbent phase so that the solvent front moves forward quickly and has less time to spread out. Because the liquid is forced at high pressure over the solid, the technique has also been referred to as high-pressure liquid chromatography.

However, in "The Case of the Dueling Drugs," before the chemist started the exacting procedure for certifiable results with more elaborate techniques, she acted on Dr. Incision's request to fax the preliminary TLC results, and they proved interesting.

Case Closed

"What do I need to do?" asked the detective.

"I think we better start looking for the husband," the coroner told the detective. "When we find him, I think we need to ask him some questions."

The coroner grabbed a book off his shelf, *Physicians' Desk Reference*, and put his phone on speaker. He turned to the information on the antidepressant and soon found what he suspected.

"Those medicines were separated by TLC, but in the bloodstream they were together. There is a known, potentially lethal interaction of the antidepressant and the cold medicine and the symptoms are hypertensive crisis."

The detective interrupted. "But you said that she had been taking the antidepressants for a long time. She must have known about adverse interactions and would have avoided them—"

"Unless a trusted professional advised her otherwise," answered Dr. Incision. "Such as a pharmacist. Such as her husband."

The coroner paused, then added, "Check how much insurance is involved—and see if you can get someone to take care of the bird. I don't think the husband is coming home soon."

DEMONSTRATION 5
A CASE OF FRICTION

Change means movement. Movement means friction. Only in the frictionless vacuum of a nonexistent abstract world can movement or change occur without that abrasive friction of conflict.

Saul Alinsky, ca. 1950[1]

Atoms coalesce into molecules, and molecules coalesce into materials. In the last chapter we discussed the bonds that join atoms into molecules, and here we will discuss the intermolecular forces that bind molecules into materials. These intermolecular forces consist of intermolecular attractions, which bring molecules together, and intermolecular repulsion, which keeps materials from coming too close. The following is a demonstration of the importance of these forces in keeping things afloat.

Obtain two 2-inch or 3-inch (5- or 7-centimeter) square pieces of aluminum foil and fold up the edges to make the sides of the foil look like boats. The edges need to be one-quarter inch to one-half inch up from the bottom of the boat, and the bottom needs to be as flat as possible. When the boats are finished, they should be about the size of inverted bottle caps. Now put on your safety glasses.

Obtain two shallow bowls or deep saucers and fill one with water and one with isopropyl alcohol (rubbing alcohol). Label each bowl as "water" or "isopropyl alcohol" (though the odor should give the alcohol away). Now take the boats and make several holes in the flat bottoms with a pencil. Push into the bottom of each boat from the outside so that the pushed-in foil is inside the boat. The holes can be as large as the pencil but do not have to be.

Reflatten each boat bottom using your fingers so that it once again resembles a bottle cap. Take one of the boats and place it in the water sample, noting what happens. Push it around in the water with a pencil or your finger to convince yourself that it is floating even though there are holes in the bottom. The intermolecular forces that form in a collection of water molecules are strong enough to form a "skin" over the surface that prevents water from running through the holes.

Now take that boat out of the water, place it on a paper towel to dry it slightly, and place it in the alcohol bowl. The boat should sink fairly quickly. The intermolecular forces that form in the rubbing alcohol are not nearly as advantageous as those in plain water and so less "skin" forms over the alcohol surface. The weight of the boat is able to force alcohol up through the holes and sink the boat.

The second boat can be placed directly in the alcohol as a control. Watching this boat sink, too, tells us that water on the first boat did not influence its behavior in alcohol.

Now try this: tear a small square of aluminum foil and lay it on a countertop. Smooth it out so that it is flat and has very few creases. Place a drop of water on the foil and observe how the water responds. For reasons we will outline below in "The Chemistry of the Case," the foil provides very little attraction for the water molecules. Because the water molecules are much more attracted to each other through their very strong intermolecular forces, they pull themselves inward, into a sphere. A sphere is the most stable form for the water drop because a sphere has a smaller amount of surface area than other regular geometrical forms. By forming a sphere, the water molecules are in more contact with each other and in less contact with air or aluminum foil. Only the bottom of the bead of water is in contact with the foil.

Place a few drops of water on a clean glass surface and observe how the water responds in this case. Again the water draws into itself, but to a noticeably lesser extent. The glass has a much stronger attraction for the molecules of water than the foil did, so there is less beading up of the water drop. As we will see in the following chapter, this behavior is a result of a difference in intermolecular forces. Intermolecular forces will also play a role in "The Case of the Sticky Situation."

CHAPTER 5

FATAL ATTRACTION: INTERMOLECULAR FORCES MAKE THE CHARGES STICK

> *Terror is as much a part of the concept of truth as runniness is of the concept of jam. We wouldn't like jam if it didn't, by its very nature, ooze. We wouldn't like truth if it wasn't sticky, if, from time to time, it didn't ooze blood.*
>
> Jean Baudrillard, *Cool Memories*, 1987

THE CASE OF THE STICKY SITUATION

Officer I. C. Yoo and Officer Candice B. Real arrived on the scene of a reported hit-and-run in the Nearmiss subdivision. A man in shorts was sitting on a curb with a bloody paper towel pressed to his leg. He lifted the towel away briefly so they could see that the wound was a nasty abrasion, but not a critical injury.

"I was crossing the street when this car came around the corner way too fast and hit me."

Officer Yoo started taking notes. "Did you go up over the hood?"

"No. I saw him coming out of the corner of my eye just about when he saw me. He hit his brakes but skidded into me anyway. I was able to put out my hands and push off his bumper." The man re-created the gesture with his hands. Officer Yoo looked down and noted skid marks on the pavement.

He lifted the towel again and exposed the foot-long patch of road rash centered on his knee. "When I put my hands on the bumper, it spun me around and I went sliding on my knee."

"Can you identify the car?"

"I think it was a white Toyota, but I'm not sure. He only stopped for a second—guess he wanted to see if he'd killed me or if he should back up and try again. I'm pretty sure the first letter on the license plate was a Z, but my glasses got knocked off when I went down."

After exchanging a look with Officer Yoo, Officer Real returned to the patrol car to radio in a message for all patrol cars to be on the lookout for a white car with a Z on the plate. She then checked to see if there were any cars matching that description registered to residents in the area. She requested an evidence technician be dispatched to photograph the skid marks and rejoined Officer Yoo at the curb to wait for EMS and the evidence technician. After they arrived, Yoo and Real left to check out the nearest address for a possible suspected car.

Officer Real scanned the road as they drove to the first location. "Isn't this kind of pointless? Even if the car is parked right out front, how are we going to prove it's the right car?"

Officer Yoo shrugged. "The vic did push off the bumper, so there might be some prints. There was a lot of rubber lost from those tires when the car skidded, and a tire mark where the car stopped."

Officer Real frowned. "Can we have a car impounded and tested for prints just because it's white and has a license plate starting with the letter Z?"

"If we find a car matching the description, we'll check out who-ever's in possession and look to see if there is probable cause."

They pulled up to the first house to see a white Toyota in the driveway, sparkling in the sun. They knocked, and a man in khakis opened the door.

"Is that your car?" Officer Yoo asked, pointing at the Toyota in the driveway.

"Yeah. What about it?"

"Were you driving it about a hour ago in the Nearmiss residential area?"

"No. I had my car at the car wash. What's the matter?"

Officer Real walked over to the car, noted the water in the windshield-wiper well, and nodded to her partner to confirm that the car appeared to have been recently washed. Officer Yoo walked over to the car, dipped his finger in the fresh wash water, and flicked a drop of water on the roof. He watched it spread with the metal's curve.

Real gave her shoulders a resigned shrug. "Even if this is the car," she said quietly to Yoo, "we're not going to find prints after it's been through the car wash."

Officer Yoo regarded the car. "Maybe not. But I think we need to ask more questions."

Yoo turned to the man in the doorway. "You want to tell me why you're lying?"

The Chemistry of the Case

Electrical attractions between negative electrons and positive nuclei hold atoms together. Electrical interactions also account for chemical bonds. Molecules, too, are held together in the condensed phases of material—which, of course, include us—by electrical attractions called, appropriately enough, *intermolecular attractions*. These attractions have their origin in the electrostatic interaction of like and unlike charges and the flexibility of the electron clouds.

While it is artistically convenient to draw atomic orbitals as perfect, rigid spheres, under many circumstances, orbitals behave more like shape-shifting clouds than billiard balls. Electrons, as it turns out, can never be modeled as standing still, but must always be considered in motion. As such, electrons can respond to changes in their electrical environment. We have already mentioned one such response when we noted that electrons in individual atomic orbitals might coalesce into molecular orbitals, much in the manner that two individual bubbles might coalesce to form a bigger bubble. In addition, just as a bubble responding to a breeze can be blown into different shapes, so the density of electrons can shift in a molecule in response to internal—and external—electric fields.

One internal field that helps determine shape is the repulsive field between identically charged electrons. As may be recalled from chapter 3, the number of electrons required to fill the energy levels around an atom follows the pattern 2, 8, 18 . . . even numbers. These numbers are even because electrons like to pair up. Once paired, however, they push all other electrons away. The result is a three-dimensional arrangement that maximizes the distance between any two electron pairs.

In water, H_2O, the repulsion between electron pairs lead to a V-shaped molecule in which the oxygen is at the point of the V and the hydrogens are at the tips. The V shape of water is a decidedly nonspherical arrangement of electrons, which creates an internal electrical field. Oxygen has a greater attraction for the electrons of the molecule than does hydrogen because, among other factors, oxygen has a greater number of protons. Hydrogen, with its one proton and one electron, would be just as happy to give this electron away, too, so it has a lower affinity for electrons. The result of this unequal sharing is that one end of water is more negative than the other, a condition called a *dipole*.

A molecular dipole can be compared to a magnet with a north and a south pole because the dipole has one end that is more electrically positive and one end that is more electrically negative. The attraction of two water molecules for each other through this *dipole-dipole attraction* is an intermolecular force that helps water to condense. Without intermolecular attractions, water and all other materials would exist in the gas phase only, and we wouldn't be here to talk about it.

Water condenses quite readily because of the dipole established by its V shape, but molecules without a dipole can condense, too. Condensed liquid nitrogen, N_2, cannot have a permanent electrical dipole because there can be no argument over electrons between two identical atoms. However, as we said, molecular orbitals are more like clouds than billiard balls so there can be momentary fluctuations in the distributions of electrons, and these fluctuations can cause fluctuations in the distribution of electrons in a neighboring molecule. The resulting temporary dipole-dipole attraction, called a *dispersion force*, can cause even helium to condense, if it is cooled to an ultralow temperature.

Water, however, requires no extremes of temperature to condense. Water's special ability to condense is due, in part, to its internal dipole, but also to its ability to engage in a special, strong intermolecular attraction known as *hydrogen bonding*. Hydrogen bonding in water is the attraction of the hydrogen end of one molecule for the oxygen end of another.

Other molecules are also able to hydrogen bond, but the fact that water is able to hydrogen bond to itself through both arms of its V structure imparts some rather unique properties to water. For one, it explains why water expands when it freezes, even causing rock to crumble into soil. Water expands because it needs to align each of its hydrogens with an oxygen, and vice versa. This alignment results in crystallized water taking up more space than the liquid, just as a pile of building blocks will take up more space when they are formed into a scaffold.

Hydrogen bonds also contribute to the ability of water to dissolve many other compounds. Sodium chloride, table salt, for instance, is composed of positively charged sodium ions and negatively charged chlorine ions. The positive end of water's dipole will be attracted to the negative chloride ion and the negative end of water's dipole will be attracted to the positive sodium ion. As a result, water molecules insinuate themselves between the ions, and the hydrogen bonds between the water molecules build a solvent cage around the ions, keeping them apart and thus dissolved.

Intermolecular attractions have other important consequences, too. In chapter 1, we noted the difficulty in measuring liquids precisely because of the meniscus: the curvature of a liquid in its container. We said that the downward curvature of water in a measuring cup is caused by the attraction of the water for the sides of the cup. But a meniscus can also be curved upward, too, like the curvature of mercury in a thermometer. Whether the meniscus curves up or down is determined by the trade-off between the attractions of the molecules of the liquid for each other—*cohesion*—and the attraction of the molecules of the liquid for the container—*adhesion*.

Intermolecular forces also explain why sugar dissolves in water and not in oil, and why butter dissolves in oil but not in water. Water-soluble molecules are *polar*; that is, they have a dipole in their structures that can be attracted to the dipole of water. Oil-soluble materials are *nonpolar*; that is, they do not have dipole attractions for water. Water tends to stick to itself and squeeze oily molecules out, which is the origin of the proverbial observation that "oil and water don't mix."

The region where water and oil meet is called an interface, and at an interface, *surface tension* may be observed. Surface tension is the resistance of a liquid to spreading out on a foreign surface when the liquid molecules would rather keep to themselves. Because a sphere is a structure that minimizes surface area, a liquid in this situation might bead up to minimize surface tension. In demonstration 5, the water beaded up on the foil because the foil is not polar. However, water spreads out on glass because glass is mainly silicon dioxide, SiO_2, which is a polar material and attracts water molecules. The final shape of a puddle of water on glass is determined by the balance between the water-water attraction and the water-glass attraction.

Besides throwing a complicating factor into our measurements and squeezing out oils, intermolecular forces drive other vital processes. The *capillary action* that helps lift water and nutrients against gravity in plants (and helped resolve "The Case of the Significant Other") is the result of intermolecular attractions. The paper towel that soaked up the blood from the road rash in "The Case of the

Sticky Situation" did so because of intermolecular attractions. The friction that caused the road rash and the friction that caused the skid marks were, in part, a result of intermolecular attractions.

Friction has two components. When two materials are rubbed together, microscopic ridges may impede motion, but intermolecular attractions play a part, too. That is why there can never be a truly frictionless surface. If the microscopic bumps and snags are smoothed, then there is just more surface contact and more opportunity for intermolecular attractions. So intermolecular attractions were important to road rash, skid marks, and bloody rags in "The Case of the Sticky Situation"—and it played one more role, too.

Case Closed

"Lying! What do you mean lying?" the man in the doorway demanded.

Yoo continued calmly. "You washed your car, but you didn't wash it in the car wash."

Officer Yoo's confrontational words had the desired effect. The man dropped his hands to his sides and sat down on his front steps.

"Look, I panicked. I've got DUIs. The guy wasn't hurt too bad, so I left." He dropped his head into his hands.

At Officer Real's quizzical look, Officer I. C. Yoo shrugged. "Water beads up on a clean car. The water I flicked up on the roof spread like grease on a hot griddle. He may have hosed down the sides, but he forgot that a car wash cleans the top, too. This guy's small mistake just turned into a big one."

"Yeah," sighed Officer Real. "When his life hit the skids, he should have stopped in his tracks."

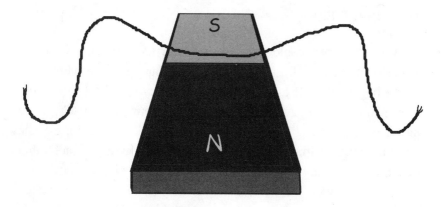

DEMONSTRATION 6
THE CURRENT CASE

Conscience is our magnetic compass; reason our chart.

Joseph Cook, ca. 1900

In this demonstration, we illustrate the relationship between an electric field and a magnetic field, which is germane to our discussion of mass spectrometry. Mass spectrometry is a fairly well-known forensic analytical technique. In mass spectrometry, an electric current formed by a stream of ions is bent in a magnetic field. In this demonstration, we will see a current-carrying wire bent in a magnetic field, an observation that relies on the same interaction between an electric and a magnetic field. *We will be working with low-voltage, low-current standard batteries, so there will be little danger of electric shock, but when electrons run through wires they create heat, so there is a possibility of batteries, wires—and fingers—getting hot enough to cause a painful burn or ignite flammable material. Please exercise reasonable caution and connect the battery for only the two to three seconds required to observe the effect.* As always, wear your protective safety glasses. We do not, however, recommend examination gloves for this experiment. They are not necessary and they could interfere with our temperature sensor—our fingers—and keep us from knowing if things are getting too hot.

To begin, clip off a 2-foot (60-centimeter) length of thin copper wire such as the 30-gauge wire suggested for purchase in "Crime Lab and Crime Solutions." Other gauges of wire will work, as long as they aren't too stiff. Strip the ends; that is, remove about a half inch (about 1 centimeter) of any insulating material from the wire.

Form a U with the wire, approximately 2 inches (5 centimeters) high, and tape the ends to a table so that the U stands up, such as we've shown in the illustration at the beginning of this demonstration. Use just enough tape to keep the U from falling over. Don't cover the ends completely with tape; leave a little of the ends of the wire exposed. Place a bar magnet, the stronger the better, on the countertop and position the magnet so that the south end is under the wire. (If your magnet is not marked north and south, don't worry. If you don't get the expected response, you can turn the magnet around.) Copper, the usual material of thin connector wire, is not a magnetic metal, and therefore the placement of the magnet should have no effect on the wire. Tip the U of wire ever so slightly toward the south end (the far end) of the magnet.

Locate the 9-volt battery and alligator clips suggested for purchase in "Crime Lab and Crime Solutions." Attach an alligator clip to each end of the wire assembly. Stand so that the north end of the magnet (the near end) is closest to you. Clip the loose end of the right-hand alligator clip to the negative lead of the 9-volt battery. At this point, do not connect the other alligator clip to the battery because as soon as you do, current will start flowing and things will heat up.

Take the other unattached alligator clip and simply touch the positive battery lead for a second. When you touch the battery, current should flow through the wire and the wire should bend toward the magnet. If you do not see the wire bend toward the magnet, you should see it push away slightly. If this is the case, reverse the magnet and try again. If you still see no response, try bending the wire closer to the magnet.

Once you have observed the wire deflecting toward the magnet, try switching the battery leads around and see what happens. Try turning the magnet around. In one configuration, the wire should bend toward the north and be repelled from the south; in the other configuration, the opposite should be true.

An electric current is a stream of negatively charged electrons. As these negatively charged electrons flow through the wire, they create a magnetic field. By switching the direction of current flow by swapping battery leads, the magnetic fields switch poles, so the interaction you just observed should have reversed.

You can also demonstrate the relationship between electricity and magnetism by using a nail and another length of wire. Wrap the wire around the nail in a series of tight coils and then use alligator clips to attach one loose end of the wire to the battery. When the other end of the wire is attached via an alligator clip, the nail becomes an electromagnet that will pick up paper clips. The magnet can be switched on and off by connecting and disconnecting the battery.

You may also find it amusing to watch the interaction of a magnetic field with a stream of electrons by using a magnet and an old, unwanted TV. We suggest an old TV for two reasons: first, *this experiment can be expensive if the TV is ruined in the process*, and second, *this experiment will not work on a plasma screen TV*.

In an old, nonplasma screen TV, the screen is lit by a stream of electrons striking a material called a phosphor. The electrons are directed to the screen by a magnetic field controlled by electricity. If you bring a magnet up to the screen, you can deflect the electron beam along alternate paths, which can produce some interesting and pretty patterns on the screen. If the screen is exposed to the magnet for too long, the effect may persist for a day or two, but it should eventually clear up. Every time we have performed this demonstration, the TV has eventually recovered, but we have not tried every TV, which is why we suggested using an old, unwanted TV.

The principle illustrated with the demonstrations above is the interaction of a magnetic field with a moving electric field, a phenomenon exploited by mass spectrometry—the forensic technique central to "The Case of the Validating Vacuum."

CHAPTER 6

VOLATILE SITUATION: MASS, GAS, AND CHEMICAL FINGERPRINTS

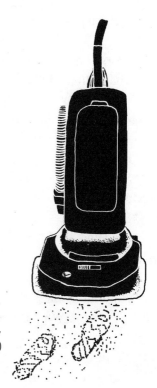

Whenever man commits a crime heaven finds a witness.

Edward G. Bulwer-Lytton, ca. 1850

THE CASE OF THE VALIDATING VACUUM

P arole Officer Mary Wanna spoke in a no-nonsense monotone, "As a condition of your parole you agreed to warrantless searches of any premises under your control at any time."

The man had been standing with the door partly open and arguing half-heartedly that he wasn't dressed, but finally shrugged and opened the door.

Officer Wanna's visit had been prompted by rumors of drug sales from this residence, so she was mildly surprised at the relative ease of the parolee's acquiescence.

Two of the patrol officers in her search team stood beside her; another had gone around to the back to prevent a hasty retreat on the part of the residents.

"Okay. Let's go. We have the resident's cooperation, so let's try not to tear things up too badly—but be thorough."

After twenty minutes, nothing had been discovered, so Officer Wanna called for the team to reconnoiter in the kitchen. She checked off a list on her notepad.

"Bedroom?"

"Searched under the bed, under the mattress, and in the underwear drawer."

"Bathroom?"

"Checked the cabinets and fixed a running toilet while I was looking in the tank."

"Kitchen?"

"Nothing in the stove, nothing in the dishwasher, and nothing in the refrigerator. What do these people eat?"

"Closets?"

"Nothing—just a vacuum."

"Did you check *in* the vacuum?"

"Yep. Completely empty."

Wanna leaned back against the counter, looking pleased. "Okay. Now I know where to look."

The Chemistry of the Case

Without intermolecular forces, as we noted earlier, everything would be in the gas phase. Now we can say that even with intermolecular forces, some things are still in the gas phase and this gas phase is essential to forensic chemistry—and to life. We walk in, talk in, and suck in sustenance from a sea of gases every day: a gas-phase soup of oxygen, nitrogen, and argon. Without it, we'd be living in a vacuum—and we wouldn't live too long.

What is a gas? The primary characteristic of a gas is mobility. All atomic-sized particles are in constant motion, but gas particles are in more motion than most. Molecules in the air, on a normal day on Earth, are zipping around at a rate of 500 meters per second, which translates to about 1,000 miles per hour. The reason we aren't bowled over by this sandstorm of air is that not all air particles are moving in the same direction at the same time.

Intermolecular attractions don't disappear when a material becomes a gas, but at these speeds they become less important. Think of catching a fast ball versus a slow ball. The glove is the same, but if the ball is moving too fast, it may not be stoppable. Because of the souped-up activity on the part of gas-phase molecules, they can expand and fill the volume of anything that tries to contain them. Solids and liquids are constrained to the bottom of the bowl.

The gas phase makes one of the classic forensic techniques possible. The technique, gas chromatography with mass spectrometry, or *GC mass spec* for short, has a place in forensic chemistry that is right up there with examining fingerprints. It also shares another trait with fingerprinting: identification is based on characteristic patterns—molecular fingerprints, if you will.

The gas chromatograph end of GC mass spec operates on similar principles as the thin-layer chromatography (TLC) described in chapter 4, but in gas chromatography the separation takes place in the gas phase rather than in the liquid phase. In gas chromatography, separation is accomplished by injecting a small amount of sample into a heating chamber exposed to a moving carrier gas. This gas blows over a viscous liquid (on a solid support) in a thin tube called the *column*. The action of the moving gas can be compared to that of a leaf blower: the lighter leaves are carried farther forward in the moving air stream and are separated from the heavier debris. In a gas chromatograph, the moving gas separates materials by carrying them at different rates along the column. The rate of movement on the column depends on the attractions of the mixture's components for the stationary phase—not gravity as it is for the leaves—but the image provides a fair analogy.

An advantage to separating a mixture with GC is that the components move out of the column in a stream of gas. This gas can be conveniently blown into a detector in which the molecular identity is established. In this manner, both operations, separation and identification, can be carried out with one setup. The detector of choice after separation by GC is a *mass spectrometer*: an instrument that sorts particles based on their mass and their charge.

A molecule has a characteristic mass based on the specific mass of the atoms that compose it. In our periodic table (see appendix), the mass for an element is the decimal number below the symbol for the element. These numbers are based on a weighted average of the masses of each element's isotopes and measured in *atomic mass units*, or *amu* for short. For instance, hydrogen, H, has a mass of 1.01 amu, and oxygen has a mass of 16.00 amu. If the formula for a compound is known, then the mass can be calculated by adding up the mass of its parts. For instance, water, with the formula H_2O, has a mass of 1.01 amu + 1.01 amu + 16.00 amu, or 18.02 amu.

Unfortunately, molecules cannot be identified on the basis of mass alone. Consider carbon dioxide and propane. These are very different materials—propane is a fuel for fires; carbon dioxide puts fires out— yet their masses are very close. The mass of carbon dioxide, CO_2, built from a carbon atom with 12.01 amu and two oxygen atoms with 16.00 amu each, has a mass of 44.01 amu. If you add up the masses of the atoms that go into propane, C_3H_8, you will arrive at 44.11 amu, which could be too small of a difference to be detected by weighing.

Fortunately, methods have been devised for finding the mass of molecules that are based on their behavior in a magnetic field rather than a gravitation field. As we saw in the demonstrations at the beginning of this chapter, magnetic fields and moving electric fields interact. The moving electrons curved toward or away from the magnet, depending on the direction of the current.

To take advantage of this curvature, the materials coming off the GC column are ionized, usually in a flame, then subjected to a magnetic field in the mass spectrometer. The magnetic field acts on the moving charged particles and causes them to curve. The amount of curvature depends on mass and charge, so the mass spectrometer effectively sorts the particles into bins, according to their mass-to-charge ratio.

This mass sorting can be understood by considering the behavior of a soccer ball and a bowling ball in a gravitational field. If each ball is launched horizontally, say, fired from a cannon with an identical impetus, you would expect them both to curve down toward the ground. We know from Galileo's famous experiment that they would land at the same time (in the absence of air resistance), but you would expect the bowling ball to be closer to the cannon when it hit the ground. If there were a row of bins in the target area, then the more massive bowling ball would land in the closer bin and the soccer ball would land in the farther bin. Essentially, that's how magnets are used to sort mass in a mass spectrometer. The charged particles curve in an applied magnetic field, and the amount of curvature depends on the mass and the charge of the particle.

Of course, sorting bowling balls and soccer balls isn't much of a trick, but objects of more similar mass, such as soccer balls and basketballs, could be sorted by our cannon mass spec, too. The advantage of the curved path is that small differences in mass are magnified. In fact, the separation of isotopes that identified the drug batches in chapter 2 was accomplished by mass spectrometry, and the mass difference between isotopes can be as little as the mass of one or two neutrons.

There are, however, complications. In the ionization process, more than one electron can be knocked off, which creates an ion with a charge greater than +1. Because the response to the magnetic field is due to the charge on the moving particle, a greater charge results in a greater response, and the amount of curvature is not only dictated by mass but also by the additional charge. To successfully ionize the majority of the material passing through, the ionization techniques can be sufficiently brutal to break up the material into several pieces as well as ionize it. Fortunately, the size and number of pieces, *fragments*, is very predictable and also characteristic of the compound. Therefore a computer is routinely linked to the detector, and the output is compared to a library of compounds for identification—just as a human fingerprint might be compared with those in a database maintained by the FBI.

Other ionizing methods include passing the material through an electron beam or introducing the material to a *plasma*, commonly called the fourth state of matter (after gas, solid, and liquid). A plasma is a gas that has been heated to such a high temperature that collisions between the gas particles are sufficient to tear off electrons and form a mélange of charged particles. When the sample enters the hot plasma (usually formed from argon), it, too, becomes ionized and can be mass analyzed by the magnetic field. Ionization by another ionic particle is sometimes used because it is a gentler ionization and thus produces less fragmentation.

Other detectors have been employed for mass sorting. A time-of-flight mass spectrometer gives a little voltage kick to the ions and then sorts them according to kinetic energy at the detector. Kinetic energy depends on mass, as can be intuitively understood by considering a bowling ball versus a Ping-Pong ball with the same velocity. Getting hit by a Ping-Pong ball traveling 3 feet per second would most likely seem inconsequential, but if you saw a bowling ball heading toward you at the same rate, you would take pains to get out of the way. Kinetic energy can be measured by the amount of voltage needed to stop the charged particle, called the *stopping voltage*: the greater the kinetic energy, the greater the stopping voltage.

New methods have also been developed for sampling. In traditional GC mass spec, the sample is injected into the gas stream as a liquid. This method, however, limits the materials that can be analyzed to those that can be put into solution form. As we will discuss later, a newer technique called *laser ablation* allows even the surfaces of solids to be vaporized and fed into the stream for separation. But there are a few reality checks that need to be made at this point. As an analytical technique, GC mass spec is very good, but it's no miracle. There is a mistaken notion that any material can be fed in one end and the detailed analysis comes out the other. This is far from the truth. Sometimes the best that can be hoped for is a list of elements that the materials contain, but no information on how they were bonded together. Even if some bonds are left intact, spectral lines may overlap or interfere. Sometimes the interpretation of the mass spec takes as much detective work as the solution of the crime.

But just as those intent on misdeeds rarely take a holiday, neither do those who would apprehend them. Mass spec techniques are continually being refined, and improvements are suggested all the time. For instance, an approach called tandem mass spec has been developed in which a front-end mass spec selectively passes on only certain materials to a second mass spec to be analyzed. The effect is to clear away interfering materials and obtain a more reliable material identity. Tandem mass specs have been known to sift through and find substances of interest in rather exotic environs, such as the residue in a vacuum bag[1]—which was what Parole Officer Mary Wanna hoped for in "The Case of the Validating Vacuum."

Case Closed

Leaving one officer inside to make certain nothing further was disturbed in the house, Parole Officer Mary Wanna went outside with the second officer and around to the back of the house.

"Good thing it's not trash day," she noted, as she popped the lid off a trash can sitting to the rear of the house.

"Good thing they keep house," said the officer.

Inside the trash can was a used vacuum bag, stuffed to the hilt with vacuumed lint and debris.

"I believe," said Officer Wanna, "this case is in the bag."

It was.

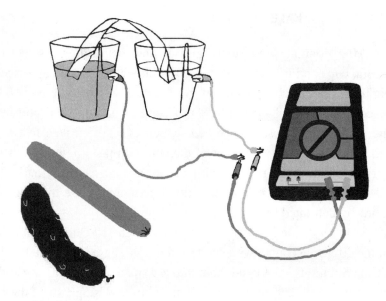

DEMONSTRATION 7
PLACE OF CONFINEMENT

The dosage makes it either a poison or a remedy.

Paracelsus, ca. 1600

The chemical reactions that determine the course of our life—and death—take place in the liquid environs of our bodies, and many forensic chemistry analyses are carried out in solution, too. An essential descriptor of any solution is *concentration*: the amount of dissolved substance in a given volume of solution. A key to understanding many chemical and physical processes of solutions is to recognize the natural tendency of these systems to move toward a state of uniform concentration. Two watery solutions poured together will tend to form an even mixture rather than segregated pools. As we will see in the following demonstration, the potential for chemical systems to equalize their concentrations can even be converted to an electrical potential, otherwise known as a *voltage*.

After donning your safety glasses and exam gloves, select two plastic cups and fill each half full with tap water. In one cup place an eighth teaspoon (about 1 milliliter) of copper sulfate, and in the other place a teaspoonful (5 milliliters) of copper sulfate. Swirl both until the crystals are mostly dissolved, which can take fifteen to twenty minutes. Notice how the color of the cup with just a few crystals is a very pale blue while the cup with a lot of crystals is a very dark blue. Color is an indicator of concentration: the more intense the color, the more concentrated the solution.

Strip all of the insulation from two 4-inch (10-centimeter) pieces of the 20-gauge copper wire suggested for purchase in "Crime Lab and Crime Solutions" and bend them into a J shape. Insert the long end of one J into each cup of copper sulfate solution. Using two of the alligator clips suggested for purchase in "Crime Lab and Crime Solutions," hook the short exposed end of each J to your voltmeter as shown in the illustration at the beginning of this demonstration. Position the range selector to a voltage range around 2 volts, and the voltmeter should read 0 volts. Later, you may have to adjust the dial to get the reading on scale.

The copper ion, Cu^{2+}, is present in both cups, as is copper metal, Cu. Copper metal can lose two electrons to become copper ion

$$Cu \rightarrow Cu^{2+} + 2e^-$$

and copper ion can gain two electrons to become copper metal

$$Cu^{2+} + 2e^- \rightarrow Cu$$

Given the chance, these two concentrations will try to equalize, somewhat like a drop of red dye will attempt to spread itself equally through a glass of water. So, in the cup that has more copper ion—the cup with the deeper blue color—the second reaction is more likely to take place, $Cu^{2+} + 2e^- \rightarrow Cu$. In the cup that has less copper ion—the cup with the pale blue solution—the first reaction is more likely to take place, $Cu \rightarrow Cu^{2+} + 2e^-$. However, in an isolated solution, any new copper ion that forms would immediately re-form the metal because of the attraction of the negative electrons for the positive ion. If, on the other hand, the electrons have some place to go and some reason to want to go there, the copper may stay ionized.

The darker solution has copper ion ready to become copper metal. The pale solution, the less concentrated solution, has copper metal willing to become copper ion. When the two solutions are connected through the voltmeter, the electrons have someplace to go: the wire of the voltmeter can facilitate the transfer of electrons.

$$Cu \rightarrow Cu^{2+} + 2e^- \rightarrow \text{electrons through wire} \rightarrow Cu^{2+} + 2e^- \rightarrow Cu$$

There is, however, a catch. The source of copper ion in solution is copper sulfate, $CuSO_4$, which dissociates to Cu^{2+} and SO_4^{2-} in solution. As such, the solution remains electrically neutral: for every $+2$ charge from Cu^{2+} there is a -2 charge from SO_4^{2-}. But if copper were to form copper ions in one solution and use up copper ions to form metal in the other, then one cup might develop a net positive charge while the other developed a net negative charge. If this were the case, they should be attracted to each other and perhaps slide across the counter and collide—a phenomenon not witnessed. As soon as a net positive or net negative charge develops, the reaction stops. So for the reaction to proceed, there has to be a way to ensure electrical neutrality, which can be accomplished by a connecting device called a *salt bridge*. A salt bridge is a salt solution held in some sort of matrix that makes it difficult for the ions to flow out too rapidly. The function of a salt bridge is to replace the charge removed from solution by reaction, but to do so slowly, without swamping the solution.

For instance, a pickle makes a good salt bridge because a pickle is permeated with a salt solution, but because of the cellular makeup of the cucumber structure, the salt solution doesn't flow. A hot dog or a sausage can be used for a salt bridge, too. Soaking a coffee filter in saltwater will also create a usable salt bridge, so we will start there.

To make your salt bridge, pour several tablespoons of table salt, NaCl, into a half cup of tap water and swirl to dissolve the salt. The NaCl will dissociate in water to Na^+ and Cl^-. Take a coffee filter, twist it into a cigar shape, and lay it in the salt solution. After a minute, remove the coffee filter, wring out any excess saltwater, and place one end of the filter into one cup and the other end of the filter in the other cup, as shown in the illustration at the beginning of this demonstration. The coffee filter salt bridge provides an ion source for the copper reaction, replacing used up positively charged copper ions with positively charged sodium ions and providing negative chloride ions to counterbalance newly produced Cu^{2+} ions.

Once you have draped the salt bridge from cup to cup, you should be able to measure a small voltage on the voltmeter. Because the only difference between the two cups is the concentration of copper ion, we can attribute the voltage produced to the concentration difference.

To convince yourself the voltage is produced by a concentration difference, pour about half of the solution from the concentrated cup into a waste receptacle and refill the cup to the original level with plain tap water. Measure the voltage again. It should be significantly less. You should be able to repeat this last step at least once more—pouring about half of the more concentrated solution into the waste receptacle and refilling it to the original level with tap water—and again observe a decrease in voltage. As the solution concentrations in the two cups approach the same value, the voltage should go to zero, which confirms that a difference in concentrations of the copper ion is causing the voltage.

Now, just for fun, start over with the original concentrations and replace your salt bridge with a pickle slice or a hot dog. These food items work as salt bridges as well. Another extension of this demonstration is to watch the voltage over time. You should eventually see the voltage slowly decrease because the salt bridge can only supply ions to the solutions for a limited time.

When you are done, dispose of the copper solutions in a commode. Be sure to throw out the emptied cups so they cannot be accidentally used as drinking glasses. Throw out the pickle and the hot dog, too.

The apparatus we built supplied a voltage, so we essentially built an electrical cell, or what is usually, though somewhat inaccurately, called a battery (a true battery is a group of connected cells). The last observation, that our cell voltage eventually diminishes, reminds us that batteries eventually run down. In this particular cell, called a *concentration cell* because the voltage is generated by a concentration difference, the voltage goes to zero as the concentrations approach an equal value in the two cups. Considerations of concentration are also crucial in "A Case of Strong Medicine."

CHAPTER 7

Too Much of a Good Thing: Establishing Concentration Levels

Cold M

Disease generally begins that equality which death completes.

Samuel Johnson, ca. 1750

A Case of Strong Medicine

Detective Buck Stopsheir sat down heavily on the couch.

"Hard day?" His wife of two months, pharmacist Ivy Prophen, joined him on the couch.

"Yep, sure was. Got the coroner's preliminary report on that poor woman found dead in her apartment."

"Oh? Did it clear your questions?"

"Not quite. If I'm lucky an autopsy determines three things—the cause of death, the mechanism of death, and the manner of death—"

"And if you're not lucky?"

"The third one is left up to me."

Detective Stopsheir passed a hand over his eyes as his wife put her feet up and asked, "What do you mean by cause, manner, and—what was it?"

"Mechanism. Cause, mechanism, and manner. The cause of death is the injury or disease that produces the fatal disruption in the body. For instance, a gunshot wound."

Ivy frowned. "Then what is the mechanism of death?"

"The mechanism is the abnormality in the body created by the cause of death. If the cause was a gunshot wound, then the mechanism might be hemorrhage, or bleeding to death."

"Okay. So what is the manner of death?"

"The manner is how the cause came about and is usually natural, homicide, suicide, accident, or—as in this case—undetermined."

"Wow. Why so exact?"

"It can make a difference as far as insurance is concerned, and it can make a difference in the nature of the charges leveled, if any. If a person has a heart attack sitting at his kitchen table, then the mechanism of death would be heart attack and the manner would be natural. But if a person suffers a heart attack in a bank because a bank robber runs in and fires off a round, then the mechanism of death is still heart attack, but the cause of death could be the gunshot. Manner of death could be homicide."

"I see. Well, what did this autopsy say about the cause and the mechanism?"

"The mechanism was apparently cardiac arrhythmia, and the cause was a combination of alcohol and an over-the-counter cold remedy, aggravated by the decedent's age, which was eighty-nine at the time of death."

His wife shrugged. "Then I don't see the problem. The death, of course, was unfortunate, but obviously accidental."

Stopshier sighed. "I wish I could be certain. Her blood alcohol level at the time of the autopsy indicated she had consumed several drinks shortly before dying—and there was a newly opened bottle of cheap wine on the kitchen counter—but her daughter seemed surprised that alcohol was involved in her mother's death."

Ivy nodded. "Did the daughter live with her mother?"

Stopshier shook his head. "No. She lives several states away and was only able to visit occasionally."

"Well, alcohol abuse is always unfortunate, but is not confined to the young. Many mature people have convinced themselves that 'just a couple of glasses of wine' is not really drinking."

Stopshier agreed, "That's true. So we searched the premises at the request of the daughter, but—"

Ivy interrupted, "The daughter asked you to search the rest of the apartment?"

"Yes . . ."

His wife frowned, "Any other items of interest?"

Stopehier shrugged. "No. Why?"

Ivy's frown deepened. "I think I'm beginning to share the daughter's concern about her mother's manner of death."

The Chemistry of the Case

"Water, water, everywhere" lamented Coleridge's ancient mariner, and he was right. About 70 percent of the Earth's surface is water. About 60 percent of the human body is water. So what caused the mariner's problem: "Nor any drop to drink"? Concentration. The mariner wasn't just stranded in water; he was stranded in the ocean: a concentrated, salty brine containing calcium, magnesium, sodium, potassium, chloride, and bromide ions. Anyone who has ever seen a pickle knows what brine does to a cucumber, and that is what the seawater would have done to the ancient mariner if he had succumbed to drinking it. In fact, out of desperation, people lost at sea have been known to drink seawater as a way of speeding their inevitable demise.

What drives the pickling of the body when seawater enters? A difference in concentration. Through a process called *osmosis*, solutions strive to mix, to attain uniform concentration. Solvent flows from dilute solutions to concentrated solutions in an attempt to gain consistency. In the case of the ancient mariner, a drink of saltwater would have drawn moisture from his body as the two solutions attempted to equilibrate their concentrations.

Solutions consist of two parts—the solvent and the solute—and concentration is a measure of the amount of solute in the solution. Nearly any water sample you might select is a solution because water is such a good solvent. Water picks up solutes from everything it passes through, which is why great effort has to be exerted to secure really pure water. This is also why patients hydrated intravenously are not given pure water but a very precisely controlled salt solution. If body cells were exposed to pure water, then water would flow into the salty cells in an attempt to dilute them, causing predictable disruption.

Chemists have different ways for measuring concentration, depending on the application. Forensic chemistry is, for the most part, a specialized branch of analytical chemistry, and in analytical chemistry, it is often convenient to measure concentrations in terms of parts: parts per thousand, parts per million, parts per billion, and a favorite standard, parts per hundred, or *percentage*.

A *part* can be volume, number, or mass, but usually it is measured in mass. Thus 1 gram of salt in 100 grams of saltwater would be a one part solute per hundred parts solution, or 1 percent.

A 1 percent solution, however, is a pretty hefty solution by forensic standards. A gram is about half the mass of a dime, and a hundred grams of water is a little less than a half cup (120 milliliters). Make an approximately 1 percent solution of salt by adding a gram of salt to 100 milliters of water, and then drop a bit on a dark surface and let it dry. See the salt residue? That's a salty solution.

The ocean water in which the ancient mariner languished is less salty than our test solution mentioned above, but still pretty salty by forensic standards. The salt of ocean water is about 30 to 40 parts per thousand, which is sometimes given the symbol ‰. Note the similarity of the symbol for parts per thousand to the symbol used for percent, %. We mention it here because it helps to emphasize the meaning of our familiar "per-cent," which is parts per hundred.

The ancient mariner may have asked (if he had the strength), Why is the ocean so salty? The ocean is salty for the same reason the drop of water in our test solution showed no salt when it was still a solution but a salty residue when the solution evaporated. Rivers contribute their dissolved salts to the ocean, but the oceans' only outlet is evaporation. When moisture evaporates from the ocean and leaves behind salt, the ocean becomes more concentrated.

There are several circumstances under which forensic chemistry concerns itself with concentration. One of these is alcohol consumption. The *proof* of alcohol is a measure of the concentration of ethanol, the alcohol in alcoholic beverages. Historically, the concentration required for an alcohol to "prove" itself, to be able to ignite, was designated 100 proof. Later it was shown that this is about 57 percent by volume ethanol. In the United States, proof has been dictated to be exactly twice the percent by volume. In other parts of the world, proof is still determined by the concentration required to ignite. So there is at least one area in which the United States has gone metric—we're metric when we measure our spirits.

Forensic chemists, however, are less interested in the concentration of alcohol before consumption and more interested in the measure after—the *blood alcohol concentration*.

Traditionally, the concentration of alcohol in the blood is measured by a mass/volume ratio, the grams of alcohol per milliliter of blood. But because blood and water have approximately the same density, and 1 milliliter of water weighs 1 gram (a wise choice on the part of our metric ancestors), blood alcohol concentration can be interpreted as percent by mass. Interestingly, alcohol is the only drug for which there are established intoxication levels in the United States: adults are considered legally intoxicated if they have 0.08 percent blood alcohol, which corresponds to less than a tenth of a gram of alcohol per 100 grams of blood. This limit is fairly liberal given international standards that range from zero tolerance in countries such as Japan to 0.09 percent in South Korea.

The idea of zero tolerance is problematic from a forensics point of view. "Zero" for a forensic chemist means the lowest concentration that can be detected, and forensic chemists can go pretty low. Depending on the analyte—the material being analyzed for—materials can often be detected in the one-part-per-million (ppm), one-part-per-billion (ppb), or even one-part-per-trillion (ppt) range. One part per million is about one drop of ethanol in a 6-foot fish tank—the type you might see in a pricey seafood restaurant. This much alcohol would not normally be noticed, even by the fish. So if someone says you are one in a million, you really are pretty special. One part per billion is about one drop of ethanol in five railroad tanker-car loads. Talk about a needle in a haystack. One part per trillion (ppt) is one drop of ethanol in five thousand tanker-car loads. Forensic analysts routinely measure concentrations down to the ppm level and the ppb level, and when called upon to do so, can usually detect down to the ppt level. So if zero tolerance is the rule, the actual legal limit could be a matter of instrument capability.

Upper-limit alcohol concentration is also problematic forensically because alcohol affects people differently. Some people may be drunk with much less alcohol, some people may be sober with much more. A common measure for potentially toxic substances is the LD_{50}, which means the lethal dose for about 50 percent of the people. Interestingly, anything in a large enough quantity can be deadly, but not everything has an established LD_{50}. Unfortunately this omission can lead to the assumption that over-the-counter medicines are safe and usage guidelines need not be strictly followed. But any substance has potential for harm, as was the situation in "A Case of Strong Medicine."

Case Closed

Detective Buck Stopshier regarded his wife narrowly, "What do you mean by saying you're beginning to share the daughter's concern about her mother's manner of death?"

Ivy Prophen raised her hand thoughtfully to her chin, "You said you found a newly opened bottle of cheap wine on the counter."

"Yes . . ."

"How could you tell it was cheap?"

"It was sealed with a screw-on cap."

"Then how could you tell it was newly opened?"

"There was only about a glassful gone—"

Stopshier stopped midsentence, stared hard at his wife, and then supplied her next question for her, "If her blood had an alcohol concentration equivalent to several drinks—where did the additional alcohol come from?"

Stopsheir sat forward abruptly and grabbed a cell phone from the table on which his feet had formerly been resting. He flipped open the phone, punched several buttons, and then looked over at his wife.

"You know," he smiled at her. "We make a good team."

"Sure do," she winked in reply. "When we concentrate."

DEMONSTRATION 8
SOLID EVIDENCE

*Let the punishment
fit the crime.*

W. S. Gilbert and
Arthur Sullivan, *The
Mikado*, 1885

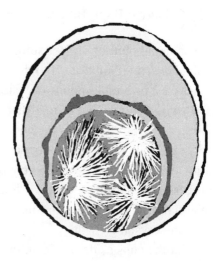

I n forensic chemistry, the gas
phase and the liquid phase are
important, but the solid phase is
no less significant. A *crystal* is a highly ordered arrangement of a solid
chemical, with each atom or molecule in a specific position. We are all
familiar with the crystalline form of carbon called a diamond and the
crystalline form of silicon dioxide called quartz. These two crystals
are *minerals*, naturally occurring crystals. There are more than twenty-
two hundred types of minerals, but only about forty can be considered
common, so identification of the type, size, and distribution of minerals in a soil sample can help identify the soil's origin.[1]

Many illegal drugs can be made into crystalline compounds at
room temperature and are more easily packaged, handled, transported,
and stored in the solid form. As a complementary test to accompany a
presumptive color test, forensic chemists can sometimes identify
drugs such as cocaine by crystal structure. In this demonstration, we
will grow crystals of different materials to show how their crystal
structures differ.

Put on safety glasses and then take three small see-through plastic
cups and label them as "copper sulfate," "table salt," and "caffeine."
Grind up a caffeine tablet as you did in the demonstration accompanying chapter 1, being careful to remove any colored coating. Add this
to the cup labeled "caffeine." Add a small quantity (about half of a teaspoon or 2 milliliters) of table salt to the "table salt" cup and add about

the same amount of copper sulfate (obtained as suggested in "Crime Lab and Crime Solutions") to the "copper sulfate" cup.

Add 2 or 3 tablespoons of water (30 to 45 milliliters) to each cup and swirl the contents to mix them thoroughly. If too much water is used, the caffeine crystals may not grow properly. The salt should dissolve quickly whereas the copper sulfate may take fifteen to twenty minutes to dissolve. Swirl the copper sulfate periodically to help the process. The caffeine tablet has filler material in it, and not all of that material will dissolve. This insoluble material should not interfere with the crystal growth.

Set the cups aside in a location where they won't be disturbed. As the water slowly evaporates, crystals of salt, copper sulfate, and caffeine should grow. If crystals do not form, simply redissolve the solid with some more water and try again, but this time you might cover each cup loosely with some plastic wrap so the water evaporates more slowly. The key to growing these crystals is slow-but-steady evaporation of the water. If the water evaporates too quickly, the compounds in each will not have a chance to settle into the orderly and extended arrays of crystals.

Once all of the water has evaporated and the crystals have grown, you should be able to observe three distinct forms of crystals. Table salt grows in rectangular prisms. Copper sulfate grows in an offset rectangular-sided form. And caffeine crystals grow in the nice long fingerlike crystals often associated with organic compounds. Take out a high-powered magnifying glass and examine their beauty up close.

We will examine some facets of crystals in "The Case of the Sweet Surrender."

CHAPTER 8

CRYSTAL-CLEAR CRIME: MICROCRYSTALLINE IDENTIFICATION

> Nobody saves America by sniffing cocaine . . .
> when it snows in your nose you catch cold in your
> brain.
>
> Allen Ginsberg, ca. 1950

THE CASE OF THE SWEET SURRENDER

Patrol Officer Pat Down set down her coffee mug and grinned at her lunch companion, the neighborhood mail carrier, Levon DaPorch. "Yes, I guess I've seen some strange stuff."

Levon shook his head. "You say you almost missed the crack cocaine?"

"Yep. But then my partner said we must have interrupted a party because they had cool drinks sitting on the table with ice in the bottom of the glasses."

"But ice floats . . ."

"Exactly. And crack sinks."

Levon nodded in approval.

Pat cleared her throat. "But they almost got me in the last house we were in."

"How's that?" Levon asked.

"We were backing up the detectives with a no-knock warrant, but the suspects must have known something was up because we could hear scrambling before we even opened the door. As soon as we got in, we secured the place, but it looked more like a scene from *Father Knows Best* than a crack house."

"In what way?"

"They had cartoons on the TV, chips and soda on the coffee table, and someone had a box of cake mix poured out in a bowl in the kitchen. Looked like they'd just added a cup of sugar."

Levon laughed aloud. "Well, you've got to give them credit for trying!"

Pat smiled. "So you see it, too?"

The Chemistry of the Case

When materials form solids, they do so in a number of ways. Some materials collapse like a house of cards: molecules falling and folding every which way in a hodgepodge called an *amorphous solid*. For example, rubbers are amorphous. Many plastics are amorphous. But other solids, more orderly solids, resemble the house of cards before it collapses. These solids, called *crystalline solids*, are significant in the forensic sciences for many reasons, including the fact that many illegally manufactured drugs are crystalline.

Water, of course, is important in all situations, legal and illegal, and we have already discussed some aspects of water crystallization. Previously we said that the hydrogen bonding between water molecules is responsible for the rigid grouping of water molecules as they solidify: the frozen molecules occupy more space than the liquid, which is why ice is less dense than water and floats. Ice cubes from the freezer, however, are not a good example of orderly crystals. The smooth, nondistinct edges of ice cubes result from rapid freezing and the fact they are formed from relatively impure water. We like to think of our ice cubes as clear, but on close inspection, common ice cubes have a cloudy center. This cloudiness is due to the gases that were trapped in the water and are now trapped in the ice cube. As the ice cube freezes, the gases are squeezed to the center. In contrast, snowflakes have an orderly, highly recognizable structure. The six-pointed stars of snowflakes originate in the hexagonal lattice of water molecules that come together to form the solid unit of ice, such as shown in figure 8.1. Frozen slowly in the upper atmosphere, snowflakes are able to retain their delicate, fine-edged crystalline structure.

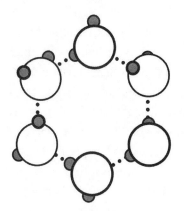

Figure 8.1 The six-pointed star of a snowflake originates in the hexagonal lattice formed when water molecules come together to form a six-sided unit of ice.

Other *molecular crystals* are held together by intermolecular forces as well. Sugar is a covalent compound, and in crystalline sugar, the sugar molecules are held in place by intermolecular attractions. Salt, on the other hand, is an *ionic crystal* formed from an extensive network of ionic bonds. But even under a magnifying lens there is precious little to distinguish a typical salt crystal from a sugar crystal. Our tongues, however, can tell the difference.

Other materials, notably cocaine, heroin, and methamphetamine, exhibit characteristic crystalline structure, as evidenced by the monikers "snow" for cocaine, "rock" for crack cocaine, "brown sugar" for heroin, and "crystal meth" for methamphetamine.

Cocaine, heroin, and methamphetamine are *organic compounds* like sugar. An organic compound is a compound formed primarily from covalently bonded carbon and hydrogen, not just "unadulterated" or grown on a special type of farm, which is the more popular usage of the word *organic*. Cocaine and heroin, however, are natural products, coming from the coca plant and the opium poppy, respectively. Usually when one thinks of an "organic" material, one thinks of mush and slime rather than crystals, and that intuition is generally correct. Organic materials tend to be oily and fatty and pretty insoluble in water. For ease of handling, cocaine is made into a crystalline solid by a specific process we will discuss in more detail later.

For microcrystalline identification, cocaine, heroin, methamphetamine, and other drugs may be recrystallized in the forensics lab. As shown in the demonstration preceding this chapter, different materials can form different types of crystals, and in the right hands and under the right conditions, the form of the crystal can be characteristic of the drug. Now the question might be: why would someone want to go through all the trouble to use microcrystalline identification when there are instruments such as the GC mass spec that are capable of quickly and definitively identifying the material under question?

As we illustrated with demonstration 1, presumptive tests and screening tests are able to give results that are either consistent or inconsistent with the presence of a certain drug, but they need to be backed up by further tests. The word *tests* is used in the plural because two positive tests are better than one. GC mass spec is indeed a wonderful confirmatory test, but it is also a destructive test. Microcrystalline analysis is an identification method that allows for the possibility of further tests.

Of course, drug dealers prefer crystalline cocaine for other reasons. The crystalline form of cocaine can be inhaled and is convenient to package and distribute. The crystalline form is also easy to dilute with sugar, caffeine, flour, baking soda, or other white powders. Dilution must be done with care because a too-dilute product will elicit complaints from customers, but a too-concentrated product will cut down on profits or kill off the consumers. There is another trade-off. Sentencing is based on the amount of drug confiscated, not the purity of the drug. So being caught with a small amount of pure cocaine can result in a lighter sentence than being caught with the same amount that has been diluted to a kilo: 5 grams of cocaine versus 5 grams plus 995 grams of sugar to yield 1,000 grams of "product." This last consideration came into play in "The Case of the Sweet Surrender."

Case Closed

"When I saw them all sitting around like innocence personified, I knew something was up," Pat Down continued. "The reports of drug deals from that house were too reliable. They had to have stashed the stuff somewhere. But all we found was a scene of domestic tranquility, complete with a box of cake mix in the kitchen, a cup of sugar having just been added."

Levon DaPorch laughed. "Any cake mix I've ever used came with all the dry ingredients and only required oil, water, or an egg, at most, so I can only guess that the crystals you saw dumped on the cake mix weren't out of the sugar bowl."

Pat Down nodded. "They took a gamble, and they lost—big time. By dumping the drugs on the cake mix, the entire mixture became the stash. Now instead of one gram, they could be charged with five hundred. When it comes to drugs, it's the quantity, not the quality, that counts. Do you see what I mean?"

Levon shrugged. "It's crystal clear."

PART II
FELONIOUS
INTERACTIONS

Procure for us some iron for the barrels, steel for the hammers, saltpeter, coal, and sulphur for powder, mercury and nitric acid for the fulminate, and lead for the shot. . . .

Jules Verne, *Mysterious Island*, ca. 1875

In part I, we discussed the nature of forensic chemistry and showed how knowledge of atomic structure, molecular structure, phases of matter, and intermolecular forces enter into the art of forensic science. But chemistry isn't just about materials; it is also about the reactions these materials undergo. Now that we've established some basic principles concerning materials, we are ready to begin our discussion of the chemical reactions that are at the heart of chemistry.

Chemical behavior is distinguished from physical behavior by one criterion: if the result of an action is a new material, then the interaction is chemical. If no new material results, then it is physical. Water boiling, for example, is a physical change because the water molecules, H_2O, could be captured from the steam and turned back into liquid water. It's the same material, just in two different physical forms. Vinegar mixed with baking soda, however, is a chemical interaction because carbon dioxide gas, a new material, is produced and released in bubbles.

In a chemical reaction, starting materials, called reactants, undergo a rearrangement of elements and bonds to form new materials, called products. This rearrangement can be summarized in what is called a chemical equation:

$$reactants \rightarrow products$$

Because we have to respect the law of conservation of mass, we know that the mass of the final products will always equal the mass of the initial reactants; in other words, the total weight of the final mixture will be the same as the total weight of the starting mixture.

Note we use the term starting and final *mixture* because, as we will see, chemical reactions do not always go completely from reactants to products but instead interact until they reach *equilibrium*, a state in which there is a mixture of some reactants and some products. The extent to which a chemical reaction takes place will depend on the nature of the reaction, the relative masses of the starting materials, the temperature, and the circumstances under which the reaction takes place. The composition of the equilibrium mixture will also depend on a couple of interesting concepts called *energy* (something we are all familiar with) and *entropy* (something that may be a bit less familiar). We will investigate these factors and their effect on equilibrium, and we will discuss the application of this chemistry to solving crime.

We begin this next part by examining the factors that differentiate chemical from physical changes and then we will focus on some classic classes of reactions. We will examine, in succession, precipitate-forming (solid-forming) reactions, acid-base reactions, redox reactions (a term we will explain), gas-forming reactions, and heat-producing and heat-consuming reactions. We will conclude with a discussion of some of the principles that govern the rate of reactions, the extent of these reactions, and their resulting equilibrium.

DEMONSTRATION 9
PHYSICAL EVIDENCE

*This I conceive to be the chemical function of
humor: to change the character of our thought.*

Lin Yutang, ca. 1960

There are two types of changes materials undergo: chemical and physical. In a chemical change a new material is formed. For instance, baking soda (which is solid sodium bicarbonate) mixed with vinegar (which is an aqueous acetic acid solution) will produce bubbling and fizzing that is carbon dioxide gas, a new material. Physical change can happen in the absence of any other ingredient and does not result in a new material. For instance, boiling water produces water vapor—steam—but capturing and condensing that steam convinces us that it is still just water, not a new material. Sugar dissolves in tea, but the sugar can be recovered by evaporating the liquid. In the following demonstration we will see other illustrations of chemical and physical changes.

Physical Change—Nothing New

After outfitting yourself with safety glasses and hand protection, take a see-through plastic glass and place about 60 to 70 milliliters (4 or 5 tablespoons) of water in it. With a disposable plastic spoon, begin adding small amounts (a quarter teaspoon or a milliliter or two) of baking soda into the water, while stirring. Once the baking soda has dissolved, add more, and continue stirring. Proceed in this manner until no more baking soda will dissolve. There should be a residue on the bottom of the glass, even with stirring.

Heat the solution gently by holding the glass in a container of hot, but not boiling, water or use your double boiler. You should see the residue on the bottom of the glass dissolve. Has the baking soda undergone a chemical change and become a new material or is the baking soda still there but in a different physical form? Set the glass aside while performing the second half of this demonstration, after which we will address this question.

Chemical Process—A New Player

Pour the same amount of water in another see-through plastic glass and again add baking soda and stir until no more will dissolve. Allow the solution to settle and then gently decant the clear liquid above the settled solid into another clean, see-through plastic glass. In the decanted solution there should be only clear liquid, no solid at the bottom. Into this clear solution, add a single drop of copper sulfate solution that has been prepared as directed in "Crime Lab and Crime Solutions." You should see a cloudiness in the solution from the formation of copper carbonate, a new compound. Copper carbonate is not very soluble in water, so when it forms in solution, it should eventually settle out as a solid.

This latest change is a chemical change because a new material, copper carbonate, has formed.

Now let's revisit the demonstration of a physical change. What if we said that when we heated the sodium bicarbonate it stayed in the same form, just dissolved into solution. If this is true, then we should be able to find evidence for the sodium bicarbonate in solution.

Drop a couple of drops of copper sulfate solution into the first glass. You should see the same new compound, copper carbonate, forming, which would be consistent with sodium bicarbonate still being in solution. Note we say "would be consistent with" rather than "proves," because we know that this is a presumptive test for sodium bicarbonate, and a confirmatory test would be necessary to be more certain. It may seem a fine point, but one that chemists, including forensic chemists, must always keep in mind.

The above demonstration illustrates the difference between chemical and physical change—a necessary distinction in "The Case of the Physical Flaw."

CHAPTER 9

A CHANGE FOR THE WORSE: WHEN IT GETS PHYSICAL

> We can make inspired guesses, but we don't know
> for certain what physical and chemical properties
> of the planet's crust, its ocean and its atmosphere
> made it so conducive to such a sudden appear-
> ance of life.
>
> Isaac Asimov, *Omni*, 1983

> No one owns life, but anyone who can pick up a
> frying pan owns death.
>
> William S. Burroughs, ca. 1960

THE CASE OF THE PHYSICAL FLAW

Detectives Wanda Who, Rodger That, and Howard Thow sat at a table that was almost too large for the small conference/coffee room in police headquarters.

Detective Who opened a file and passed out photos of a crime scene that included one of the nude body of a young woman. Wanda Who cleared her throat. "The cause of death was asphyxiation, the mechanism was compression of the trachea by ligature—probably a standard nylon rope in this case—and the manner of death was ruled homicide."

Her two colleagues looked at the photos and then over at the rest of the file expectantly, but Wanda shook her head. "Other than that, there is precious little to go on."

Wanda straightened in her chair. "Let's review what we know."

She lifted out a thin stack of papers and flipped through them, reciting a line or two from each. "The body was found in the alley . . . moved from the original scene . . . dumped very cleanly . . . whoever strangled her took care not to leave fingerprints and they compromised any trace evidence by dumping her in a littered alley." She handed copies of the report to her colleagues.

Detective That snorted. "And trace evidence is no good unless you have someone to trace it to."

"Do we have the rope?" asked Rodger.

"No," answered Wanda, "but the marks on her throat were consistent with a braided rope, and there were no traces of hemp or other fiber—which would be consistent with a nylon rope. And there were some burns that could be rope burns."

"Was she assaulted?" asked Rodger.

"No. There were no bruises or evidence of much of a struggle. The strangulation must have been accomplished fairly quickly."

"At least we have her ID'd," said Howard.

"Yes. A missing-persons report came in and we had her identified in six hours."

Detective That consulted the case file. "Do you have any theories?"

Detective Who shrugged. "Well, she was a young, good-looking college student. So I naturally thought of boy trouble."

"Did she have a boyfriend?"

Wanda shrugged and sighed. "Several. Her roommate said she was dating a pre-med, a lifeguard, and a college dropout who worked at a fast-food place by their apartment."

Howard fidgeted. "That's not much help!"

But Rodger looked thoughtful. "I think it is. At least it tells us where we should concentrate our efforts first."

The Chemistry of the Case

Much has been written about the "gut instinct" that guides police work, but this is, of course, fiction. If police officers continuously followed the feeling in their guts, then arrests would depend on what the detective had for lunch. Detective work is, and must be, much more systematic, and in this regard, chemistry and crime solving have a lot in common. There are, of course, flashes of insight in both criminal and chemical investigations, but most often progress is made by careful collection, categorization, and correlation of facts.

In the sciences, a method called, appropriately, the *scientific method* is often cited as the systematic process by which scientists proceed from question to conclusion. In criminal investigations, a similar process is employed. But while the scientific method is usually presented as a series of steps, it must be immediately acknowledged that these steps *describe* a thought process rather than *dictate* a thought process. No scientist approaches the lab with these steps written on a clipboard, and no detective carries a checklist of steps next to his or her badge and Miranda card. But awareness of the process, even on a subliminal level, assists in the organization of thought.

In the scientific method, the first step is really not a step, but a precipitating event: an observation is made. For a scientist, this might be an unexpected result, such as a cloud of gas where no gas was expected. For an investigating officer, the event is a possible crime. Here the two circumstances may momentarily diverge. In science, many times the question is open-ended. In crime solving it is not. Science is concerned with why a thing happened, but in crime solving, motive is important only if it leads to whodunit. After the arrest, though, motive may be used to determine the charges.

In the scientific method, as it is generally understood, the next step is to form a working hypothesis to explain the event, and here the philosophies converge again. In police work, this hypothesis is usually called a "theory." Semantic purists may find this objectionable because, in science, a hypothesis is a best first guess whereas a theory is an explanation that has been substantiated by experiment. But in police work when one asks "What's your theory?" the question is understood to be "What is your working hypothesis?"

Whether you call it hypothesis or theory, the structure is helpful because it focuses the investigation in a specific direction. At this point, the scientific and forensic investigations become very much alike. Evidence is gathered and tested, and based on how it fits, the working hypothesis is revised, refined, or rejected.

The painstaking analysis of evidence, either criminal or scientific, requires time. Police and scientific investigations may require hundreds of personnel hours, and many of these hours may be spent sifting through reams of irrelevant and immaterial data, looking for the one piece that fits. Obviously the more organized the incoming information is, the easier it will be to sort through, so in the criminal as well as the chemical sciences, close attention is paid to systematic categorization. For the criminalist, this may consist of the categorization of criminals by modus operandi, first-time versus repeat offenders, and type of crime, such as known sex offenders or drug users. For the chemists, the categorization may be by types of materials and types of reactions.

The first categorization for chemists is the division of the world into energy and matter, the famous E and m of Einstein's equation $E = mc^2$. For chemists, there are two abiding principles concerning energy and matter: the *conservation of energy* and the *conservation of mass*. Conservation of energy means that energy is neither created nor destroyed in a chemical reaction, and conservation of mass means that matter is neither created nor destroyed in a chemical reaction. The question, of course, might be how these conservation principles align with Einstein's equation: the interpretation of Einstein's equation is that matter and energy can be interchanged, $E = mc^2$. The saving grace for chemists, however, is the c in Einstein's equation, which stands for the speed of light. Chemists are hard workers, but they don't work at the speed of light, so for the purposes of chemistry, energy and matter can be considered separate and immutable. In the world of bench-top chemistry, the principles of the conservation of mass and the conservation of energy are firmly in place.

Matter can further be subdivided into mixtures and pure substances, and the difference between mixtures and pure substances is variability. The ratio of parts in a pure substance, say, in H_2O, water, cannot be varied without changing the nature of the substance. Water has a ratio of two hydrogens to one oxygen, and if this is changed to two hydrogens to every *two* oxygens, a new substance results, H_2O_2, hydrogen peroxide. Hydrogen peroxide has obvious chemical differences from water. If you wash your hair with water, it gets clean. If you wash your hair with hydrogen peroxide, it changes color. Mixtures, on the other hand, can have variable composition. Sand is a mixture of silicates, carbonates, phosphates, and other minerals. But even though the composition can vary from black sand to white, it is still all sand. Sugar water can be made in any proportion from slightly sweet water to syrup, the ratio of sugar to water being infinitely variable between these extremes.

Mixtures such as sand and sugar water can be further subdivided into *heterogeneous* and *homogeneous* mixtures. Homogenous mixtures are uniform throughout, such as sugar water. A sample from the bottom of a glass of sugar water should have the same composition as a sample from the top. The situation is different for sand. The composition of sand varies widely from spot to spot. The sifting of sand from natural movement accounts for the concentration of lighter elements in the Earth's crust, which makes the Earth's soil a heterogeneous mixture.

Pure substances, likewise, can be subdivided into compounds and elements. The elements are the separate pure substances on the periodic table. Each element is composed of like atoms, each with the requisite number of protons. Compounds are materials that are formed from specific combinations of elements. Copper, Cu, is an element, but copper sulfate (root killer or ceramic glaze) is a compound.

Classification helps explain another important concept in chemistry: the difference between physical and chemical processes. A *chemical process* is one in which a new material is formed, with different physical characteristics and different reactivity. For instance, when hydrogen peroxide, H_2O_2, a disinfectant, decomposes into hydrogen, H_2, and oxygen, O_2, on contact with blood, this is a chemical change. The substances produced are an explosive gas (hydrogen) and a gas necessary for life (oxygen). A *physical change* is a change wherein the material may change form or phase, but it is still the same chemical substance, with the same reactivity. For example, when sugar is recovered from sugar water by allowing the water to evaporate, you start with sugar and water and you end with sugar and water, so the separation is a physical change. When a reaction changes color or produces bubbles or light or heat, then it is probably a chemical change. In the chapters that follow, we will categorize various chemical reactions based on the chemical changes they undergo, but in this chapter we first distinguish what is chemical and what is physical. It is often vital to separate the physical from the chemical, as we see in "The Case of the Physical Flaw."

Case Closed

Detectives Wanda Who and Howard Thow regarded Detective Rodger That curiously.

"You have a theory?" Wanda asked. "Does it have to do with the rope?"

"Not the rope," answered Rodger. "The rope burns—or rather the burns that you attributed to the rope."

"How's that?" asked Howard.

"I don't think they're rope burns. You said there didn't seem to be much of a struggle, and rope burns require the physical movement of the rope back and forth over an area."

Wanda frowned. "But the marks looked like burns—"

"I think they were," interjected Rodger, "but not physical burns. I think they were chemical burns."

"Chemical burns!" Howard pushed back in his chair. "Where would the chemicals come from?"

"Swimming pool chemicals," Rodger said simply. "A lifeguard would have routine access to nylon rope, and might pick up rope that has been contaminated with concentrated swimming pool chemicals. The type that can burn your skin."

Wanda brightened for a minute, but then frowned. "But is that physically possible?"

Detective That shrugged. "Chemically it is."

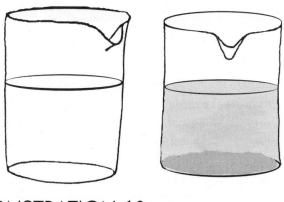

DEMONSTRATION 10
PRECIPITATING EVENTS

The first thing that dissolves in alcohol is dignity.

Attribution unknown

When there is a chemical reaction, there is evidence. A new material is formed, so sometimes there are bubbles, sometimes colors change, sometimes heat or light is produced, and sometimes a *precipitate*, or solid, is formed. In this demonstration, we present a chemical reaction evidenced by a color change and the formation of a precipitate.

Adjust your safety glasses securely over your eyes and pull on your examination gloves. Take a small plastic cup (the kind recommended in "Crime Lab and Crime Solutions") and place one-half to two-thirds of a tablespoon (7 to 10 milliliters) of citric acid (sour salt) in it. Fill the cup about halfway with distilled or bottled water and swirl the contents to mix. The solution should cool noticeably: this mixing is an example of an endothermic process, as we will discuss in chapter 14.

Add about a half teaspoon (2 to 3 milliliters) of baking soda with a plastic spoon and stir. When the fizzing stops, add more baking soda, and continue adding small quantities of baking soda while stirring until additional baking soda does not cause additional fizzing. Work slowly and patiently; you only want to add baking soda until the fizzing stops. If you overshoot, it may interfere with the subsequent reaction.

Add one more small quantity of baking soda (a quarter teaspoon, or 1 milliliter) and stir to ensure that this reaction is finished.

Now add about a teaspoon (5 milliliters) of copper sulfate and stir this solution until it is a rich deep blue color. If the solution appears pale, you may want to add a few more crystals of copper sulfate. The resulting solution is called *Benedict's reagent* and will be used later.

To another half-filled cup of water add a glucose tablet, crunch it up, and stir the solution to dissolve the glucose. There will be filler material in the tablet that will not dissolve and will either sink or float. Don't worry about the presence of this filler; we will work around it.

Find a small glass vessel (sufficient to hold about 8 ounces or about 240 milliliters) that can be heated. The jelly jar we suggested you acquire in "Crime Lab and Crime Solutions" would work. Pour in some of the Benedict's reagent, being careful not to transfer any solids left at the bottom. To the same glass vessel add some of the glucose solution from the center of the solution. To do this, squeeze the bulb of an eye-dropper to expel the air and insert the tip into the middle of the solution. Draw up solution from here, while being careful not to disturb the sediments. Put in about the same amount of glucose solution as there was Benedict's solution in the glass.

Using the double boiler, heat this mixture with boiling water in the double boiler arrangement described in "Crime Lab and Crime Solutions." Do not place the glass vessel directly on a burner or flame because glass can heat unevenly and crack. Heat the mixture for at least fifteen minutes while the reaction develops (as described in the next paragraph). More heating may be required if results are slow to develop.

The sample solution should darken, and eventually a brick red precipitate should form. As the precipitate settles out of the solution, a greenish tinge will be seen in the blue Benedict's reagent solution. If you compare this sample glass with pure Benedict's reagent, you should see a clear difference between the two.

The brick red precipitate is cuprous oxide—also called copper(I) oxide—Cu_2O, which forms in the presence of certain sugars. Benedict's reagent is used in a test for the presence of glucose, an essential tool in the management of diabetes.

To convince yourself that the reaction described below results from the presence of glucose and not just from warming the Benedict's reagent, you could warm some of the Benedict's reagent without glucose, too. As an additional control, you could try the reaction with table sugar instead of glucose from glucose tablets, as follows.

Take about a half teaspoon (3 milliliters) of refined table sugar and dissolve it in about a half cup (120 milliliters) of water in a glass jar. Add an equal volume of freshly prepared Benedict's reagent and heat the mixture in the same double boiler as above. Heat the solution until it is steaming, and then remove the solution from the heat and allow it to cool. You should observe none of the changes that accompanied this same test with glucose. Sucrose, table sugar, is a *disaccharide*, which means it is a compound formed from two simple sugars. The two simple sugars that make up sucrose are glucose and fructose; however, the glucose in sucrose is bound up with fructose and not free to react with the Benedict's reagent.

It is possible, however, to set up a reaction that will liberate the simple sugars from sucrose. This reaction is called *hydrolysis* (*hydro-* meaning water and *-lysis* meaning to cut) because water is involved in cleaving the bond.

Take about a half teaspoon (3 milliliters) of refined table sugar and place it into a glass jar or cup. Add enough aquarium pH-lowering solution so that all of the sugar dissolves, which should be about 2 to 3 teaspoons (10 to 15 milliliters). Be patient because sugar dissolves slowly. Once all of the sugar has dissolved, add five more drops of the pH-lowering solution to ensure a sufficient quantity remains during heating.

Heat the solution gently for ten to fifteen minutes to promote the cleavage of the disaccharide. The heating should be sufficient to make the glass hot to the touch. Do not allow the sugar solution to boil or heat too long: if the solution turns dark brown, you have heated it too much. Slightly brown is okay.

Allow the solution to cool slightly then sprinkle in about a quarter teaspoon (1 milliliter) of baking soda and stir. Continue adding quarter teaspoons of baking soda with stirring until absolutely no more fizzing occurs. Add in one or two more quarter-teaspoon (1 milliliter) portions of baking soda to ensure the reaction is finished.

To this neutralized sugar solution add an equal volume of the fresh Benedict's reagent. Heat the mixture of sugar and Benedict's reagent until the combined solution is steaming. As this solution heats, it should begin to produce the signs of the glucose reaction demonstrated in the first Benedict's test, which confirms the hydrolysis of table sugar to glucose. The solution should begin to appear green as the brick red precipitate, Cu_2O, forms in the blue Benedict's reagent. Eventually the precipitate will settle out and the blue color will return to the solution.

The Benedict's test for glucose is especially pleasing because it offers such a clear result with its precipitate formation and color change. Several similar color-changing and/or precipitate-forming chemical reactions have been harnessed by forensic chemists, as we will see in the chemistry behind "A Case of Nerves."

CHAPTER 10

CHEMISTRY UNDER THE INFLUENCE: COMPOUNDING THE CRIME

Everything in moderation, including moderation.

Mark Twain, ca. 1880

A CASE OF NERVES

E na Fogg rolled down her window as the uniformed officer dismounted the patrol motorcycle behind her and approached her car.

"Yes, Officer? Was I going too fast?"

"No, ma'am," replied Officer Ona Honda, leaning down to the open window. "But I observed you crossing the center line several times and you veered onto the shoulder back there. May I see your license?"

Ena complied, digging through the large purse on the seat beside her until she produced a wallet. Officer Honda took the license and walked back to her motorcycle to radio in for wants and warrants. While the officer waited, she considered her options. The woman was probably intoxicated; her driving had been erratic and there was the odor of alcohol in the car. But no open containers were visible, just the purse on the front passenger seat, so there was no telling the last time Ms. Fogg had taken a drink. Officer Honda would have to call for backup to transport the driver to the station, and that would take time. If the driver became argumentative and refused to take the field test, that would take time. They might have to wait in the station for the blood alcohol analyzer. By the time they were able to test the driver, her blood alcohol level might have fallen below the legal limit.

Officer Honda listened as wants and warrants radioed back clear. She observed the woman in the car adjust her rearview mirror and rest her elbow on the open window and drum her fingers on the side of the car.

Officer Honda stood, thinking. Should she run her in? Would there be any benefit from a good scare? Was it detrimental to let her "beat the system" with a negative test? As Officer Honda weighed her options, she watched as the woman temporarily disappeared, leaning over to the passenger seat.

Officer Honda considered, and then knew what she should do.

The Chemistry of the Case

Chemical reactions generally fall into two broad classes: reactions in which something is broken down and reactions in which something is made. The reaction described in demonstration 10 falls into the second category: the Benedict's test is a *synthesis* reaction; it forms a solid, a *precipitate*, that settles out of a mixture of two solutions.

Benedict's test is used to detect glucose, a fundamental food for both animals and plants. As we will see when we discuss DNA, enzymes, and proteins, the molecules of human construction are amazingly large, but glucose, the energy source for all this construction, is very small. Ethanol, the alcohol found in alcoholic beverages, is composed of only two atoms of carbon, one atom of oxygen, and six tiny hydrogens, as shown in figure 10.1. The way these atoms are arranged, however, packs a punch.

Organic molecules are made up of a covalently bonded carbon and hydrogen, *hydrocarbon*, underlying structure, with other covalent groups attached. When these other covalent groups are added to a basic hydrocarbon scaffold, the resulting compound has an altered reactivity. An *alcohol* is a member of the family of organic compounds that contains an added OH group, an oxygen bonded to a hydrogen, and this group has the effect of making the organic molecule more able to mix with water—among other effects. Members of this family include isopropyl alcohol (rubbing alcohol), methanol (a chafing dish fuel used with camp stoves and buffet tables), and, of course, ethanol, the alcohol in alcoholic beverages. Ethanol for recreational consumption has a fascinating history and a fascinating chemistry, from its production via the digestive systems of microorganisms; to its storage, refinement, and flavoring; to its ultimate metabolism in the digestive systems of macroorganisms, namely, humans. It is this consumption by humans that holds the most interest for forensic chemists.

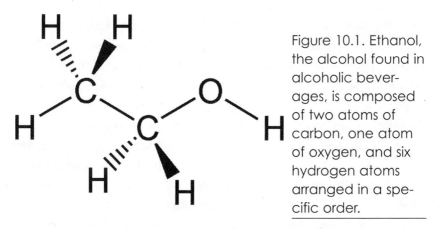

Figure 10.1. Ethanol, the alcohol found in alcoholic beverages, is composed of two atoms of carbon, one atom of oxygen, and six hydrogen atoms arranged in a specific order.

Ethanol is produced industrially by adding water to ethylene, the basic unit of polyethylene. But ethanol produced in this manner is generally used as a solvent or for perfumes, lacquers, or other unappetizing applications. To increase the unappetizing aspect, industrial ethanol will often be *denatured*; that is, small amounts of certain chemicals are added to produce digestive discomfort, to change the color or odor, or to make the taste more disagreeable (though it is difficult to see how someone bent on consuming undiluted ethanol would find any taste disagreeable).

The vast majority of the ethanol produced for consumption is made the old-fashioned way: by allowing yeast to digest glucose in the absence of oxygen. The chemical equation for this reaction is

$$C_6H_{12}O_6 \rightarrow 2CH_3CH_2OH + 2CO_2$$

The above equation can be deciphered as follows. The molecule on the left side of the equation is glucose, a sugar, which is also shown on the left in figure 10.2. The subscript 6 on the carbon, C, indicates that there are six carbons in glucose. Similarly, the subscript 12 on the H in the formula for glucose indicates there are twelve hydrogens in glucose, which are shown in figure 10.2. Following this same logic, there should be six oxygens in glucose as indicated by the formula. When we consult figure 10.2, all six are there.

Glucose is broken down into two ethanol, CH_3CH_2OH, molecules and two carbon dioxide, CO_2, molecules as indicated by the 2 in front of the formulas for ethanol and carbon dioxide in the above reaction. As can be seen in figure 10.2, the original sugar had six carbons and there are a total of six carbons in the product molecules. As written, all the material in the reactant is accounted for in the product. Each ethanol molecule has two carbons, as can be seen in figure 10.2, and each carbon dioxide molecule has one. By having two molecules of ethanol and two molecules of carbon dioxide, there are six carbons total. All the carbons in the reactant show up in the product. This accounting is necessary to have a *balanced chemical equation*: a chemical equation that obeys the law of conservation of mass; that is, mass is neither created nor destroyed in a normal chemical reaction.

The chemical process that produces ethanol, however, is often followed by a physical process called *distillation* to concentrate the alcohol to interesting levels. Distillation takes advantage of the fact that the boiling point of ethanol is lower than that of water, so a heated mixture will produce a vapor that is richer in ethanol than water. The

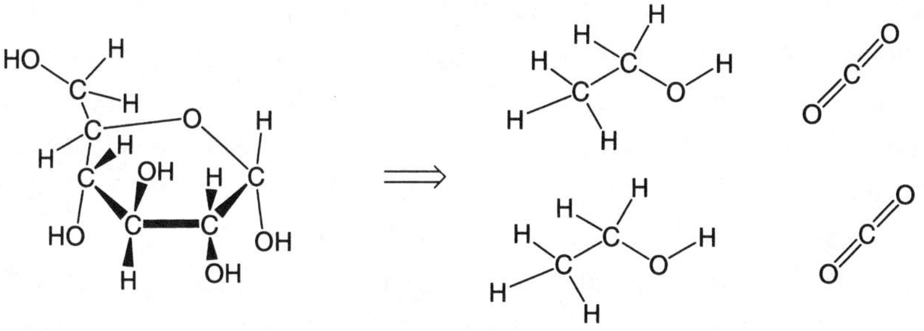

Figure 10.2. Glucose (on the left of the arrow) can be broken down into two ethanol, CH_3CH_2OH, molecules and two carbon dioxide, CO_2, molecules (right) as indicated by the 2 in front of the formulas for ethanol and carbon dioxide in the chemical equation. The original sugar had six carbons, and there are a total of six carbons in the product. The original sugar had twelve hydrogens and six oxygens, and there are a total of twelve hydrogens and six oxygens in the product molecules.

liquid that condenses from this vapor can be reheated to effect a further separation. By subsequent applications of this method, fairly concentrated ethanol can be extracted. The metallic coil that is usually associated with illegal ethanol distillation apparatuses—"moonshine" stills—is a way of accomplishing these multiple distillations in one continuous setup. The liquid in the bottom of the coil is vaporized and moves to the next coil before condensing to a more concentrated form. Absolutely pure ethanol is not easy to obtain, however, because water and ethanol enjoy strong mutual intermolecular attractions. But any material that even approaches pure is generally considered too strong for recreational consumption.

The type of reaction that glucose undergoes to produce ethanol is called a *decomposition reaction*. In the human body, ethanol undergoes another decomposition reaction, which is why ethanol levels have to be replenished to maintain intoxication. Unfortunately, the decomposition reaction occurs as a series of steps, as many reactions do, and one of the steps produces acetaldehyde, the toxin that is responsible for the morning-after feeling of having been poisoned.

The body attempts to break down acetaldehyde as fast as it can, but if enough alcohol is consumed, enough acetaldehyde remains to fuel a hangover. In fact, the drug used to deter drinking, Antabuse, doesn't have to do anything more than block the metabolism of acetaldehyde to make the drinker red in the face, short of breath, headachy, nauseated, weak, and light-headed. As a rule, however, the undigested alcohol can still be found on the breath for some time after drinking. Law enforcement takes advantage of this fact when they test to see if more than the legal amount of ethanol has been consumed by a vehicle operator.

There are now several types of alcohol detection instruments, such as the penlight sensor we encountered in the introduction to this book. But the pioneer method for determining blood alcohol content is the classic Breathalyzer. The basis for alcohol detection by the Breathalyzer is a chemical reaction in which potassium dichromate, a reddish orange compound, reacts with ethanol in the presence of a catalyst and sulfuric acid (the acid in lead-acid car batteries) to produce a chromium ion that lends a green color to the solution. This same chromium ion is responsible for the green color of minerals such as emerald. The intensity of green color is directly proportional to the amount of alcohol in the breath.

Although the trademark instrument, the Breathalyzer, has become synonymous with blood alcohol detection, the Breathalyzer has been largely supplanted by blood alcohol detectors that use the interaction of ethanol with light, a notion we will explore in chapter 18. Newer instruments are more efficient and minimize the need to keep chemicals on hand. The word *breathalyzer*, however, has entered our language as a genericized trademark, a suitable tribute to a landmark device.

But whatever detection method is used, it cannot go backwards in time. And although alcohol does take some time to digest, it does digest, so the detectable amount of alcohol will decrease steadily with time after the last drink is taken. This was the dilemma facing Officer Honda in "The Case of Nerves." She knew that waiting for a squad car and transporting the driver to the station to test for blood alcohol content (BAC) would take time. While it was apparent the driver had been drinking, it was possible that by the time they got to the station, she would no longer test above the legal limit. There was, however, a solution. An alcohol solution.

Case Closed

Watching the driver's head disappear again as she leaned over to her purse in the passenger seat, Officer Ona Honda keyed the radio.

"I need backup," Officer Honda announced into the handset. "One to transport to the station for BAC testing."

Ona Honda walked back to the car and bent down to talk to the driver through the open window. "Have you been drinking tonight, ma'm?"

"Well, yes, but only a few."

"I'm going to have to ask you to step out of your car."

"Why?"

"I need to do a field sobriety test."

"I'm not drunk!"

"Maybe. But your odds of convincing me would have been better if you hadn't just taken a swig to calm your nerves."

DEMONSTRATION 11
SEEING RED, WEARING BLUE

Anger: an acid that can do more harm to the vessel in which it is stored than to anything on which it is poured.

Seneca the Younger, ca. 30 CE

Although it may seem ridiculous to again read the instruction to put on safety glasses and examination gloves—especially when the demonstration involves cutting an apple on a paper plate and pouring wine—please do. Scan down the demonstration and see that we will ask you to test with vinegar and ammonia. If you have ever gotten pure vinegar in your eyes, or on a fresh cut, you may understand our precautions.

As we will discuss in more detail below, acids are a class of chemicals that have been described as having a sour taste, like that of citric acid or vinegar. But this definition has been replaced by a safer one that does not require the dangerous practice of tasting chemicals. Though it may seem like a circular definition, an acid is probably best described as a material that reacts with a base to form a neutral compound. A base is another class of chemicals that was once described as having a bitter taste, such as soap, but is better described as a material that reacts with acid. Another somewhat circular definition might be to say that an acid is a chemical that turns blue litmus paper red. A base is a chemical that turns red litmus paper blue. Litmus paper is paper that has been permeated with an *indicator*: a chemical that changes color in different environments; that is, it indicates whether the solution is acidic, basic, or neutral. Purple cabbage juice makes an excellent indicator, but it can have a bit of an odor. In this demonstration, we will use red wine and red apple peels as indicators.

With safety glasses and gloves in place, obtain a small glass that you can see through and fill it a quarter of the way with tap water. Place 1 to 2 teaspoons of red wine in the water. It should be enough wine to give a distinctive red-wine color to the water.

Add a teaspoon (5 milliliters) of household ammonia. The molecules that give the wine the red color now respond to the basic environment caused by the ammonia. The solution should now appear dark blue-green.

Add 2 teaspoons (10 milliliters) of vinegar. The solution should return to its original wine color as the basic environment is neutralized by the addition of the acidic vinegar. (We will be discussing this neutralization reaction you've just witnessed in the chapter that follows.) Try tipping the scale even further by adding even more vinegar and see what happens. You should see another color change, but the color will depend on the wine.

Obtain an apple with a very dark red peel, such as a Red Delicious or a Rome, and an inexpensive paper plate. We are not asking you to use an inexpensive paper plate out of sympathy for your budget; the experiment will probably work better on an inexpensive plate than on a more costly plate. The manufacturing process for the inexpensive plates usually results in a slightly basic paper.

Keeping your safety glasses in place, slice the apple with a knife so that the knife makes a cut into the paper plate. Make several apple slices so that there are several cuts into the paper plate. Remove the apple and note the color of the slice mark on the plate.

The skin of the apple initially appears red because it contains a naturally occurring dye, an organic molecule, that acts as an indicator. The red dye in the skin of the apple is forced into the plate with the sharp edge of the knife, and on the plate it should appear blue to purple.

Now pour a small amount of distilled (clear) vinegar onto a paper towel and wipe the blue cut marks. Observe what happens to the blue color as the chemical environment becomes acidic as a result of the vinegar. You should see the dye develop a greenish color.

The dye in the apple skin is acting as an indicator because its color indicates its chemical environment. It will be blue in a basic environment and turn greenish in the more acidic environment of vinegar.

Acids and bases will indicate the resolution to "The Case of the Cracked Case."

CHAPTER 11

ACRIMONIOUS ADVERSITY: ACID-BASE CHEMISTRY

'Tis melancholy, and a fearful sign
Of human frailty, folly, also crime,
That love and marriage rarely can combine,
Although they both are born in the same clime;
Marriage from love, like vinegar from wine

Lord Byron, *Don Juan*, ca. 1820

THE CASE OF THE CRACKED CASE

Forensic chemist May B Wright reached across the restaurant table and took the hand of her husband, elementary school teacher Reed Story.

"I'm sorry, honey. I know I've been spending a lot of time at my new job lately, but it's all for a good cause."

"You've been catching lots of bad guys?"

May withdrew her hand and grunted. "Well, if I am, I'd be the last person to know. On TV they give the impression that one technician does all the tests—and the detective work—but in reality there can be as many as seven to ten technicians involved in different aspects of a crime scene investigation, and piecing together the big picture is left to the detectives. As for me, all I do, day after day, is run one test after another—and, oh, yes, stop and calibrate the instrument every time I get a new sample."

"So it's not exactly what you thought it would be?"

"Well, actually, it is what I thought it would be. I knew with a bachelor's degree I would have to start off as a technician running routine tests. But if you work hard and are good at what you do, they support you when you get ready to go for your master's—maybe even a PhD. With those credentials I should be able to move into the research side or become a specialist in an area that is more directly involved."

Reed smiled. "They're not going to find anyone who works harder than you."

The eatery the couple had chosen was a small, quiet, out-of-the-way Italian restaurant and at the moment they were the only customers. They reached across the table and touched hands in silent acknowledgment of this rare luxury.

May sighed. "It's a good long-term plan, but I'll be glad when I get to see the faces of the police officers who bring in the samples instead of just case numbers!"

Reed frowned. "Wow. Do they have you locked up in a closet somewhere?"

May laughed. "They may as well have. The room has my instruments, my samples, a fume hood, a computer, a sink, a bench, and that's about all. But this detachment from the case is for a good reason. The technicians are only human. If they knew the detailed facts of the cases, it might influence their interpretation of their results."

"So what do you do on a typical day?"

"The first thing I do is pick up my samples—materials that have been tested with presumptive tests—"

"Presumptive tests?"

"Little prepackaged tests—sort of like pregnancy tests. The patrol officers use them in the field to determine if a substance might be a drug."

May leaned down and fished in her purse. "Here, let me show you with my portable pharmacy!"

May pulled out a packet of headache powder and a packet of powdered antacid. Reed watched with interested amusement as she emptied a bit of each powder on a white square of the plastic-coated checkered tablecloth. She dipped a finger delicately into her Chianti and dropped a bit of the wine on each powder.

"There!" May announced triumphantly, waving her hands over the powders.

Reed leaned over to study the tablecloth. "I think I see what you mean. Both white powders look alike, but when you drop wine on them, the aspirin stays pretty much the same color, but the antacids turn a dark purple, almost blue."

May nodded. "The aspirin is an acid and the antacid is a base, so they react with the wine differently. The presumptive tests act in a similar way with a drug such as heroin or crack cocaine."

Reed regarded the piles thoughtfully and then asked, "But if the samples have already tested positive with the presumptive tests, then why do you have to recheck them?"

"There are several reasons. First, there are substances that can cause false positives. And the dilutants can affect the results . . ."

Reed frowned. "Dilutants?"

May opened her hands to the piles of powder on the tablecloth. "Prescription and over-the-counter medicines almost never come in pure form, mainly because the part of the pill or powder that is actually a drug is so small that it could get lost when you tried to take it! The pill is mostly 'carrier' or 'inactive ingredients.' In the illegal drug world, the same principle is at play: the drugs may be transported to dealers in pretty pure form, but the dealers cut the drugs with dilutants before they are sold on the street. These dilutants or other possible contaminants could skew results."

Reed nodded.

May continued, "And while the presumptive tests can provide probable cause for arrest, a confirmatory test is necessary for prosecution. The bottom line is 'beyond a reasonable doubt,' so evidence has to be checked and double checked."

"How do you run your confirmatory tests?"

"Well, first I calibrate my instrument—"

"Every time?"

"Every time. Then I do a spot check on the sample to see if I agree with the officer's conclusion."

"Have you ever found that the officer was wrong?" Reed interrupted, a gleam of intrigue in his eye.

May smiled, "Funny you should ask. Just recently, I had to report a result that conflicted with the officer's report."

"Was the presumptive test done incorrectly?"

"Unlikely. These are straightforward tests with an unmistakable color change."

"Was the officer color-blind?"

May laughed, "Color blindness would be discovered pretty quickly in the rigorous screening these officers undergo—if that were the case they'd have their backup read the test!"

"Did *you* make a mistake?"

"I checked and rechecked, even going to a second instrument and procedure."

Reed leaned forward conspiratorially, "Did the officers take some of the confiscated drugs for themselves and replace them with some other white powder? I saw a TV show once—"

May grinned. "Nope. Check your facts . . ."

The Chemistry of the Case

Acids and bases are the yin and yang of chemistry. They are opposites, yet they complete each other. Earlier we discussed valence electrons— the outer electrons available for bonding. And earlier we talked about covalent bonds being formed by sharing of two electrons. When both the bonding electrons come from one of the bond participants, then this electron-pair donor would be termed the *base*. The bonding entity that accepts the electron pair is called the *acid*.

To act as a base, a chemical entity (molecule or ion) has to have a pair of electrons available for bonding. The structure of the hydroxide ion (see figure 11.1a and b) shows three separate pairs of electrons available for bonding, so the hydroxide ion is an excellent candidate for a base. Another common base is ammonia. The structure provided in figure 11.1c indicates the nitrogen in ammonia also has a lone pair of electrons that it can donate. The positively charged hydrogen ion, H^+ (see figure 11.1d), is bereft of electrons. The hydrogen ion is therefore an excellent electron pair acceptor, which makes it an excellent acid. Although there are many types of acids, the hydrogen ion, for the sake of simplicity, will be the only acid we will consider here.

Figure 11.1e also depicts the bottom-line definition for an acid and a base: an acid is a material that reacts with a base, and a base is a material that reacts with an acid. Our examples of acid and base, the hydrogen ion, H^+, and the hydroxide ion, OH^-, as we see in figure 11.1, can react to form water, a neutral compound that is neither acid nor base. This reaction, the acid-base reaction, is called, appropriately enough, *neutralization*. In the demonstration with which this chapter began, common household chemicals were evaluated for their acidic

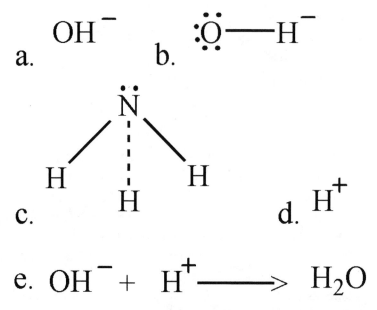

Figure 11.1. The hydroxide ion (a) can be written in expanded form (b) to show its three separate pairs of electrons available for bonding. Because it has these unbonded pairs, the hydroxide ion is an excellent candidate for a base. Another common base is ammonia, NH_3. The expanded form for ammonia (c) shows a pair of electrons on the nitrogen that are available for bonding. The positively charged hydrogen ion, H^+, has no electrons around its nucleus (d) and is therefore an excellent electron pair acceptor and an excellent acid. Our bottom-line definition of an acid is a substance that can react with a base, and our definition of a base is a substance that can react with an acid. An example of this acid-base reaction—neutralization—is shown in part (e).

or basic nature, and we saw evidence of these two types of materials undergoing a neutralization reaction.

Acid-base chemistry is found in many everyday situations: swimming pool chemistry, fish tank chemistry, personal hygiene chemistry, gardening chemistry, and food chemistry, to name a few. Acids, such as vinegar or grapefruit juice, tend to be sour. Bases, such as soap, tend to be bitter. Taste, as noted earlier, is never recommended as a method for classifying unknown chemicals and is unnecessary if there are indicators such as cranberry juice or red wine available.

When acid-base chemistry is vital to a process, the term *pH* will often be associated with it. For instance, the pH of swimming pools must be tested and adjusted on a regular basis. A personal care product may be pH balanced. The pH of a material, which normally ranges from 0 to 14, is a measure of its acid or base nature. The larger the pH value, the more basic. For instance, household ammonia typically has a pH of 11 to 12. Saturated sodium bicarbonate solution will have a pH of around 8.5 at room temperature. The lower the pH value, the more acidic. Black coffee has a pH of 4.5 to 5.5, and lemon juice typically has a pH of about 2.5. Battery acid, not a mixture to be trifled with, has a pH of about 1. Acid-base chemistry plays a significant role in much of forensic chemistry, including drug chemistry—an area of major concern to law enforcement.

Not all drugs, of course, are a cause for legal concern. The structures of two of the more innocuous, drug-related compounds, salicylic acid and caffeine, are shown in figure 11.2. The drug aspirin is a slightly modified form of salicylic acid, and salicylic acid is, as the name implies, an acid. It is an acid because it can dissociate in aqueous solution to release H^+. Salicylic acid was originally obtained by chewing willow bark, but when the material was purified, it was found that the acidic nature had to be tempered (buffered) to avoid stomach upset.

Caffeine is another drug with herbal origins, but this drug is a base. Although caffeine use is common in many parts of the world, caffeine is a stimulant, and in some areas and cultures, its use is prohibited. Thus caffeine, in these cultures, is an illegal drug.

Several drugs that are currently considered dangerous were once thought to be harmless. Tetrahydrocannabinol, or THC, the active ingredient in marijuana, is an acidic drug that has had a rather erratic legal history. It apparently does have at least some recognizable medical utility in reducing the nausea associated with chemotherapy and

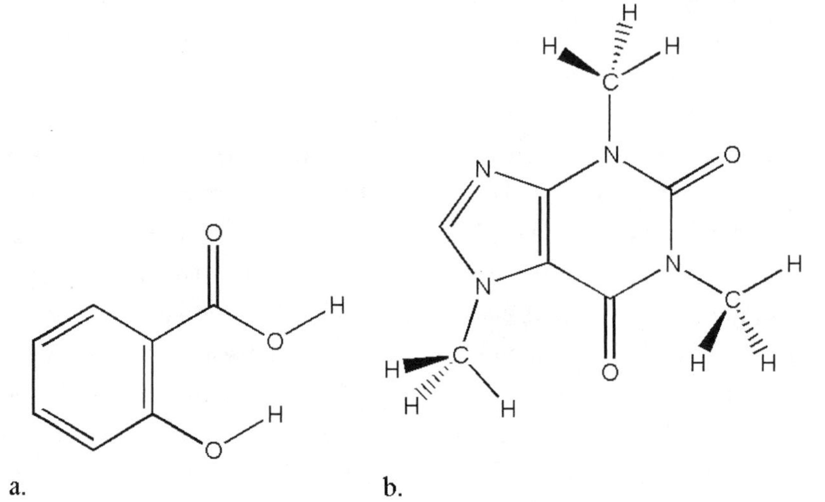

Figure 11.2. (a) Salicylic acid and (b) caffeine.

can combat the wasting associated with cancer. But there are synthetic mimics that have similar effects but are not subject to abuse, so the controversy surrounding the use of marijuana continues.

On the other hand, the big three—cocaine, heroin, and methamphetamine—are incontrovertibly illegal in virtually all countries. The structures of cocaine, heroin, and methamphetamine are shown in figure 11.3. These three compounds contain nitrogen with a non-bonded pair of electrons, which allows these compounds to act as bases. The compounds have other structural similarities, but cocaine and methamphetamine are stimulants, whereas heroin is a *narcotic*, a drug capable of inducing narcosis (a deep stupor or unconsciousness).

Heroin is a synthetic derivative of the compound morphine. Opium, the natural product from which morphine is derived, is harvested from unripened opium-poppy seed pods. Raw opium has strong narcotic properties when ingested. Crude heroin is relatively simple and cheap to produce in a process that involves treatment of opium extract with lime (calcium oxide), ammonia, acetic anhydride (a chemical used in the production of aspirin), sodium bicarbonate (baking

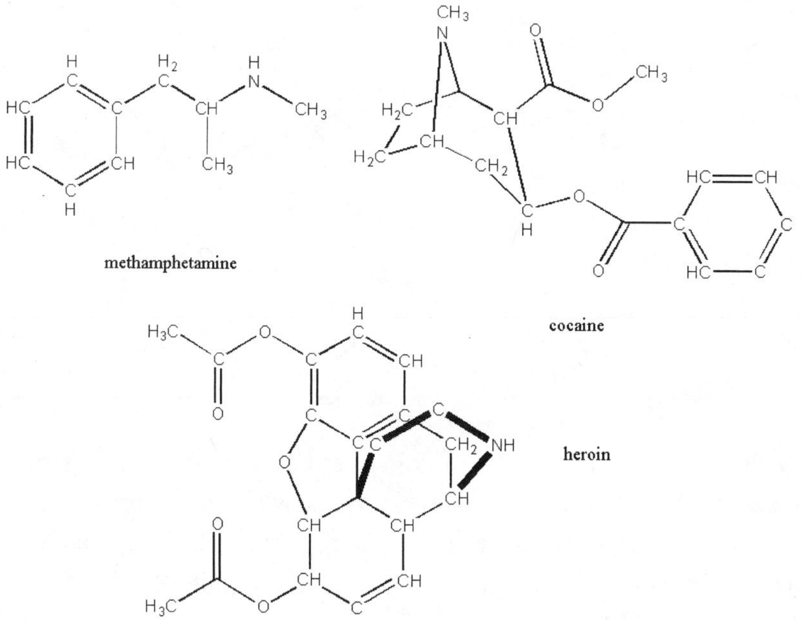

Figure 11.3. The structures of cocaine, heroin, and methamphetamine. Note that for these more complicated structures, some bonds have been omitted and some carbons are not explicitly shown. Groups such as CH_3 may be written in condensed form.

soda), alcohol, and activated charcoal. But the quality demanded by addicts is more expensive and involves a more complicated chemical procedure.

To create a crystalline form that is soluble in water and therefore easier to inject, the heroin base is neutralized with hydrochloric acid. The reaction and the resulting hydrochloride salt are shown in figure 11.4. Though still used in some countries as a painkiller for terminally ill patients, chronic heroin use suppresses natural endorphins, the body's own chemicals that attenuate pain. Once the body's production of endorphins has been stopped, then withdrawal of the heroin will result in acute pain, even when there is no physical cause.

Interestingly, this withdrawal and the dangers associated with dirty needles used for injection remain the most dangerous aspects of heroin

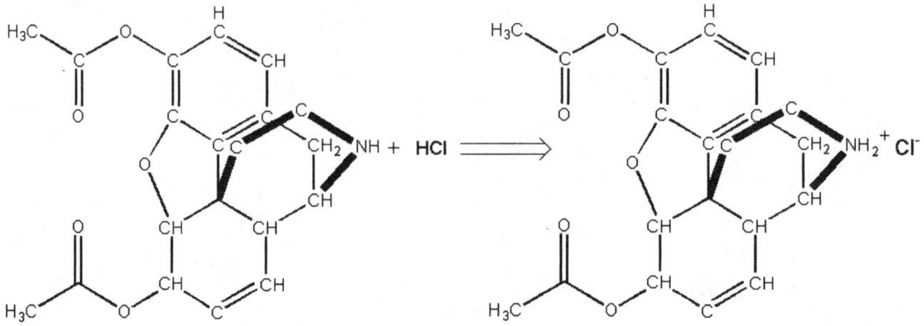

Figure 11.4. The reaction between heroin and hydrochloric acid and the resulting salt.

use. The legendary deaths by heroin overdose are often attributable to poisoning by the dilutants or interactions with other drugs, such as alcohol or cocaine. Because cocaine and methamphetamine are stimulants, they may be used to moderate the sedation of heroin, compounding the ill effects.

Amphetamines are stimulants that can be used medically for attention deficit disorder and to treat depression, obesity, or narcolepsy. Abuse can lead to severe psychosis, including symptoms associated with schizophrenia, though usually temporarily, and withdrawal can cause depression. *Methamphetamine*, or methylamphetamine, is a strong stimulant that has been used by militaries to energize troops and as a treatment for depression and obesity, though even its legitimate use has been curtailed because of its potential for abuse. Adverse effects of methamphetamine are similar to those of amphetamine, compounded by the debilitation of sleep deprivation and malnutrition. Methamphetamine is not directly derived from a natural product, but it can be synthesized by several relatively straightforward processes, and most of the necessary chemicals are available in over-the-counter products. The 1960s saw the rise of bootleg methamphetamine "cooks" and "kitchens." In 1986 the United States government attempted to curb the production by controlling the distribution of the chemical precursors for methamphetamine synthesis.

Cocaine is a stimulant that derives from the coca plant. As an herb, coca leaves were chewed and enjoyed for centuries by the indigenous peoples of South America and, later, their European conquerors. In pure form, cocaine is a white, smooth-surfaced material. It can be made into a crystalline salt in a manner similar to that used for heroin, as shown in figure 11.4. *Freebase* cocaine is the original, basic form of cocaine as opposed to the crystalline salt. The salt is soluble in water, but the freebase is not. Freebase is preferred by some users because it vaporizes at low temperatures and is therefore suitable for smoking. The salt is not smokable, but can be dissolved for drinking or injecting. It can also be taken in through nasal inhalation or simply eaten. The high from inhaling the freebase is more immediate and intense but does not last as long. Freebase cocaine can be obtained from the crystalline salt by dissolving the salt in water, filtering off any dilutants that are insoluble in water, and neutralizing it with a base such as ammonia or sodium bicarbonate. As the freebase, the cocaine is insoluble in water and forms a fine suspension. An oil-like substance, such as diethyl ether, is used to extract it. As we discussed in chapter 5, oil and water do not mix, and the freebase, being more soluble in the ether than the water, is transferred to the ether and separated. Oil-like substances, however, can also be more flammable. In addition, the fumes can be heavier than air and show up in unexpected places in unexpectedly high concentrations. As a result, the danger of flash fires always exists with the use of ethers, as does the danger of explosion.

To avoid the dangers (and bother) associated with the ether extraction step, *crack cocaine*, another form of freebase cocaine, is prepared by simply removing the water after the salt has been neutralized. The dry residue contains freebase cocaine, any dilutants that were in the original salt, and leftover base, such as sodium bicarbonate. The crusty mixture resembles water pipe scale and can be broken into small chunks called "rocks." The name "crack cocaine" comes from the crackling noise that is made when the material is smoked: the trapped water evaporates with pops and crackles.

Chronic use of cocaine can lead to alterations in brain chemistry that cause depression, which promotes dependency. Habitual nasal use can lead to tissue damage because the salt can dissolve in the mucus and liberate hydrochloric acid. The stimulant effect of cocaine can cause aggression, paranoia, and psychosis. Feeling as good as Superman is good for Superman, but bad in the hands of us mortals.

Experimentation with psychoactive materials began with the evolution of the human psyche and will continue as long as the psyche seeks to be altered, but because of their potential for aggravating antisocial behavior, these drugs are usually controlled by law and confiscated when found in illegal possession. It is the job of chemists such as May B. Wright in "The Case of the Cracked Case" to analyze samples of illegal drugs brought to her to confirm their content. To accomplish her job in the most efficient, economical, and accurate manner, May must be aware of the acid-base properties of the samples, the best method for analysis, and how possible contaminants might affect a spot test. In fact, it was a spot test that was the cause of May's concern in "The Case of the Cracked Case."

Case Closed

Reed Story regarded his wife's enigmatic smile. "Let's see. You received a sample that was reported to have a positive presumptive test. You did a spot check on the sample and got a negative result. You checked your instrumentation and confirmed your negative result. So what happened . . . ?"

"In forensic labs," May hinted, "everything is checked, checked, and rechecked."

"Aha!" Reed leaned back in a triumphant gesture. "I get it! They were running a spot check on you!"

"Yep," May conceded. "And I passed!"

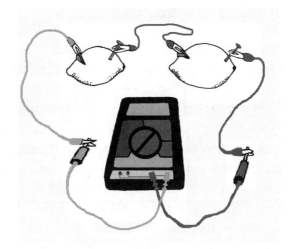

DEMONSTRATION 12
REDUCED TO ESSENTIALS

*"As a rule," said Holmes, "the more bizarre a thing is
the less mysterious it proves to be. It is your commonplace, featureless crimes which are really puz-
zling, just as a commonplace face is the most difficult to identify."*

Sir Arthur Conan Doyle, *The Red-Headed League*,
ca. 1890

The work of chemists and criminalists have many characteristics
in common, including their sorting, respectively, of chemicals
and criminals into classes so as to better analyze their behavior. The
reactions that we will be discussing here, *redox reactions*, are useful
in analysis and synthesis. For this reason, chemists keep a catalog of
oxidizing agents and *reducing agents* that can be used, respectively, to
induce *oxidation* and *reduction*: the reaction pair that make up the category of redox reactions.

After securing your safety glasses over your eyes, obtain the following items described in "Crime Lab and Crime Solutions": eight fresh lemons (place them into a small box or a pan so that they don't roll around easily), eight fairly clean pennies (you can clean pennies by placing them in a vinegar–table salt mixture, swirling, waiting a few minutes, then rinsing), eight zinc-coated nails (called galvanized nails at the hardware store), and nine alligator clip connector wires.

Take a small knife and cut a single slit into each lemon long enough to accommodate a penny and about a quarter inch (not quite a centimeter) deep. Place a clean penny into each slit. At a separate location on each lemon, gently push in one zinc-coated nail. Take one alligator clip wire and attach it to the penny of the first lemon. Take a second alligator clip wire and attach it to the nail on the same lemon. Attach the other end of this same wire to the penny of the second lemon. Attach another wire from the nail of the second lemon to the penny of the third lemon, and so on, until each nail from a previous lemon is attached to the penny on the next lemon. If the lemons are in a line, then each lemon will be connected to the next lemon in line with one wire, and the connections will alternate from nail to penny. This arrangement is shown in the illustration at the beginning of this demonstration for two lemons; your arrangement should look the same, but with more lemons.

On your voltmeter, you will probably have one red lead and one black lead. The black lead should be fitted to the voltmeter connector marked "ground" or "common" or "COM" or "–" or perhaps just the ground symbol, which is usually an inverted triangle, either solid or striped. The red lead should be fitted to the voltmeter connector marked "volts" or "+" or "V" or "DCV" or "VDC," depending on what your voltmeter's designers chose to indicate direct-current voltage (as opposed to alternating-current voltage). Attach this red lead to the open connector on the penny of the first lemon and attach the other lead, the ground, to the other open connector on the nail of the last lemon. Turn on the voltmeter and switch the selector knob to voltage, choosing a range that will accommodate 5 volts. You should observe approximately 4.5 V on the meter. If it reads –4.5 volts, switch the voltmeter leads. If nothing happens, make sure all of the lemon connections are secure and that the nails or pennies have not worked their way loose. Make sure the connectors run in an alternating pattern: nail to penny to nail to penny to nail to penny, and so on.

The reaction that is producing the voltage is similar to the reaction we saw in chapter 7, except that now the zinc nail is providing the electrons instead of copper wire. Because the lemon is a more complicated environment than a copper-ion solution, many reactions may occur once electrons reach the penny. The hydrogen ion, present in the acidic lemon juice, is a likely candidate for reaction. Because positive ions are present and able to accept electrons, and zinc is present and more willing to donate electrons, electrons will migrate from zinc to the copper wire, where they react.

$$Zn \rightarrow Zn^{2+} + 2e^-$$
$$2H^+ + 2e^- \rightarrow H_2$$

The path of least resistance for these electrons is through the wires, and the voltage that we measure is the push of the electrons through the wire trying to get from zinc to copper. The push of the electrons is similar to the push of high water trying to flow over a dam to a lower level, and in fact the analogy of the flow of electrons (electric current) and the flow of a stream (water current) is a good one in many ways. Each lemon individually provides less than a volt, but hooked together in a series, each voltage adds to the next. So by the time you get to the eighth lemon, you have enough voltage—enough water going over the dams—to provide 4.5 volts.

Four and a half volts is enough to perform some simple electrical tasks. If you have an old, inexpensive digital watch that still works but the battery has long since died (or if you invest in a cheap watch and remove the battery), you could try opening the battery compartment and touching the open jumper wires from the lemons to the two leads where the battery used to be.

It is a little tricky to find the right leads. You could try putting the battery back and using its position to decide which are the right leads, or you could just poke around until you get the digital display to light up. It may be necessary to switch the leads unless you know which side calls for positive and which for negative.

In "Crime Lab and Crime Solutions," we suggested you visit an electronics shop to purchase a small, light-emitting diode (LED) that requires less than 4 volts to operate. You can now attach the open wires from the lemons to the leads of this LED. If it doesn't light up, try switching the leads. We found that the yellow LEDs work best.

Either way, left or right, reduction or oxidation, redox reactions lead to the resolution of "The Case of the Reducing Rat."

CHAPTER 12

BURNING PASSION: RUNAWAY REDOX REACTIONS

The many men, so beautiful!
And they all dead did lie:
And a thousand thousand slimy things
Lived on; and so did I.

The cold sweat melted from their limbs,
Nor rot nor reek did they:
The look with which they looked on me
Had never passed away.

Samuel Taylor Coleridge, *The Rime of the Ancient Mariner*, ca. 1798

THE CASE OF THE REDUCING RAT

Detective Barry Bodie straightened up from his crouch near the steps leading into the cellar and looked into the anxious eyes of the property owner standing beside him. He dusted off his hands. Removing a notebook from his jacket and retrieving a pencil from his pocket, he asked, "Can you describe how you found the deceased?"

"This property was abandoned for years before I bought it. The previous owner had tenants from time to time, but the tenants didn't do much in the way of upkeep. There hasn't been an occupant in the house for quite a while. The guy I bought it from said the cellar and outbuildings have been sealed for years, but I think I've seen signs of vagrants. I got it for a song. I am—was—going to restore it as a bed and breakfast, but now I don't know—"

"The body?" Detective Bodie interrupted.

"Yes. Well. I took possession two years ago, but I can only do repairs on weekends, so I just got around to the cellar. I was in the process of clearing out the rubble when I came across the box and took the lid off."

"Why did you take the lid off?"

"Curiosity, I guess. As soon as I saw the body I dropped the lid and called the police—called you, that is." The young man pointed down into the cellar to where a long board rested beside a similarly long box. The box contained a plainly visible human skeleton and showed equally plain signs of vermin activity in the form of at least two access holes gnawed into the wooden sides.

Detective Bodie regarded the owner. "These vagrants you spoke of—"

Their conversation was interrupted by the arrival of the coroner, Luce Grip, and the evidence technician from the state crime lab, Rusty Nale. After a brief exchange of information, the coroner and the technician descended into the cellar and began their work. After concluding his interview with the young man, Detective Bodie joined Grip and Nale in the cellar.

"Got anything yet?" Bodie asked.

"There's a bullet hole in the skull," explained Luce Grip. "And from the pelvis, I'd say the vic was male, but that's not positive yet."

"Anything in the pockets? Any ID?"

"Nothing but a couple of quarters, an empty bag of chips, and a chewed-up wallet," said Nale. "The rats got to everything even remotely edible. The ID is gone from the wallet."

"Can you tell how long this guy's been dead?"

"Not without going to the lab," said Grip. "Between the rats and the bugs, there's not much to go on. It'll take some time. We're pretty backed up."

Detective Bodie frowned. "Can't you give me something? Now the cat—er, rat—is out of the bag, pertinent people might start to evaporate. The new owner places the closed box here for at least the last two years . . ."

Rusty Nale looked up. "Well, don't let him out of your sight. Even from the little evidence I've found, I can tell you this body has been here less than two years."

Detective Bodie frowned. "How?"

The Chemistry of the Case

So far, our survey of chemical reactions has covered precipitation reactions and acid-base reactions. Now we add a third class of reactions: redox reactions.

The defining characteristic of a redox reaction is the exchange of electrons. In the lemon battery (demonstration 12), we saw an exchange of electrons doing the work of lighting an LED. You may have observed that the penny was shinier where it had been in the lemon, which is evidence of the acid, the hydrogen ions, from the lemons. These hydrogen ions would very much like to regain their electrons and form hydrogen gas. When connected to zinc with a wire, the hydrogen ions exert a pull on zinc electrons, and zinc, which is less attached to its electrons than the hydrogen ions are, gives up electrons to hydrogen. This exchange of electrons was represented by the two partial, or *half reactions*,

$$2H^+ + 2e^- \rightarrow H_2$$
$$Zn \rightarrow Zn^{2+} + 2e^-$$

We call half reactions that have electrons on the product side *oxidation reactions*. The zinc half reaction in the lemon battery is an oxidation reaction because it gives up electrons to the hydrogen ion. Half reactions in which electrons are on the reactant side are called *reduction reactions*. The hydrogen-ion half reaction in the lemon battery is a reduction reaction because it gains electrons to form hydrogen gas. A popular mnemonic for remembering this terminology is *LEO the lion says GER*. LEO stands for Lose Electrons Oxidation. Gain Electrons Reduction is the GER. The term *redox* is shorthand for reduction-oxidation and serves to remind us that these reactions must occur in tandem. The electrons can be exchanged only if there is an electron source and the electrons have some place to go. Besides making cute mnemonics, the terms *oxidation* and *reduction* have historical origins in metallurgy. When metals are found naturally in ores, they are in an ionized state. For instance, a common iron ore, iron pyrite or fool's gold, is the combination of an iron ion, Fe^{3+}, and the sulfide ion, S^{2-}. Cuprite is a copper and oxygen ore, and when cuprite is smelted, the copper ion loses its oxygen, gains electrons, and becomes copper metal. Because the pure copper metal has been relieved of its oxygen, it has been *reduced* in weight, and so the reaction is termed *reduction*. A reducing agent, such as charcoal, has to be present in the smelting process so that the oxygen has some place to go. The carbon reacts with the oxygen to form carbon dioxide; thus, a process that facilitates reduction has come to be called *oxidation*, even if no oxygen is involved.

Although redox reactions are perhaps most easily envisioned in batteries because of the obvious flow of electrons through wire, other redox reactions occur in combustion, corrosion, bleaching, putrefaction, respiration, metabolism, electrolysis, and the process by which food goes stale. The etchant used in our very first demonstration is an iron compound that removes copper from circuit boards by oxidizing the copper to soluble copper ions. Understanding redox reactions is essential to forensic chemists because of their omnipresence, but also because of specific reactions of interest. These reactions range from the curious— for instance, crack cocaine is smoked on steel wool so that the iron will preferentially oxidize and the cocaine will not alter its character or psychoactive properties—to the commonplace, such as combustion. Combustion, however, is not commonplace when it becomes arson.

Arson is defined as the crime of setting a fire with the intent of causing damage. While the notion of a serial arsonist, a "pyromaniac" or "firebug," is an intriguing one, this type of individual is actually quite rare. With arson, as with other crimes, the motivation is usually more mundane: revenge or profit. In fact, arson is very often committed to conceal another crime. But whatever the motivation, an understanding of redox reactions is essential to an arson investigation.

The primary reaction of an ordinary combustion process involves the redox of a hydrocarbon-based molecule and oxygen to form water and carbon dioxide. Methane, CH_4, the simplest hydrocarbon, is the principle component of natural gas and swamp gas because it forms when organic material rots (a redox reaction). When methane combines with oxygen, it can burn according to the following combustion reaction:

$$CH_4 + 2O_2 \rightarrow CO_2 + 2H_2O$$

The products of this combustion, carbon dioxide and water, are two fairly innocuous materials. The problems arise, of course, with the nonmaterial product of this redox reaction: heat. Although the heat generated and consumed in chemical reactions will be treated later on, heat cannot be omitted from any discussion of combustion. Heat, oxygen, and fuel are the big three—the fire triangle—necessary for burning, which is a sustained redox reaction.

To initiate and maintain a hydrocarbon combustion that is vigorous enough to produce light as well as heat—in other words, a flame—the hydrocarbon fuel needs to be in the gas phase or volatile enough to be promoted to the gas phase. When these conditions don't exist, an arsonist might use an *accelerant*, such as gasoline, paint thinner, or some other hydrocarbon derivative that is easily vaporized. Accelerants work to get the fire "started," that is, they provide sufficient heat so that solid materials undergo *pyrolysis*: breakdown into smaller, more volatile pieces that can then ignite. For example, in a wood fire, it is not the solid cellulose of wood that is burning but the pyrolysis products at the surface of the wood.

Because accelerants are often needed to initiate a vigorous fire, arson investigators and firefighters are taught to be alert to odd odors at the source of a fire. Dogs are used to sense accelerants, too. But the task of identifying a specific accelerant is complicated by many factors. To begin with, to be a good accelerant, the material must be volatile, so it is apt to vaporize and blow away. Residue, if it remains, is probably pyrolyzed, which means the investigators need to identify the original material from its pieces. Innocent items made from petroleum products—such as furniture, adhesives, carpet, clothing, toys, and tools—can confuse the issue by contributing their own pyrolysis products to the mix.

Because of its volatile nature, accelerant evidence must be collected in an airtight metal container. Plastic (made from petroleum products) can give off its own fumes, which might contaminate the evidence. In addition, an accelerant such as paint thinner or acetone might react with a plastic container, or a plastic or rubber seal, which could further complicate the investigation. Control samples, samples from areas not contaminated by the suspected accelerant, are essential to sort accelerant from any ambient hydrocarbon-based materials. But there's good news, too: when collecting evidence, arson investigators can exploit the fire triangle in reverse: heat, oxygen, and fuel are necessary to sustain a fire, and exclusion of any one of these will retard the fire. Therefore an investigator will search for intact accelerant in cracks or under carpet or anywhere a liquid might flow, but the oxygen supply would be restricted. Retarding fire by oxygen starvation, however, is not always a good thing. In a closed room where the oxygen supply has been effectively consumed, the intense heat might still create superheated pyrolysis products that can flash as soon as oxygen is admitted.

For other, slower oxidation reactions, however, excluding oxygen can be an effective redox retardant. Corrosion is a redox reaction; therefore, iron covered with paint or oil to exclude oxygen will resist corrosion longer. Food susceptible to oxidation can be stored in airtight containers, though an airtight state is never fully realized. Some foods, such as potato chips, are sealed in nitrogen-filled bags to retard spoilage but are also supplied with expiration dates, which acknowledges this method's limitations. The other limitation, of course, is that oxygen gas is not the only reagent that can cause oxidation. Nitrates serve as the oxidizing agent in gunpowder mixtures. Some heated plastics can release oxidizing agents. Some bacteria can grow even in the absence of oxygen, so it is better to dry evidentiary material such as biological samples before storage. Considerations such as these would eventually lead to the resolution of "The Case of the Reducing Rat."

Case Closed

Detective Bodie rubbed his chin in his hand. "Hmm . . . if you're right, he found an unusual way to conceal his crime. 'Discovering' the body himself would allow him to explain any fingerprints or trace—and avoid the embarrassing questions that would come up if someone else should happen to find it first. By keeping the body hidden for so long, he has obscured a lot of evidence. But how the heck can you narrow it down to less than two years?"

"It has to do with a redox reaction."

"The action of the bacteria on the bones?"

"No."

"The corrosion of the fittings on the box?"

"No."

"The rot of the wood?"

"No."

"Then what?"

"Food spoilage. Oily food like chips will only last about six months even in the best of packaging."

"Spoiled chips? I thought you said the rats ate all the food!"

"They did. But they didn't eat the package—or the expiration date stamped on it."

DEMONSTRATION 13 INCRIMINATING CHEMISTRY

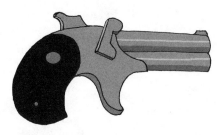

No weapon has ever settled a moral problem. It can impose a solution but it cannot guarantee it to be a just one.

Ernest Hemingway, ca. 1945

Another important class of chemical reactions produces gas as a product. Among the most famous—and infamous—is the explosion of gunpowder. In the following demonstration, we will show how the residue of reacted gunpowder, commonly called GSR for gunshot residue, might be collected. We will use impact caps as a stand-in for gunpowder in this simulation, but the dynamics of the explosive reaction are similar. The biggest difference is that the caps produce only a small amount of residue whereas an actual gun would produce much more. With care, however, the cap gun residue can be detected and the basic mechanism of the process can be appreciated.

Put on your safety glasses and examination gloves, but this time the gloves are not so much for your protection as they are to keep you from contaminating the test. Bring out the pack of lotion-free tissues, cap gun with caps, and total-salt aquarium test kit that we suggested for purchase in "Crime Lab and Crime Solutions." Take a tissue and moisten it with distilled or bottled water. Load the cap gun with caps so that you can fire at least four shots.

Cover as much of the barrel and cylinder of the cap gun with the damp tissue as possible. If you can, cover up the trigger and hammer areas as well. Discharge the cap gun at least four times and allow the smoky and gaseous residue to settle on the damp tissue. When you are done, place the tissue into a small plastic cup and pour in another tablespoon (15 milliliters) of water so that the tissue is completely soaked. The cap gun shot residue will dissolve in the water. After a minute, remove the tissue, squeezing out as much water as possible. This water is the sample to be tested with the total-salt test kit.

Read the directions on the total-salt test kit. Handle the materials carefully, as the label no doubt suggests. Then run the test on the water in which the tissue was rinsed. You should get a positive result, but to confirm your findings you need to compare your result with a control.

To obtain your control, clean your hands thoroughly and put on a new pair of examination gloves. Soak a clean tissue in the same amount of water as before and run the total salt test again. The sample obtained from the cap gun shot tissue should be about twice as rich in total salts as the blank sample of water.

Cap-gun impact caps are made from chlorine-containing compounds, which is why the residue can be found using procedures that test for salt. Regular GSR contains nitrogen compounds, usually in the form of nitrogen-oxygen compounds called nitrates. At one time, tests specific for nitrates were used to indicate that an object—a hand, a body, or clothing—had been exposed to gun smoke. The presence of nitrates from sources such as foods, fertilizers, or personal care products, however, led to too many false positives, so the presence of nitrates is no longer used as *inculpatory*, or incriminating, evidence. Present-day analyses for gunpowder check for a pattern of metal fragments, unreacted gunpowder, and other compounds and nitrates to ensure a more definitive assessment. Patterns, as it turns out, will also be meaningful in "The Case of the Material Witness."

CHAPTER 13

THE SMOKING GUN: EXPLOSIVE CHEMICAL REACTIONS

Consistency is contrary to nature, contrary to life.
The only completely consistent people are dead.

Aldous Huxley, ca. 1950

THE CASE OF THE MATERIAL WITNESS

The private investigator stepped forward and shook hands with the police detective.

"Chase Kars," he said, by way of introduction.

"Glad to meet you," replied the detective, seating himself behind a desk placard that read Detective Manny Douts. "Please, have a seat. How can I help you?"

"Well, as I said on the phone, the family is very upset about the delay in the disposition of this case and they have asked me to contact you to see if there is any way the matter can be expedited." Investigator Kars took his seat.

Detective Douts nodded his head sympathetically. "I certainly understand. It must be very trying for them. But the scene investigation, blood work, and toxicology reports take time, and we need all that information before we can proceed."

Kars nodded in response. "I understand. But is all this really necessary? As difficult as it is for the family to accept, it appears that the gunshot was self-inflicted. I don't think there is any benefit to be gained by putting them through more than they've already been through."

Detective Douts opened his hands. "I assure you I understand, but I believe it would be in the family's best interest to be thorough."

Chase Kars frowned. "But wasn't the weapon found in her hand?"

"Yes."

"And you found the bullet?"

"Yes. Two of them, in fact. One was in the wall."

Kars offered, "Hesitation isn't uncommon."

"No, it's not."

Kars continued. "Wasn't the fatal injury a close contact wound?"

"Yes."

"And wasn't there gunpowder residue on her hand?"

"Yes. All over her hand."

Investigator Kars met the detective's direct gaze.

"Oh," he said quietly, "I see."

The Chemistry of the Case

As we noted earlier, there are usually indications when a chemical reaction takes place: color change, precipitate formation, light production, and/or bubbles. This last sign, the formation of bubbles, is favored by many reactions. Mixing baking soda and vinegar forms enough bubbles to make science-fair volcanoes. A mixture of cream of tartar and baking soda, called baking powder, creates enough bubbles to turn batter into cake. Dropping a zinc-coated nail (also called an *anodized* or *galvanized* nail) into vinegar produces a lovely stream of bubbles. A gas-producing chemical reaction inflates lifesaving airbags in automobile accidents and the carbon dioxide produced in the fermentation of glucose produces enough bubbles to give beer a nice foamy head.

In short, if a reaction can form bubbles, it will. The question is, Why? The answer is entropy.

The official definition of *entropy* is the tendency for systems to move toward a state of maximum disorder, but the unofficial manifestations of entropy are everywhere. Soups mix, they don't separate. Perfumes waft, they don't congeal. Gunpowder explodes, it doesn't implode.

These systems act in the manner that they do because of entropy. A mixed soup is more disordered than the separated soup mix and water. Like kids let out for recess, perfume fumes spreading across a room are more disordered than when they are localized in a bottle.

There is a tendency to think of entropy as just an interesting theoretical construct, but it is as much of a driver in nature as energy. For instance, even without an input of energy, food dye spontaneously mixes in water. An input of energy is required to separate a mixture, to overcome entropy. The word *gas* derives from the word *chaos*, and the association is an apt one. Reactions that produce gas are driven forward because of the entropy inherent in the gas-phase product: the bubbles.

Entropy is a factor in the formation of bubbles, and it is a factor in how bubbles behave. In the absence of outside forces, gases expand uniformly in all directions. Floating freely in the air, bubbles are round. No one direction is more probable than another. In the presence of a force, such as a strong breeze, a bubble may distort in a given direction, but there is always a portion of the gas in the bubble moving in the opposite direction, too. Though the majority of the propellant in the cap gun was moving away from the shooter in the above demonstration, cap powder residue was detected on the tissue behind the muzzle. So at least some of the propellant moved in the opposite direction, too. Gas particles tend to spread in all directions.

Until they are constrained, gases continue to expand. A gas-phase sample fills its container, and if the container is not strong enough, the container bursts. A container bursting forcefully enough and quickly enough is called an explosion.

Gunpowder is a historically famous exploding gas-producing reaction. Although the recipes have evolved and permuted over the years, the original mixture contained carbon in the form of charcoal, solid sulfur, and a mixture of sodium nitrate and potassium nitrate, $NaNO_3$ and KNO_3, which is also known as saltpeter. When provided with a spark, this mixture reacts to produce at least potassium sulfate, a salt; potassium carbonate, a salt; carbon dioxide, a gas; and nitrogen, a gas. The last two help provide the explosive expansion. Besides being a gas-producing reaction, the gunpowder reaction can also be categorized as a redox reaction, like combustion. But whereas the combustion reactions of chapter 12 used oxygen gas for the oxidant, gunpowder uses an oxygen-containing salt such as potassium nitrate, KNO_3. A salt is easier to pack into a cartridge than a gas.

Gunpowder formulations were known in ancient China and were prepared routinely by at least the first century of the Common Era because the ingredients are relatively straightforward and easily obtained. Native sulfur is found in natural deposits near volcanoes and hot springs and has been known to add an odor to water in nearby streams. Charcoal is produced when wood burns. Sodium nitrate and potassium nitrate, saltpeter, is a by-product of the decomposition of animal waste and it can be harvested from manure piles.

The historic recipe for gunpowder is a formulation called *black powder*, but black powder produces clouds of black smoke, which can be a double liability: smoky clouds could make it difficult to see where you are shooting, and make it easier for others to aim at you.[1] Modern mixtures called *smokeless powder* consist of nitrated organic compounds. Smoke is an aerosol of large particles resulting from incomplete combustion. The nitrated organic compounds are so reactive that their combustion is essentially complete. The explosive power of these types of compounds is attested to by the notoriety of TNT, trinitrotoluene, although this particular nitrated organic compound is not used in gunpowder.

An impressive amount of chemical engineering has gone into the formulation of modern gunpowder, and its recipes are constantly being improved—with the main concern being the rate of explosion. The heat of the ignition needs to cause the gases formed by the reaction to expand rapidly enough to project the bullet, but not so rapidly as to blow up the barrel. Gas needs to be produced quickly, but at a steady rate. Just like a follow-through in tennis, bowling, or baseball, the longer the force of the explosion can be applied to the bullet, the higher the ultimate velocity, which is the muzzle velocity in this case. Nowadays, the size and shape of the grains of the gunpowder are controlled for burn properties. Some are even coated with a substance to delay the burn. If the particles do not all burn at once, gas production can be prolonged and the force sustained.

High-speed photography shows that gases exit the barrel in a ring like a smoke ring. The gases themselves are invisible, but they carry residue from the incomplete combustion of the grains and primer that was used to start the explosive process. The gun smoke can also carry *bullet wipe*, lubricant from the bullet itself, and particles of gun propellant, such as nitrates, but it is the particles of the primer that are most characteristic of gunshots and most useful for gunshot identification.

Like a smoke ring, the gun smoke ring spreads and dissipates to the extent that it is no longer detectable at about 18 inches (45 centimeters) from the muzzle. But if the target is close enough, the size of the ring imprint on the target can be used to estimate the distance between the target and the gun at the time of firing.

In the primer, a commonly used oxidant is barium nitrate. The fuel used in the primer is usually an antimony-sulfur salt, antimony sulfide, because in the primer a fast burn rather than a slow burn is desired. The reaction between the oxidant and the fuel in the primer can be like a bowling ball atop a ladder: the slightest nudge and down it goes. When the nudge is provided by the firing pin, the heat from the breakdown of the primer ignites the gunpowder.

Gunshot residue can be identified by the presence of metals—antimony, barium, and lead—in ratios that would result from a primer being fired. In addition, if a gun is fired at close range, GSR patterns can sometimes be used to estimate the distance of the gunshot or the proximity of a particular object to the gun as it fired. The patterns from GSR, for instance, provided pertinent information in "The Case of the Material Witness."

Case Closed

Investigator Kars surveyed the faces of the family members before him and then spoke as gently as possible to the older woman seated in the group's center. "The detective was not able to share all the information with me regarding the progress of the ongoing investigation, but I saw, when he summarized it for me, that there are still some questions that need to be answered regarding your daughter's assumed suicide."

A young woman put her hand on the arm of the older woman as she wept quietly into a tissue. "What questions?"

Kars spoke slowly. "We had supposed that a first shot was fired before the fatal shot, which is not unusual for someone preparing, but hesitating, to self-inflict a wound. But now there may be indications that the second shot was fired after her death."

There was an audible intake of breath.

"There was gunpowder residue found on her hand, but it was all over her hand. If she were holding the gun herself when it was fired, some parts of her hand should have been shielded. There should have been a distinct pattern to the residue. There may be several possible explanations as to why the residue was found where it was, but I think your best course would be to allow the police to conclude their investigation."

DEMONSTRATION 14
THREE STRIKES AND A
FOUL

*Franz remembers the
Inspector told him casts
could be taken from
footprints in snow. It
seemed so miraculous, like walking on water, that
Franz hadn't pressed him for details at the time.
Now he knows snow is added to the plaster instead
of water, so the liquid will be at the same temperature as the footprint. Franz also learned that paste,
suet, wet breadcrumbs, and porridge can be used
to copy footprints in an emergency, when plaster
isn't available.*

Jody Shields, *The Fig Eater*, ca. 2000

emonstration 14 is really four demonstrations because we have
four concepts to show. The first is that heat is produced by some
chemical reactions; the second is that certain chemical reactions cool
as they proceed. The third is that the amount of heat absorbed or given
off can influence the forensic utility of reactions, and the fourth is that
heat added to, or taken from, a chemical reaction can dictate its course.

The Heat Is On

With safety glasses and exam gloves in place, fetch the very fine steel
wool that was suggested for purchase in "Crime Lab and Crime Solutions." Putting on garden gloves just long enough to handle the steel
wool, carefully pluck a clump of steel wool from the package and soak
it in a small amount of vinegar. The vinegar facilitates an oxidation
reaction that rusts the steel wool. Pull the steel wool out of the vinegar

and place the thermometer into the middle of the steel wool clump. Close your hand around the clump and the thermometer. Note the initial temperature. Continue to monitor the temperature and notice the extent to which the temperature rises. We were able to observe about a 2.5°C (4.5°F) increase.

The oxidation of steel wool (rusting) is an *exothermic* process, which means it gives off heat as it proceeds.

For a control, make a cotton ball the same size as your steel wool sample and soak the cotton ball in vinegar. Remove it from the vinegar and place the thermometer in the middle, just as you did with the steel wool. You may still see a temperature change, but a much smaller one. This smaller temperature change is caused by the warmth of your hand and was a part of the larger temperature change seen earlier. As such, this addition to the effect would be called the *background* temperature change.

The Heat Is Off

With your safety glasses and flexible gloves still in place, put 2 to 3 tablespoons (30 to 45 milliliters) of citric acid (sour salt) into a small self-sealing sandwich bag. Place a quarter cup (60 milliliters) of cool tap water into a second sandwich bag. Place the water bag across the inside of your wrist where you can easily sense differences in temperature.

After you have a sense of the temperature of the bag, pour the plain water from this bag into the bag with citric acid and mix so that the citric acid begins to dissolve. Replace the mixture bag across the inside of your wrist and wait. The bag should begin to cool as the citric acid continues to dissolve.

The dissolution of citric acid is an *endothermic* process, which means that heat is transferred into the citric acid/water mixture from the surroundings. In this case, the surroundings are the water, the bag, and your skin. As heat is drawn into the dissolving system, it is removed from the surroundings, which causes the surroundings to cool.

Other materials such as "lite salt" (potassium chloride) and baking soda (sodium bicarbonate) also dissolve by an endothermic process, but we chose citric acid for this demonstration because the change is more noticeable.

In the Cold Light

With your safety glasses and exam gloves in place, take three glow sticks of the same color that were suggested for purchase in Crime Lab and Crime Solutions." Start them glowing by breaking the membrane and mixing the chemicals, keeping your treatment of the glow sticks as identical as possible. The light that you observe is the result of a chemical luminescent reaction and is considered a product of that reaction. Put one of the glow sticks in the freezer for two hours and note that the light becomes dimmer as the glow stick becomes colder. Once the two remaining glow sticks have died out (this should take several hours), wrap one of them in a paper towel and put it in the freezer. After twelve hours, bring it out and allow it to warm up. You should see it start glowing again, though perhaps not as intensely. Cold restores the glow sticks to some extent. You can compare it with the other glow stick that was not put in the refrigerator, but the comparison is not as clean as most controls because there are other factors at work (such as we will discuss in chapter 15).

A Villainous Cast

Plaster casts of footprints or tire marks have always been forensically important. Casts can be made using plaster of Paris, but plaster of Paris heats up—considerably—when water is added, which is why we will not be using it for this demonstration. Heat can change the physical form of the material, such as soil, in which the print was made, which could change the print. Cooling the material in which the print was made could be just as detrimental. Evidence technicians normally have several types of materials from which to choose when making plaster casts. Dental casting material (also called "dental stone") is often chosen because it does not change temperature much during the solidifying process.

Retrieve the dental casting material that you secured from your dentist or over the Internet as suggested in "Crime Lab and Crime Solutions." After putting on your safety glasses and examination gloves, mix the plaster with just enough water to make it easy to pour. Select shoes that have a pronounced tread and step into some soft soil to make a nice footprint. Pour your plaster into the imprint while being careful not to disturb the soil around the print. An attempt at this process should convince you that it is a delicate art and it takes a trained technician to perform it well routinely. Allow the cast to set at least overnight and then lift it out and clean it. Compare the print with the shoe that made it. Can you pick out the shape of the manufacturer's tread? Can you find any marks that came from wear? Markings that are unique to the history of that particular shoe are called *accidental marks*. A cast of the treads can help to identify the shoe type and manufacturer, but it takes a comparison of accidental marks to tie a particular shoe with a particular print. Casts of tire prints can be collected in a similar manner and their accidental marks examined. Accidental marks, we will see, were the crux of the matter in "A Very Cold Case."

CHAPTER 14

IN HOT WATER: THERMOCHEMISTRY

Solving a crime required the Inspecting Officer to determine the error in the situation.

Jody Shields, *The Fig Eater*,
ca. 2000

A VERY COLD CASE

The lecturer, Kurt Nod, spoke to the convention of forensic science professionals in a voice as crisp and clear as the equations he had written on the board.

" . . . in summary, identifying evidence—evidence that can be used to uniquely identify a suspect—is very important. But case evidence— evidence that can be used to develop a theory for the case—is extremely valuable, too. What I have presented here is the newest development in case evidence analysis. Are there any questions?"

A hand went up in the back of the hall.

"Yes?"

A young woman stood and identified herself. "Misty Chance, evidence technician." She addressed the podium. "May I say, your lecture was fascinating . . ."

Dr. Nod acknowledged the compliment.

"But," the young woman continued, "I notice that you left one thing out of your review of evidence collection techniques—footprint casting. Haven't there been some new developments in materials for making casts of footprints?"

"Well, yes." Dr. Nod answered. "Chemists are working on new materials and techniques all the time. Materials that are more plastic and thermally neutral. Methods for mixing the plasters to keep them at a compatible temperature, methods for cleaning the cast once it is made. . . . But let's face it. These techniques still rarely work well, and when they do, the best information they can provide is the approximate shoe size and maybe its make."

The young woman looked thoughtful, but continued. "What about accidentals? The random marks that appear on shoes from use? Doesn't the history of the shoe make every footprint unique?"

The lecturer coughed back a short laugh. "Yes, accidentals. Well, I'm afraid the utility of accidentals has been a bit overrated. Matching accidental markings on a footprint to a perpetrator's shoe can make a good plot for a crime drama, but in reality such evidence is rarely definitive and often challenged in court."

The lecturer went on. "In fact, I recall one case in particular in which we had quite abundant footprint evidence, but we were never able to make any use of it. The footprints were left by a voyeur—a Peeping Tom, if you will—who was terrorizing a particular neighborhood in the winter. At every scene, he left quite clear footprints in the snow. He must have thought we wouldn't be able to collect the footprints so he didn't bother to cover them up. However, with the new materials that are available, such as a plaster that mixes at low temperature, we were actually able to recover several footprints from the snow. But it didn't do any good. We weren't able to discern any accidentals in any of the footprints."

Dr. Nod began to look around for more questions when the young woman spoke up again.

"Excuse me, sir. But about those footprints . . . I think I know where you went wrong."

The Chemistry of the Case

Thermochemistry is the study of the role of heat in chemical reactions. To address the role of heat in chemical reactions, it is necessary to define our terms precisely, beginning with heat.

Heat is the flow of energy. When a system "heats up," energy flows into the system. When a system "cools down," energy flows out of the system. So the next logical question is, What is energy? Energy is the ability to do work, and energy comes in two basic forms: *kinetic energy* and *potential energy.*

Kinetic energy is energy in motion. All atomic- and molecular-sized particles are always in some state of motion. For an atom, there is only one mode of motion possible and that is the motion of the atom as it flies across the room or bounces off other atoms or molecules. This mode of motion is called *translational motion.* For a molecule, two other modes of motion may become available: *rotational motion* and *vibrational motion* (as illustrated in figure 14.1). The inherent motion of molecular-sized particles is evident when a drop of food coloring is placed as gently as possible on the surface of an apparently still glass of water: the food coloring spreads with the minute movements of the molecules of the liquid.

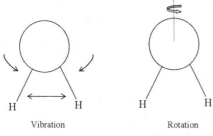

Figure 14.1. Molecules can move laterally (translational motion) and can also rotate and vibrate.

Potential energy is stored energy—energy waiting to be released. A compressed spring is a good representation of potential energy. On the molecular scale, potential energy can be stored in the bonds that hold atoms together in molecules. In a chemical bond, positively charged nuclei are held together by the intercession of a cloud of negatively charged electrons. If something should happen to disrupt the density of electrons between the nuclei, the bond would be broken, and the atoms would fly apart as though released from a compressed spring. In this event, the potential energy of the bond would be converted into the kinetic energy of atoms in motion.

Every chemical system, from moon rock to mayonnaise, contains some amount of energy in its chemical bonds and/or in the motion of its atoms and molecules. When energy is added to a normal gas, liquid, or solid, the energy tends to distribute itself in a uniform, statistical manner among the various translational, rotational, and vibrational modes. Temperature is solely a measure of the translational mode because the thermometer can register only the motion of molecules that collide with it. But energy tends to be uniformly distributed, so the temperature of a sample tends to increase linearly with the amount of heat added—unless the system is going through a phase change. When heat is added to a pot of water, the temperature will go up until the boiling point, but heat added at the boiling point goes into promoting molecules to the gas phase rather than increasing translational motion, so the temperature stays constant.

The essence of chemistry is the rearrangement of atoms from one molecular material into another, which requires breaking and re-forming bonds. The question now is, Why do some chemical reactions heat up their surroundings (such as the reactions in hot packs) and why do some reactions cool down their surroundings (such as the reactions in cold packs)? The answer is in the trade-off between the potential energy stored in the bonds of reactants and products. If the original bonds, the reactants, have more stored energy than the energy stored in the new bonds—the products—there will be a net release of energy. If the new bonds have more stored energy than the old bonds, then the reaction will require an input of energy, which it may absorb from the environment.

In other words, energy is part of the overall chemical balance. From demonstraton 14, we may surmize that temperature sensitivity could be a problem for presumptive tests such as the ones illustrated in chapter 1. In chapter 1, we did not have the tools to discuss the details of the chemistry, but now we have enough information. Caffeine and acetaminophen are bases. When the aquarium indicator is added to samples of these two compounds, the color shifts from yellow to green, indicating a base. But this reaction must be at least somewhat endothermic because cooling the reactants inhibits the reaction. Try it.

In chapter 11, we discussed illicit methamphetamine kitchens, and in these kitchens, the methamphetamine cooks use all the reactions we've talked about so far: precipitation, redox, acid-base, and gas formation. Heat is also involved.

The starting material for methamphetamine is ephedrine, an ingredient that used to be readily available in over-the-counter cold medications, but that is now more closely controlled. One of the several methods that methamphetamine cooks have to choose from requires the use of red phosphorus, which can be obtained from match heads. If the phosphorus reaction is overheated, a poisonous gas, phosgene, may form, turning a dangerous enterprise into a deadly one. One of the steps in another of the methods is so exothermic that burns are a common hazard of the trade. So, it would seem, attention to detail is as essential to crime as it is to crime solving. It was attention to a small detail that led to the resolution of "A Very Cold Case."

Case Closed

Dr. Kurt Nod's impassive face met the eyes of the frowning evidence technician.

"You know where I went wrong?" asked Dr. Nod. "Do you think the footprints in the snow were incorrectly collected?"

"No, sir," said Misty Chance. "Incorrectly interpreted."

Dr. Nod's eyebrows rose. "How so, young lady?"

"Well, sir, accidental markings come from the history of the shoe. If there were no markings, maybe the shoe had no history. Maybe the perp knew that footprints could be collected from the snow but still didn't worry because each time he wore a brand-new pair of shoes."

Dr. Nod's face registered momentary surprise, but then he shrugged. "If that were true, then it proves my point: footprint evidence is useless!"

Ms. Chance nodded politely and then added, "But it might have helped develop a theory for the case. Maybe you could have looked for multiple purchases at a local shoe store or a shoe store robbery—"

Dr. Nod interrupted. "Well, as it turns out, neither one of those was true."

He shuffled the papers in front of him, and then looked back up, frowning.

"When we arrested a suspect, he gave his occupation as shoe store owner."

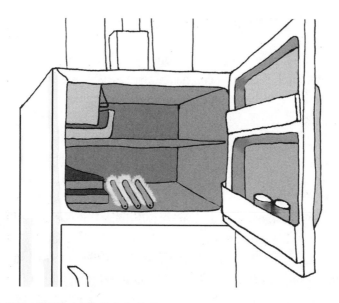

DEMONSTRATION 15
SEQUENCE OF EVENTS

Tobacco, coffee, alcohol, hashish, prussic acid, strychnine, are weak dilutions; the surest poison is time.

Ralph Waldo Emerson, ca. 1860

My candle burns at both ends;
It will not last the night;
But ah, my foes, and oh, my friends—
It gives a lovely light!

Edna St. Vincent Millay, *First Fig*, ca. 1920

hemical reaction rates, or chemical *kinetics*, factor into several processes of interest to the forensic chemist. For instance, one of the objectives of gunpowder engineering is to control the rate of reaction. The goal is to produce a sustained, yet adequately vigorous, burn. The following demonstrations show first how two seemingly similar chemical reactions can have vastly different reaction rates, and second, how an ambient factor, such as temperature, might influence a reaction rate.

Put on your safety glasses and flexible exam gloves. Use a prepared solution or make a new solution of copper sulfate (described in "Crime Lab and Crime Solutions") in a plastic cup by filling the cup about halfway with distilled or bottled water (about a cup, or 240 milliliters) and pouring in about a teaspoon (5 milliliters) of copper sulfate crystals. You will have to swirl the solution for several minutes to dissolve the crystals. Once the crystals are dissolved, the solution should be a sky blue color. Pour half of this solution into a second plastic cup.

Making sure your hands are protected by garden gloves, tear off a pinch of steel wool. Take a 6-inch-by-2-inch (15-centimeter-by-5-centimeter) strip of aluminum foil and fold it over several times so you end up with a stiff strip 2 inches long and about a quarter inch wide (about 5 centimeters by a half centimeter). Put the steel wool in one cup and the aluminum foil in the other.

You will see a very rapid redox reaction with the steel wool. You will observe copper metal plating out on the surface of the steel wool within minutes of its introduction into the solution. The aluminum foil will need to sit overnight before you can observe clear evidence of copper metal forming on the surface of the foil. This reaction is very slow compared to the steel wool reaction, although on the surface they appeared the same—copper plating out of solution and onto a metal.

Now, with your safety glasses and gloves in place, select three glow sticks of the same color and break the inner chamber in all three to start the reaction. Set one glow stick aside as a control. Wrap another glow stick in a paper towel and put it in the freezer for an hour. When the hour is up, warm some tap water in a pan (do not bring it all the way to a boil) and dip the third glow stick into the warm water for a minute or so. Remove this glow stick and compare it with the control. The warm glow stick should be glowing with more intensity. Take the other glow stick out of the freezer and compare it with the room-temperature glow stick and the warm glow stick. You should see three different intensities of glow, going from low intensity (cold) to high intensity (warm).

As the heated glow stick cools down to room temperature, the intensity should return to that of the control glow stick, but the glow stick that was heated should also die out sooner. Temperature is often a vital factor in chemical reaction rates, and time will be a crucial factor in "A Matter of Timing."

CHAPTER 15

DOING TIME: THE IMPORTANCE OF CHEMICAL REACTION RATES

The lost child cries, but still he catches fireflies.

Ryusui Yoshida, date unknown

A MATTER OF TIMING

Time is of the essence when a child is missing. Patrol Officer Al Swell responded to the 911 call and secured the scene immediately upon assessing the situation. He called his sergeant, who arrived shortly and initiated a search. When Detective Helen Gone arrived, she ran a hand through her habitually disheveled hair and stepped from her car. She brushed cookie crumbs and pet hairs from her dark suit as she straightened. Patrol Officer Swell walked over to her and gave her a brief description of the situation.

Officer Swell nodded to a young woman standing by the side of the road wringing her hands and occasionally raising a tissue to her eyes, "Ms. Hope Livson allowed her ten-year-old son to ride his bike to a friend's house, about a half mile away. When her son failed to call to let her know he had arrived, she called the friend's house. When she learned they had not seen him, she went on foot to look for him. She found the bicycle," Patrolman Swell indicated the boy's bike lying on the sidewalk, "then she saw the stains on the cement that appear to be bloodstains." Here Swell pointed toward a patch of sidewalk a few feet from the bike but well within the yellow tape that had been stretched around the scene.

Officer Swell took a deep breath then continued. "And she saw her son's T-shirt—stained with what also appears to be blood."

Detective Gone met Officer Swell's worried eyes and frowned.

"Did you get the boy's description?"

"Four foot six. Slender. Short sandy hair. Brown eyes. No distinguishing marks. Had on a white T-shirt, sneakers, and blue jeans and was carrying a backpack with a sandwich and a bottle of soda."

"Did she handle the bike or the T-shirt?" Detective Gone asked.

"She says she backed away used and her cell to call 911 as soon as she saw the blood."

Detective Gone thanked Officer Swell and then moved over to Ms. Livson to assure her that she had done the right thing and that they would be doing everything possible to locate her son.

Ms. Livson was ashen and obviously shaken. She sobbed into the tissue. "We just moved here last year because we wanted our son to grow up in a small town and learn small-town values. Respect for people. Respect for life. Some place where he would be safe . . ." Her voice was lost in a convulsion of grief.

Detective Gone patted the mother's arm then walked decisively to her car to get started.

She opened the trunk and removed an evidence collection kit. She slipped a pair of disposable booties over her shoes and pulled a pair of latex gloves over her hands. She selected a pair of tweezers from her kit and studied the ground as she approached the scene. She lifted the yellow tape and stepped in carefully.

Detective Gone stepped around the footprints scattered on the ground, noting very small prints, which could have been made by a small boy, and slightly larger prints, which she ascribed to the mother. She made her way to where the bike and an empty soda bottle lay. There were indeed brown stains resembling blood on the cement and on the T-shirt, and there was also a copious soda spill. The soda had washed over some of the stains on the cement and the stains on the T-shirt had run. One of the darker stains on the sidewalk seemed to have trapped several short, fine brown hairs. Detective Gone straightened up and called to Officer Swell.

"What time did the boy leave the house?"

The officer consulted his notebook. "Two o'clock. Ms. Livson says she looked at the clock so she would know when to expect his call from the friend's house."

Detective Gone consulted her watch. It read three thirty. She looked down at the sidewalk again and then straightened up and made her way carefully back outside the yellow tape. She crossed over to where the patrol officer waited.

"I'm going to my car to make some calls. I have a theory—"

Officer Swell lowered his voice. "Kidnapping?"

Detective Gone smiled sardonically. "No, not quite."

The Chemistry of the Case

In forensic chemistry, as with all forensic sciences, *when* a thing happened is often as significant as *where* and *what* happened. Chemical reaction rates are used by forensic chemists to establish time lines for events, times of injuries, and times of death. But in all these cases, the best that can be hoped for is a good estimate of time because a chemical reaction is not like a ticking clock. Chemical reaction rates vary influenced by availability of reactants, ambient temperature, physical state of the reactants, catalysts, or all of the above. Those involved in the forensic sciences must understand these factors to correctly interpret reaction-rate evidence.

Chemical reaction rates vary because, in many ways, a chemical reaction is like a random automobile accident. As with a crash, the first order of business is for reactants—the atoms or automobiles—to encounter each other. The probability for an encounter increases with the concentration of reactants or the number of cars there are on the road. Rush hour is when the most accidents occur. Similarly, there must be a sufficient concentration, or availability, of reactants for the reaction to proceed at a given rate. For instance, everyone knows that steel can rust, but steel-jacketed bullets have been found well preserved underground because the rust reaction requires oxygen, and the concentration of oxygen is lower underground. Fires go out when oxygen is excluded, and newspapers refuse to decompose in landfills for the same reason.

In addition, the more the reactants are in motion, the more likely they are to collide. In the last chapter, we asserted that atoms and molecules are constantly in motion, and this motion increases as heat is added to the system. Increasing the temperature, then, can increase the rate for a reaction. Arsonists use accelerants to generate enough heat to advance the reaction rates of materials with lower combustibility into the self-sustaining range. Fires will burn two to three times faster for about every 10 degrees Celsius (18 degrees Fahrenheit) increase in ambient temperature.

But chemical reactions are different from auto collisions in that there also has to be an attraction. Nitrogen and oxygen molecules in the air experience billions of collisions per second, but the attraction just isn't there. (This is a good thing for us: we would not do well breathing an atmosphere of nitrogen oxides.) The molecules also have to be aligned so that the proper orbitals overlap. As we considered earlier, electron orbitals can act like shape-shifting clouds, adjusting their form to their environments. They blend and build, but to do this they first have to overlap, as shown schematically in figure 15.1. Molecules that collide in random orientations may not have the right orientation for reaction.

Figure 15.1. Molecular bonds are formed when atomic or molecular orbitals overlap.

Moreover, even if there is an encounter and the orientation is correct, there are additional constraints. When potential reactants run into each other, they must do so with sufficient energy to achieve reaction. If two cars bump at a stop sign, drivers may get out, inspect their bumpers and shrug, get back in their cars, and drive off. There is no "car crash" to report. If they bump with more energy, the damage will be different, and the encounter will qualify as a crash.

This last consideration carries a qualification of its own. Statistically, at a given temperature, in a collection of identical molecules, only some of them will have the energy sufficient for a reaction. To help picture this statistical distribution, watch a pot of boiling water. At a boil, bubbles break through the water and splash up off the surface. But only occasionally will a small amount splash up high enough to jump out of the pot. So it is with the energy distribution for molecules: all molecules have energy, but only a few of them will have enough energy to react.

The number of molecules with sufficient energy to react always increases as the temperature increases, as noted earlier. Therefore, almost all reaction rates, with the exception of a few exothermic reactions, increase with increasing temperature. Increasing the temperature increases the number of encounters and the energy of individual encounters. This fact is taken into account when attempting to determine the rate of the set of biological reactions known collectively as *rigor mortis*.

To understand the origins of rigor mortis, we first consider metabolism. *Metabolism* describes the set of reactions by which the body converts food into energy. The most common route for metabolism relies heavily on the input of oxygen. However, in oxygen-deprived circumstances, such as when the body is exerting itself to the point that oxygen is used faster than the lungs are taking it in, metabolism can proceed by an alternative, anaerobic route. The situation is less than optimum, and as a result the brain registers "pain" to convince us to slow down and let the lungs and heart catch up. Under these oxygen-deprived overexertion conditions, muscles become sore and stiff. Likewise, in death, when the lungs cease to function altogether, some of the body's metabolic reactions can continue anaerobically for a space of time. After death, the soreness caused by these anaerobic reactions is not an issue, but the stiffness can be used to establish an approximate time of death.

Rigor mortis can set in anywhere from one to six hours after death. The onset is faster at higher temperatures and slower at lower temperatures. The onset can also be quicker if the deceased had engaged in rigorous physical activity before death: the anaerobic reactions were already under way.

Rigor mortis usually peaks after about twelve hours and then recedes. To get a better estimate of the body's progress in rigor mortis, and thus a better estimate of time, the extent of rigor mortis is compared with the temperature of the liver. The liver is nicely insulated and cools at a fairly constant rate after death. Of course, extreme environmental conditions can also affect the cooling of the liver.

Another tool that has been used successfully to estimate the time of death is entomology, specifically the life cycle of carrion-feeding insects such as the blowfly. Because the development from egg to adult is only a matter of days and is highly dependent on temperature, the presence of eggs or larvae can provide an excellent estimate of time lapsed. The rate of decay is significant in another aspect of forensic science and that is the preservation of biological materials prone to deterioration. As we stated above, the rates of chemical reactions depend on the mobility of the reactants. And the reverse is true. Inhibiting reactions can be achieved by inhibiting mobility, which can be realized by removing the medium: water. Biological samples are best preserved when they are dried before storage. On a TV drama, a technician might be shown using a cotton swab to collect a biological sample, but what is not shown is the ten to fifteen minutes that the technician patiently waits for the swab to dry before transferring it to the evidence bag. And when the sample is ready, it is nearly always stored in paper, not plastic. Plastic can lock in residual moisture or contribute to organic contamination. On crime shows, evidence is often displayed in plastic bags for dramatic effect. In reality, however, paper is nearly always the better choice.

Biological samples must also be dried because water can act as a catalyst for many of the reactions that degrade these materials. A catalyst is a substance that increases the rate of reaction without being consumed in the reaction, as rain might increase the rate of automobile accidents without the amount of rain being changed in the least. In an earlier chapter, we used vinegar as a catalyst for the rusting of steel wool. Steel wool will rust in water, but it will rust much more quickly in vinegar-acidified water. Biological samples also must be dried because physical state can influence reaction rate. We alluded to the influence of physical state in chapter 13 when we said that the size and shape of the grains of the gunpowder control the rate of gas production. But it is always the collection of factors—temperature, concentration, physical state, and catalysts—rather than one individual factor that determines rate, so it is exceedingly difficult to assign an absolute time line on the basis of chemical or biological processes. Luckily, however, sometimes relative time can be established, and this can be vital information, too. It was relative time that led to the resolution of "A Matter of Timing."

Case Closed

Officer Al Swell was talking quietly to Ms. Hope Livson when Detective Helen Gone stepped from her car and rejoined them on the side of the road. The detective's face bore a satisfied smile.

"We found your son and he is all right."

Officer Swell steadied Ms. Livson as she slumped in relief. "Oh, thank goodness! Are you sure?"

Detective Gone nodded. "A boy answering your son's description, last name Livson, walked into a veterinary clinic two blocks from here, about an hour ago."

Ms. Livson frowned and shook her head. "A veterinary clinic! Why?!"

"Because your son learned the values you wanted him to learn, including valuing life. He found an injured kitten on the side of the road and is trying to help it."

Officer Swell raised an eyebrow. "So instead of kidnapping it was kitten-nabbing?"

Helen Gone smiled. "Exactly."

Ms. Livson shook her head. "But how did you know?"

"I was as worried as you were at first. Bloodstains on a T-shirt are not good. But when your son spilled soda on the stains, he helped us out. The stains on the T-shirt ran but the ones on the cement did not, which meant the cement stains were older than the others—and that told me your son had likely come across a preexisting injury."

Ms. Livson now looked more frustrated than worried. "But what does that have to do with a kitten?"

"The hairs in the dried blood—and the new blood." Helen Gone took a quick swipe over her suit with her hand. "I know how kittens can shed. And scratch!"

DEMONSTRATION 16
EXTRACTING THE TRUTH

Any organism in equilibrium with its environment is dead.

Bruce Averill and Patricia Eldredge, *Chemistry*, 2005

In chapter 9, we made the distinction between chemical reactions and physical changes. Here we make use of the distinction between chemical properties and physical properties. A chemical property is a property that can be detected only by the chemical's interaction with other chemicals. Take, for example, the property of flammability: the flammability of a substance can be determined only by mixing that substance with an oxidizer (such as oxygen), adding heat, and seeing if the substance flames up. A physical property is a property that a material displays all by itself, sitting alone on a shelf. For instance, the shiny yellow color of gold is a physical property because no other chemical is needed to detect it.

An analogy might be found in human behavior. A physical human property might be the color of one's hair. One could determine the color of one's hair by looking in a mirror. A chemical human property might be akin to charisma. One does not know how charismatic one is until experiencing a human interaction.

In this demonstration, we will be examining some physical and some chemical properties of soil and showing how these properties might be used to distinguish soil samples of forensic interest. Along the way, we will encounter a new concept, one that will be of importance in all of our subsequent discussions: the concept of equilibrium.

Adjust your safety glasses comfortably over your eyes and put on your examination gloves. Get three similar small glass drinking cups and place them side by side. Obtain two tablespoon-sized samples of different soils, such as one from your backyard and another from a local park. The soils do not have to look drastically different for the demonstration to be successful. However, as you go down into the earth, the layers of soil quickly change character. So try to skim just the top quarter inch (a half a centimeter or so) and try to find a patch that is relatively uniform. It will be difficult, however, to find a patch that is completely uniform, which is what gives soil its forensic value. Different soil samples can sometimes be profiled to determine if they could be—or could not be—from a specific site.

The first procedure is a simplified demonstration of a test that is sometimes used forensically to profile soils according to the densities of various components.[1] For instance, sand will have a fairly high density; that is, it will have a fairly high mass in a given volume, such as a bucket. Anyone who has ever carried buckets of sand can attest to its heft. Loam, on the other hand, is not very dense. Loam makes for rich, fertile topsoil. Given the choice, most people would prefer to haul buckets of loam rather than buckets of sand because there is less mass in the bucket volume—it is less dense.

In this demonstration we will use liquids of different densities to analyze soil. Because the liquids have different densities, the components of the soil will distribute themselves in different liquid layers. This distribution can be used to qualitatively characterize the soil, and the resulting soil profile can be compared with other soils.

Place water to a depth of about three-quarters of an inch (about 2 centimeters) in each glass, followed by the same-sized layers of canola oil (or other liquid vegetable oil), and mineral oil. There should be three distinct layers in the glasses because these materials have different densities and are immiscible, or incapable of mixing (see chapter 5 for a discussion of intermolecular forces and an explanation of why some liquids do not mix). For instance, we found that water settled to the bottom, the mineral oil went to the top, and the canola oil situated itself in the middle, though it was a little difficult to see a completely clear separation. In a forensic laboratory, forensic chemists build a similar *density-gradient tube* by mixing solvents in various ratios to form a more elaborate ladder of densities.[2]

Place a teaspoon (5 milliliters) of one of the dirt samples into one glass and then a teaspoon of the same dirt sample into another glass. Label these two glasses as "dirt A," or something similar. Put a teaspoon (5 milliliters) of the second dirt sample into the remaining glass and label it something like "dirt B." Get three plastic spoons or forks (forks actually work better for mixing but a spoon will do) and stir the contents of each glass vigorously. Use one stirring utensil per glass because exchanging the utensils can cause cross-contamination. When stirring, make sure that the entire dirt sample is thoroughly exposed to each of the three liquids in the glass.

Allow each glass to sit for at least fifteen minutes while the liquid layers separate again. The longer you wait, the more well formed the layers will become. You may want to set up this demonstration in the evening and wait until the morning to make your final observations.

You should see some components of the soil suspended in each liquid layer. Some other materials may simply fall to the bottom of the glass since our simplified demonstration does not have a great enough range of densities to separate everything. Although intermolecular forces are also a consideration, the layer the components choose will depend largely on their density: materials of like density will tend to be in the same layer.

The result of the several influences, however, is separation, and that is what we want. The glasses with different soil samples should show a different distribution of materials in the various layers. This distribution can be used for a partial characterization. The two glasses with the same soil sample should appear the same, which serves as your control. If the two glasses with the same sample were different from one another, then the test would be useless for distinguishing between samples.

We say "partial characterization" because this demonstration shows how soil samples can be compared, but you no doubt recognize that this type of comparison is qualitative at best and could be used only to indicate if two soils *possibly* could, or could not, come from the same source. To better characterize the soil sample at least one other test should be run, such as the test we offer in the next part of this demonstration.

For this part you will need the soil test kit (or kits) we suggested for purchase in "Crime Lab and Crime Solutions" and, of course, your safety glasses and protective gloves. Since soil test kits differ, we now defer to the manufacturer and suggest that you read the instructions thoroughly. Acquaint yourself with the suggested procedure and then choose several convenient tests to perform on the soil samples that you set aside when you prepared for the density test.

The tests that best illustrate the principle that is the subject of the subsequent chapter—physical equilibrium—are the water extraction tests; that is, tests that involve soaking the sample in water first, and then testing the water. For the soil test kit we used, the water extraction tests turned out to be the tests for nitrogen, phosphorus, and potassium.

Keeping your two soil samples well separated and labeled, perform the water extraction tests. When you run the tests, allow for at least a quarter hour of settling time, waiting until the water at the top of the sample is relatively free of debris. Extract your water sample for testing from the middle of the water layer, so it will be as clean as possible. Add the reagents as directed (usually powders) and record the results (usually a comparison with a color chart) for each sample. For more consistent and reliable results, you should place both the color chart and the sample against a white background. Now take the soil sample and the test that gave the most obvious positive result (for us it was the potassium test on our loamlike soil) and run the test again on the same sample. This time pour off all the water from the sample and replace it with fresh water. You should see another positive result, though perhaps a slightly weaker response. The presence of the second, albeit weaker, response tells us that the first water extraction did not remove all of the *analyte*, the substance being analyzed for, from the soil.

We won't go into the specific chemistry that produces the color in these test kits because the objective is to compare samples rather than extract a specific numerical measurement. Numbers would vary depending on the soil test kit, the conditions of the water extraction, the purity of water used for extraction, and so on. However, the two different soils should show a unique pattern of results that can be compared. Given the four results—nitrogen, phosphorus, potassium, and density gradient—each of the soils should be sufficiently characterized that a chemist might be comfortable saying the results are consistent with the soils being from the same or different locations.

Note, once more, the strongest statement that can be made is that the results are *consistent* with a finding, not that they *prove* anything. After performing these tests, you may have a better feel for both the delicacy and the inherent murkiness of soil tests. In fact, as with many other types of evidence, the results of a soil test are perhaps strongest when they eliminate a possibility rather than prove one, but elimination is enough to point the way in "The Case of the Perfect Grime."

CHAPTER 16

The Clue Is in the GUE: Physical Equilibrium

Anyone who has proclaimed violence his method inexorably must choose lying as his principle.

Aleksandr Solzhenitsyn, ca. 1970

The Case of the Perfect Grime

Professor Doug Dert frowned as he formulated his question, "Are you sure about these soil samples?"

"Collected them myself," answered Detective Justin Tyme.

The professor ran his finger down a page of the binder on his desk and looked up at the bottled soil samples on the wall to his left. He held up a small capped vial with a bit of dark brown matter in the bottom and regarded it thoughtfully.

"Well, based on the analysis done by the state crime lab, I believe I can tell you what you've got."

Detective Tyme reached into his breast pocket for his notebook. "What is it?"

"The analysis is consistent with potting soil."

"Potting soil? That's all?"

"Yes. That's all."

Detective Tyme put his notebook back in his pocket.

Professor Dert asked, "Can you tell me any more about the case?"

"I didn't want to prejudice your evaluation beforehand, but it doesn't matter now. Mrs. Notta Tall was the victim. She had lived alone for a number of years, but recently her nephew had become a houseguest. We interviewed the boy, but he said he spent the day at the beach and a neighbor said she saw him leaving that morning. The neighbor said she had been in the habit of looking in on Mrs. Tall before the nephew arrived and took over, and she still keeps an eye on the place.

"That morning, the gardener mowed the lawn and that afternoon the housekeeper came and went. The nephew says he got back from the beach at four o'clock, parked his car, and walked immediately back to the garden looking for his aunt. He found her in her gardening shed, stabbed by pruning sheers."

"Oh!" said Professor Dert. "How awful! But now I know where I've heard that name before. Mrs. Tall grew hydrangeas and usually submitted her best to the gardening show. Never won, though. Tricky plants, hydrangeas. The color of the flower depends on the pH of the soil. An acidic soil results in a blue flower, a neutral soil will produce a pale, creamy flower, and an alkaline soil will cause the flower to be pink. But that's not as easy as it sounds. The quality of the color depends on the variety, the parentage of the bush, the weather, and the health of the plant as well. The soil also must contain aluminum if a blue color is desired. You usually can't control the color without potting the plants. When a hydrangea is planted too close to a house's foundation, rainwater may leach lime from the cement and change the pH of the soil around the plant . . ."

The professor's voice trailed off as he regarded the vial in his hand. "She probably mixed her own potting soil using a commercial stock, which is why it doesn't match any of the soil samples I have in my collection."

Detective Tyme sighed. "Well, I knew it was a long shot, but I found that soil spread around where she had fallen, so I thought I'd try. There was a footprint in the soil, but it turned out to be the nephew's. He trampled all over the scene before he called 911. It was an outside chance that the soil had been brought in by the perp. Are you sure it's potting soil? If it didn't match any of your samples . . . "

Professor Dert held up his hands. "I'm sure. When the lab did the extraction, the organic phase contained insecticide and the inorganic phase contained synthetic fertilizer. The amount of vermiculite pretty much confirmed it."

"Vermiculite?"

"It's a mineral added to potting soil to improve the drainage. As sand would do in natural soil."

"If it acts like sand, then why not use sand?"

"Good question. The vermiculite also retains some moisture so it's sort of dual purpose. And there is always availability, consistency, and convenience to consider—natural sand would have to be sterilized before it could be used. Still some purists add sand, too—but I guess not Mrs. Tall."

Detective Dert frowned and then sat up abruptly. "May I have those samples back? I think I have a warrant to obtain."

The Chemistry of the Case

Equilibrium is the balance of forces. These forces can be electrical (a lightning strike is nature's way of equilibrating electrical forces); areas of pressure (a tornado is nature's way of equilibrating atmospheric pressures); chemical differences (a chemical reaction is nature's way of equilibrating chemical forces); or physical differences, such as the differences we examine in this chapter.

One equilibrium at play in the preceding demonstration was the balance between gravity and the buoyant force caused by the soil's particles displacing the liquid. When the soil particles were surrounded by a liquid with a similar density, the gravitational force was balanced by the buoyant force, and the particles were suspended in equilibrium. Another example of physical equilibrium in the above demonstration is found in water extraction. When we ran the test the first time, most, but not all, of the analyte was extracted into the water. An equilibrium amount remained in the soil. We know this because the second extraction collected more analyte.

Extractions are important when analyzing samples called *general unknowns*. When Detective Tyme submitted his sample to the state crime lab for a general unknown examination (GUE), he was hoping some bodily fluids or other trace evidence could be extracted, or that a detailed analysis would allow him to narrow down the origins of the sample. To perform a general unknown examination, one of the first steps is to separate the organic materials from the inorganic materials. Separation and isolation is as essential in chemical analysis as it is in police work. It is generally understood that witnesses and suspects need to be separated and isolated as soon as possible if their account of events is to be considered trustworthy. If they are not separated, their stories will become cross-contaminated or collaborated. There will be interferences. So it is with chemical analysis. The chemicals must be separated before they can be analyzed.

The separation of organic materials from inorganic materials is usually accomplished by a technique called *solvent extraction*, which we illustrated in the previous demonstration. In solvent extraction, a solvent is allowed to come in contact with the substance being analyzed so that anything soluble will dissolve in the solvent. Relying on the principle of "like dissolves like," we can be assured that ions and polar materials will dissolve in a polar solvent, such as water, and nonpolar molecules, which include organic compounds, will dissolve in nonpolar solvents, such as oil. (The ether extraction mentioned in chapter 11 in connection with freebase cocaine could have been classified as an organic extraction.)

Once separated from inorganic materials, organic mixtures can usually be broken down into separate components by techniques such as thin-layer chromatography (TLC), which we discussed in chapter 4, or by mass spectrometry, as we discussed in chapter 6. Inorganic materials may be analyzed by colorimetric techniques (methods that depend on a color change) such as in the above soil test, or they may be analyzed by another type of chromatography: ion chromatography.

Extraction may also be recognized by an alternative name: *leaching*. Leaching is the term applied to the equivalent process used on farms when fertilization has caused a high concentration of salts in the soil. Extra irrigation is carried out to leach the salts from the soil. Leaching can also be an environmental concern when water leaches agricultural chemicals out of the soil and into the groundwater. Rinsing salt-cured meat under running water highlights the key to successful leaching or solvent extraction: rinsing the meat will remove more of the salt than soaking. Multiple or continuous extractions are necessary to obtain the maximum effect because of equilibrium.

Physical equilibrium, the topic of this chapter, and chemical equilibrium, which we will discuss in the next chapter, is the observation that molecular-scale interactions tend to go only so far—and no farther. When an extraction is carried out, the organic materials may be separated from the inorganic materials, but the separation is never perfect at the molecular level. This observation can be confirmed by the prosaic process of mopping a floor: the mopping will be efficient only as long as you are mopping with clean water. Once the water becomes saturated with dirt, mopping achieves no further separation. The floor stays dirty.

Equilibrium is also at play in attempts to remove blood evidence by scrubbing. Soap and water may remove all the visible blood residue, but this physical extraction is incomplete. Entropy, the tendency of systems to move toward a state of maximum disorder, dictates that whatever is soluble in water should spread into the water—but not all of it. If everything went into the water, that would result in a new imbalance, which is again forbidden by entropy. Having all of the blood in the water and none left on the wall would create order rather than disorder.

But the fact that scrubbing will remove more blood than rinsing alone reveals the other piece to the equilibrium puzzle: energy. Entropy affects equilibrium, but so does energy. As we saw earlier, some chemical processes give off energy and some require energy from the environment to proceed. The processes that give off energy are easy to understand: energy is released when a system goes from a high-energy state to a low-energy state, such as marbles rolling downhill. But processes that require energy can be understood, too, if entropy is included in the analysis. Endothermic dissolutions, dissolutions that draw energy from the environment and feel cool, can occur when sufficient disorder is created to overcome the need for energy. An equilibrium situation is one in which the two drivers—the need for low energy and high entropy—are balanced.

The fact that no extraction is ever 100 percent sets a practical limit on the amount of evidence that can be obtained from any one sample. But this limitation can be turned into an advantage if multiple tests are required. In a method called *carbon sampling*, a charcoal wire is placed in the headspace above a volatile sample, such as a fire accelerant, to absorb an equilibrium load of vapor for analysis. If necessary, this process can be repeated with additional carbon wires, something that would not be possible if all the vapor were adsorbed the first time. Once a carbon wire is saturated, it can be removed and the vapor recovered by putting the wire into a clean atmosphere. The vapor will then leave the carbon wire and can be captured and analyzed. This alternate behavior in reversed situations—the vapor absorbes into the wire in a vapor-rich atmosphere and leaves the wire in a vapor-poor atmosphere—demonstrates an important feature of molecular-scale equilibrium: the equilibrium is *dynamic* rather than static. Equilibrium is a two-way street.

The dynamic nature of physical equilibrium can be shown by carefully layering, in a clear glass jar, food coloring–tinted water, followed by mineral oil, and then clear ethanol. You must be careful not to mix the layers as you pour. Seal the jar because this demonstration takes some time, and some ethanol could evaporate and change the results. Food coloring is selected because it is soluble in water and not in mineral oil. It is, however, soluble in ethanol because ethanol is somewhat like water, as shown in figure 16.1, and is polar. Initially the food coloring will be located strictly in the bottom water layer. But within a day the food coloring will find its way, through its miniscule solubility in mineral oil and the dynamic equilibrium between the oil and water and ethanol, to the top layer, and the ethanol will become colored too. The middle layer, the mineral oil, will remain clear.

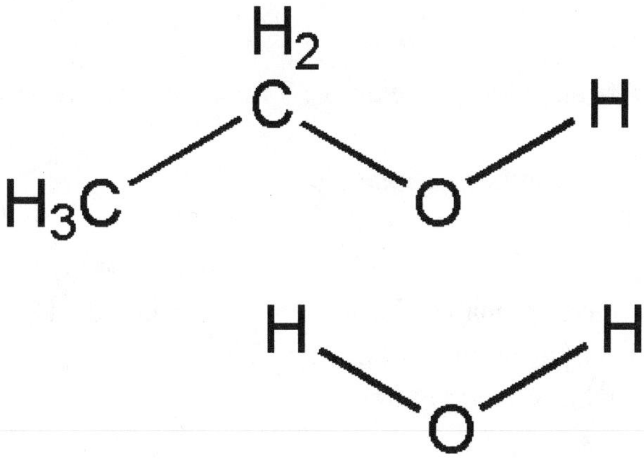

$$H_2C$$

$$H_3C \qquad O \qquad H$$

$$H \qquad H$$

$$O$$

Figure 16.1. Ethanol is soluble in water because it has a structure that is similar to that of water.

The reverse experiment can be tried, too. If clear water is put on the bottom layer, with mineral oil on top of the water, and food coloring–tinted ethanol poured carefully on top of the mineral oil, and the jar is sealed, the food coloring will make its way down to the bottom water layer, with the middle layer remaining clear.

That fact that the jar must be sealed so that the ethanol doesn't evaporate is a demonstration of another physical equilibrium: phase equilibrium. Phase changes—solid to liquid, liquid to gas, and vice versa—are equilibrium processes. Liquids have an amount of vapor associated with them, and this vapor, if not allowed to escape, will be in equilibrium with the liquid. When the jar is opened, the vapor can escape, and driven by entropy, more liquid will evaporate in an effort to restore equilibrium. This aspect of phase equilibrium helps considerably with limitations set by the extraction equilibrium. Once the solvent is saturated with the solute that it is extracting, it can be removed and some of the solvent allowed to evaporate, which concentrates the solute and makes it easier to analyze.

So it was the equilibrium of solvent extraction that allowed Professor Doug Dert to determine that Detective Justin Tyme's soil sample was potting soil—and nothing more. Nothing to anyone but Detective Tyme, that is.

Case Closed

"Wait!" Professor Dert called after Detective Tyme. "Where are you going?"

"To get a warrant to search the nephew's room."

"Didn't you do that before?"

"He wouldn't let us in and we didn't have probable cause."

"And now you have probable cause?" asked Professor Dert, making no effort to keep the surprise out of his voice.

"Yes. Because of what you *didn't* find."

"What?"

"You didn't find any sand. If the nephew just got back from the beach, there should have been some sand in that soil."

Professor Dert nodded gravely. "Yes. At least an equilibrium amount."

DEMONSTRATION 17
EVIDENCE INDICATING OTHERWISE

Despite crime's omnipresence, things work in society. . . . Order eventually restores itself, by psychic equilibrium.

Camille Paglia, ca. 1980

Having demonstrated and discussed physical equilibrium, we will now demonstrate and discuss chemical equilibrium. In physical equilibrium situations, materials do not change their chemical nature to achieve equilibrium; they change how they are distributed between different phases. In the preceding chapter, we saw that the analyte in our soil sample distributed itself between the water and the soil in the water extraction, but it remained the same substance. In a chemical equilibrium, a chemical reaction proceeds until it establishes its equilibrium distribution of reactants and products, governed by factors to be discussed below.

Because equilibrium is a balance, the balance can be shifted, as we saw with the second water extraction performed on the soil sample: the analyte that remained in the soil came out into the fresh water. Similarly removing products from a system in chemical equilibrium will cause reactants to turn into products to restore the balance. Likewise, adding more reactants will force the production of more product so that the balance remains. In the following demonstration, we will see a chemical equilibrium shift from product to reactant and vice versa by the addition of product and reactant, respectively.

Put on your safety glasses and exam gloves. In a small see-through plastic glass place a quarter cup (about 60 milliliters) of tap water and add four drops of the aquarium indicator, bromothymol blue (as suggested for purchase in "Crime Lab and Crime Solutions"). After you use a plastic spoon to mix the indicator and water, the water should be a nice pale green. This color is the appearance of the indicator in neutral solution.

Get two eyedroppers. Use one of them to add one drop of vinegar to the solution and use the spoon to mix. Vinegar is an acid and thus dissociates to provide hydrogen ion in solution. The indicator is an acid, too, but a weaker one. The large amount of hydrogen ion already in solution from vinegar "pushes" the hydrogen back on the indicator. In other words, the indicator will shift its structure in response to its new acidic environment (see figure 17.1). The indicator will appear yellow.

Use the other dropper to add one drop of household ammonia to the glass, being careful to keep the vinegar dropper separate from the ammonia dropper. Use the spoon to mix. Ammonia is a base and as such will take up hydrogen ions from the solution. The indicator should respond to the hydrogen-deficient environment by releasing its hydrogen. In other words, in the tug-of-war for hydrogen ions, ammonia will win and the indicator will revert to its nonhydrogenated form, which is blue (see figure 17.1). Adding another drop of vinegar should shift the color back to yellow. Adding another drop of ammonia should shift the color back to blue.

The original green appearance of the water was the result of a fairly equal balance of yellow and blue indicator structures. (Recall from art class that yellow and blue make green.) You can achieve that balance again if you carefully add a small partial drop of ammonia to

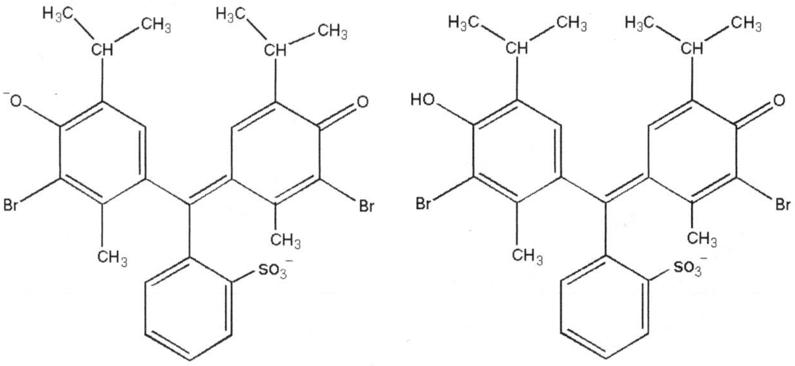

Blue structure in basic solutions   Yellow structure in mildly acidic solutions

Figure 17.1. The structure and color of bromothymol blue in basic solution (*left*) and acidic solution (*right*). When the indicator molecule is in neutral solution, both the acidic and the basic forms are present and in equilibrium, so both colors contribute to the color of the solution. Compare the left sides of the two structures. What a difference one little hydrogen makes!

the yellow form. You can do this by pushing a very small portion of ammonia out of the dropper and touching the end of the dropper to the side of the spoon. When you stir the solution, the portion of a drop that ended up on the spoon will be mixed into the entire solution. The smaller portion of ammonia should only partially convert the indicator to the blue form and you will have a green solution: a blend of both structures, yellow and blue.

The final color of the solution is not the result of one structure but rather a balance of two forms of the indicator molecule in chemical equilibrium. In the discussion that follows, we will compare some aspect of chemical equilibrium to a population in which there is a mixture of single and married people. But we acknowledge that marriage, as well as the chemistry of indicators, is a bit more complex than this simple metaphor would imply. For instance, marriage may eventually play a role for the friends in our next vignette, but first they must resolve "The Case of the Well-Handled Crime."

CHAPTER 17

EQUAL, JUST AS FOR ALL: CHEMICAL EQUILIBRIUM

One crime has to be concealed by another.

Seneca the Younger, ca. 30 CE

THE CASE OF THE WELL-HANDLED CRIME

Inspector Guy N. Charge took a long pull on his mug before meeting the eyes of his table companion and Saturday-night steady, Yvette N. Airy.

"I'm telling you, Yvette, I've seen a lot in my time, but this one got to me."

Yvette regarded her friend with concern. "Can you describe it again?"

"The bucket must have fallen on top of it and the lack of oxygen put the fire out. I moved a bucket and there it was."

Guy took a deep breath. "The outline of a hand. Just a charred patch on the ground, but the perfect outline of a hand."

Yvette frowned. "No other body parts?"

"Nope. Just a hand. And when I realized that, I breathed a little easier. A charred imprint of a hand isn't good news—but when there's no arm to go with it, it isn't as bad as it could be."

"How could you have just a burned hand? You said the import warehouse was a mess, nearly burned out. How could someone who was caught in the fire burn just their hand?"

"They couldn't. That's why I dug out the whole imprint and took it in for analysis."

"Well?"

"Combustion products of carbon compounds and some residual polymer."

"Plastic?"

"A rubber glove. Probably latex. The kind we use every day in evidence collection to avoid contamination. The kind we use every day when handling injuries to avoid infection."

"We use them at the clinic, too," said Yvette.

Guy, lost in thought, didn't respond.

Yvette propped her chin on her hand and regarded Guy with skeptical impatience. "You said the hand helped you clear the case. What the heck did a latex glove have to do with a warehouse fire?"

"Well, arson is a peculiar crime. It requires so much preparation that it is rarely a crime of impulse or passion. Personally, I have never run across a serial arsonist—there are a few firebugs out there, but they are rare. No, fires are usually set to cover another crime."

"So? What was the other crime this time?"

"Well, I was pretty mystified at first. I thought maybe the gloves were used to handle the accelerant, but the dogs didn't pick up on any accelerant—"

"Are you sure it was arson?" Yvette interrupted.

"The sprinkler system was disabled."

"Oh."

"And the fire started in the records room, a suspicious finding in itself."

Inspector Charge continued. "Then I realized whoever started the fire must have used the gloves themselves for a sort of accelerant because they burn pretty well. But I was still left with the question of why the fire was set in the first place. I needed to develop a theory so I could focus on a suspect. There didn't seem to be any evidence that they were trying to burn up in the latex fire. Then I started thinking about the nature of the business . . ."

Yvette sat back and smiled. "Aha! I see where you're going with this."

The Chemistry of the Case

It is common to think of a chemical reaction as an all-or-nothing situation: bangs, pops, flashes of light, and all the reactants turning into products. This perception is understandable because in most useful reactions there is no equilibrium to speak of. A gunpowder that exploded only partially wouldn't get the job done. If acetone attacked latex to any significant extent, then lab gloves would be useless. But in reality, many reactions proceed only partially, that is, until they reach equilibrium: a stable ratio of products and reactants. Here we will explore the factors that establish chemical equilibrium and help to explain why a gunpowder reaction goes essentially to completion and the acetone-latex reaction is a dud.

In the last chapter, we discussed physical equilibrium and noted that physical equilibrium is the result of a balance of forces, like a painting hanging on a wall with its balanced forces of gravity and tension in the suspending wires. Chemical equilibrium is also a balance of forces, but the origin and action of the forces is more subtle. The balance point of chemical equilibrium—the equilibrium distribution between reactants and products—has its basis in entropy and energy.

Earlier we said that physical equilibrium in molecular-scale systems was a result of the trade-off between energy and entropy. Intermolecular attractions pulled inorganic potassium, nitrogen, and phosphorous out of the soil and into aqueous solution because it is energetically favorable for water to dissolve these salts. But we also said that not all the salts should go into solution because that would create a new separation. Separation is a much more ordered situation than a mixture and as such would not be favored by entropy. Entropy, we said, would require at least some inorganic solute to remain in the water-soaked soil.

These same considerations are at play in chemical equilibrium. As we've pointed out, some chemical reactions are exothermic: they give off energy. If the new bonds that are formed in the products are lower in energy than the old bonds in the reactants, then the difference in energy can show up as heat. Reactions that give off heat—reactions that go downhill in energy—tend to occur very readily. The natural tendency is for processes to achieve, when possible, a lower energy state.

But as we've also seen, there are also reactions that absorb heat, so there must be more to the story. There is, and it can be found by reconsidering the ideas in chapter 13. In chapter 13, we discussed gas-forming reactions and said that these were highly favored because of the chaos that they caused. The natural direction, we said, was for the maximum entropy to be created. So if enough chaos is created, then endothermic reactions are possible—even encouraged. But then back in chapter 11, we discussed precipitation reactions, in which two materials coalesce into one—which is in the direction of order rather than entropy. So what is the deal? Sometimes entropy drives the reaction, sometimes energy drives the reaction?

Exactly. There is a trade-off between the benefits to be gained by giving off energy and the benefits to be gained by increasing entropy.

Consider, for example, latex. Latex is a naturally occurring rubber that can be found in the sap of many plants. One of its functions is to protect the plant, like scabs protect mammals, because it coagulates on exposure to air. The material made from latex sap is also called latex, but processed latex is made by separating out the rubber particles in the sap and joining them together with bonds between sulfur atoms. This process is called *vulcanizing* in reference to the fire and brimstone (heat and sulfur) involved in the procedure. The resulting material is flexible and impervious to water and many other common solvents. Because imperfections—entropy—are a part of any process, latex gloves are thoroughly tested and inspected before sale. And because of the possible catastrophic consequences of such imperfections in latex gloves, for instance, exposure to infectious agents, procurement procedures for latex gloves tend to be fairly rigorous.

At this point, however, it behooves us to add that latex has also been used for condoms as well as gloves, and rumor has it that latex condoms will dissolve in mineral oil and petroleum jelly—information that should be dispensed along with latex condoms. We did test latex gloves and found that this was at least not immediately the case, but we admit that we did not test any latex condoms. We do, however, recommend against a field test. Currently most condoms are made from polyurethane, probably at least partially in response to this concern.

There is, moreover, another interesting concern: allergies. There are people who have an allergy to latex and cannot use either latex gloves or latex condoms. In fact, the allergic reaction can be so extreme as to cause *anaphylactic shock*, a condition that can result in death. The question is this: How can people be allergic to a material like latex that is so inert that it resists attack by solvents as aggressive as acetone or gasoline? The answer is that even in the vulcanized material of latex, some minute amount of residual plant protein is in equilibrium with the bonded material and can be sufficient to cause an allergic response.

The presence of an equilibrium amount of free material, even in a substantial-looking latex glove, demonstrates the power of entropy as a driver for physical and chemical processes. So it would seem reasonable that a reaction that breaks the large strands of latex back into smaller particles of rubber would be highly favored by entropy. It might seem that latex should be a much more chemically delicate material. But in this case, energy wins. Disrupting the sulfur bonds would cost more in terms of energy than the advantage gained by increased entropy—so latex gloves resist decomposition

There is another aspect to chemical equilibrium, which we saw displayed in our opening demonstration: equilibrium on the molecular level is not static, it is dynamic. The forward reaction, from reactants to products, occurs alongside the backward reaction, from products to reactants, at rates so balanced that there is no net change. This constant exchange of partners allowed the indicator solution to respond rapidly to a new environment. The situation might be compared with a dynamic societal circumstance: marriage.

In a given population, there will be a number of married couples and a number of single people, yet the ratio of marriages will stay fairly constant over time in the absence of societal upheaval. Our green solution in the demonstration with which this chapter began was an equilibrium mixture of "single" indicator molecules (the blue ones) and "married" indicator molecules (the yellow ones). If, in our human model, there is an influx of single people for some reason (such as the return of soldiers after World War II), there will be an increase in marriages. In our chemical case, this would correspond to an influx of vinegar, which would create many more partnered molecules, resulting in a solution that is predominantly yellow. In our human analogy, if a part of the single population should be removed, say the mostly male recruits for World War II, then the population might respond by experiencing more divorces than remarriages, resulting in fewer marriages. Chemically this would correspond to more dissociations than re-associations, and the blue form of the indicator molecule would dominate.

The analogy is actually a pretty good one for our present consideration. At any one time, the percentage of married persons in this country is a result of the trade-off between the marriage rate and the divorce rate, and this percentage remains remarkably constant—at equilibrium. One of the reasons for the balance is that the people who divorce can remarry and the people that remarry can redivorce. The situation is dynamic, not static. There can be a good deal of back-and-forth. Chemical reactions can behave in much the same manner. In figure 17.2a, we illustrate a *synthesis*, a chemical marriage, and in figure 17.2b, we illustrate the opposite reaction, a *decomposition*, a chemical divorce. If we start with a high concentration of the separate reactants, then the synthesis reaction will occur. If we start with just the product, the decomposition reaction will occur. When both reactant and product are present, both reactions will occur. When the amounts of reactants and products are such that the synthesis and decomposition rates are equal, we will have equilibrium, as shown in figure 17.2c.

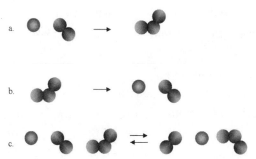

Figure 17.2. A synthesis reaction, shown schematically in (a), combines components into a compound. A decomposition reaction, shown in (b), decomposes a compound into its components. At equilibrium, shown in (c), synthesis and decomposition take place at the same rate, and the equilibrium concentrations of components and compounds stay the same over time.

The dynamic behavior of chemical equilibrium is summarized in Le Châtelier's principle. Enunciated by Henri Le Châtelier around 1885, the principle states that a chemical reaction can be "pushed" or "pulled" toward products or reactants by the addition of reactants or products, respectively. We saw this principle at work in demonstration 17. When the indicator was in equilibrium with the ammonia solution, it was in its blue form because of the base. When vinegar was added, the indicator shifted its equilibrium in response to the influx of acid, and in the process, the indicator turned yellow. In the vignette of the last chapter, we talked about the pH-dependence of the color of hydrangeas, and we may now add that this color change, too, is the result of a chemical equilibrium.

In chapter 14, we saw that altering the temperature could confound a presumptive test, and now we can add that this temperature effect is again a result of equilibrium. When heat is required for a reaction, then adding heat will cause the reaction to shift forward toward products. When heat is produced in a reaction, adding heat will cause the reaction to shift back toward reactants. The soil chemistry of the hydrangeas and the sullied chemistry in the presumptive test are examples of *complex-forming reactions*, a class of reactions we have not yet discussed but that provide a good forum for discussion of chemical equilibrium.

In a complex-forming reaction, a positively charged (therefore electron-deficient) metal ion becomes surrounded by electron-donating entities, such as water. In the complex of water with aluminum shown in figure 17.3, it can be seen that the oxygen has two nonbonding pairs of electrons to donate, so water has the ability to surround and to form a complex with a central metal ion. Note that six water molecules can fit around the aluminum ion and that the final complex still has a positive charge. The electron-donating molecules that act to create complexes around a metal ion are called *ligands*, from the Latin *ligare*, which means "to bind." Thus *ligand* shares its roots with *ligature*, which means "a rope used to bind." The ligands "bind up" the central metal ion in a metal-ion complex.

The color of the hydrangeas in "The Case of the Perfect Grime" of chapter 16 was influenced by the equilibrium amount of aluminum in the soil, and this in turn was controlled by the amount of acid, measured by the pH. When there is a sufficient acid concentration, the pH is a small number, and the complex formed by aluminum resembles the water complex shown in figure 17.3. This complex still carries a charge and is soluble enough to be absorbed by the plant. When there is a significant amount of base in the soil, the hydroxide ion will bond with the aluminum, and the resulting complex is neutral, making it less soluble and therefore unavailable to the plant. In this case, the flowers will appear cream-colored or pink, but not blue. Chemical complexes are also a concern in cooking because acidic food can leach aluminum from aluminum pots that are not protected with a nonreactive coating.

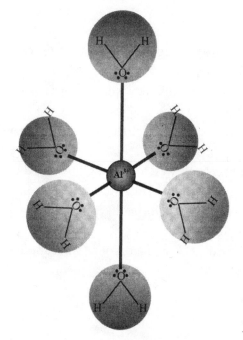

Figure 17.3. Water has the ability to surround—to form a complex with—a central metal ion.

Ligands that are especially adept at forming complexes are called *chelating agents*. Another such agent, oxalic acid, is used for radiator cleaner because it forms complexes with the radiator scale and moves it into solution. Oxalic acid works quite well in this application, but the process is still an equilibrium process, which is why the procedure is called a radiator *flush* rather than a radiator *soak*. A given amount of oxalic acid solution forms an equilibrium amount of soluble complex and must be removed and replaced with fresh solution if more scale is to be removed.

The analysis of Inspector Charge's charred handprint in "The Case of the Well-Handled Crime" also involved equilibrium. An extract of the handprint was analyzed via gas chromatography, and gas chromatography, as described earlier, is a technique that relies on an equilibrium between the gas phase and the absorbed phase to effect separation. Thus the use of gas, liquid, and solid enabled Inspector Charge, and his friend, Dr. Airy, to come up with a solution.

Case Closed

"So you think you know what was going on?" Inspector Guy N. Charge asked his dinner companion.

"Yes," answered Yvette N. Airy. "I think they were using the latex glove fire to cover up smuggling."

Inspector Charge's eyebrows rose. "Really! But what were they smuggling out?"

"Ha! Don't try to trip me up. They weren't smuggling out, they were smuggling in. Smuggling in substandard latex gloves. Some procurement agency had gotten wise and was closing in on them, so they were disposing of the evidence."

Inspector Charge smiled broadly. "I applaud your crime-solving acumen! In fact, I'll give you a hand."

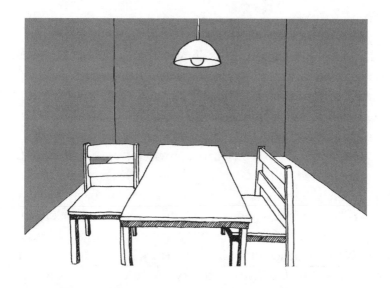

PART III
INTERROGATION LIGHTS

Truth, like light, blinds. Falsehood, on the contrary, is a beautiful twilight that enhances every object.

Albert Camus, ca. 1950

Every contact leaves a trace.

Edmond Locard, ca. 1910

Edmond Locard (1877–1966), a pioneering forensic scientist, established what has become known as Locard's exchange principle: *Every contact leaves a trace.* The idea has served forensic science well. *Trace evidence* is the potentially incriminating hair, paint, pollen, glass, fiber, skin flakes, spittle, semen, fingerprints, and such that may be present at a crime site, albeit in extremely small amounts.

Methods for trace evidence analysis are crucial to forensic science because trace evidence is the one type of evidence that persists. A carpet may be cleaned, but the blood that seeped into the cracks of the floorboard will remain. A room may be vacuumed, but hairs caught on the rough edges of wood will stay stubbornly attached. Fingerprints may be wiped away from a gun grip, but will remain on the cloth that was used to do the wiping.

Look closely at the ground in an outdoor area. You may find wrappers, coins, nails, or even bits of cloth. All of these belonged to someone at some time. What were they doing at the time? Inspect an indoor area for evidence of who has recently been in the room. You may be surprised by what you find. Try taking a strip of clear sticky tape and pressing it down on any random surface. It won't come up clean. Even if it appears clean, closer inspection will reveal particles of dust or dirt, all of which came from somewhere. Take your black light and use it to inspect an area, moving it around to different angles. New things become noticeable. Although the forensic sciences cover a broad spectrum, ranging from forensic entomology to forensic psychology, it is the forensic chemist who is most often involved in the analysis of trace evidence, and forensic chemists have become very adept at the art.

In fact, with all the new techniques for collecting and analyzing trace evidence, the concern has been voiced that savvy criminals will start covering their tracks more thoroughly. Luckily, few criminals are that clever. Many crimes occur on impulse or arise from opportunity. Most crimes are committed in a moment of passion, or under the influence of alcohol or drugs, and most criminals leave a trail such as bloody footprints or a dropped weapon. But if an attempt is made to disguise or clean up a crime, then trace evidence can be critical to an investigation. Sometimes trace evidence is left when attempting to avoid leaving trace evidence! But there are still challenges. Every contact leaves a trace, but the trace could be a smeared fingerprint or DNA that is not in any data bank. Good investigative work will always be necessary to make sense of any trace left behind.

In parts III and IV, we will make use of all the chemical principles developed in parts I and II to elaborate on the analysis of trace evidence. Because biological evidence, which can be linked to a specific individual, is such a critical kind of trace evidence, we will devote part IV to the discussion of bodily materials. Here, in part III, because trace evidence is, by definition, hard to see, we will focus on light.

Light can be characterized as an *oscillating electromagnetic field*, a description that may still leave us in the dark, so we will elaborate on the concept. A *field* is an effect that extends out over a region of space. For instance, if there is a bonfire in the middle of a backyard, it will create a temperature field: the temperature will be highest where the fire is centered, then extend out and gradually diminish with distance from the fire. An *oscillating field* is a field that varies regularly with time. An oscillating fan blowing over a block of ice could serve as an example of an oscillating temperature field. If you were standing in front of the block of ice, you would feel a periodic burst of cool breeze that would vary regularly with time.

An *oscillating electromagnetic field* is an oscillating electric field accompanied by an oscillating magnetic field. In demonstration 6, we illustrated the relationship between electricity and magnetism when we ran current through a wire and created a magnetic field. A moving magnet can also create an electric field, which is the basis for light: a moving electric field, such as a spark, generates a magnetic field, which in turn generates an electric field, which in turn generates a magnetic field, and so on, which is what we call light.

Atoms and molecules have electric fields associated with them because they are made up of separated electrons and protons, both of which carry an electrical charge. Light can originate from an oscillation in a molecular field caused by the movements of molecules with heat. Atoms or molecules may also interact with an external oscillating electromagnetic field of light. We say light *may* interact with atoms and molecules because the interaction depends on the type of light.

Light comes in many varieties, each of which can be described by its characteristic *frequency*. The frequency is a measure of how often a oscillation cycle repeats itself in a given period of time. If we turn our oscillating fan on high, it will pass over the block of ice more often, creating a high-frequency oscillating field. If we turn it on low, we'll have a low-frequency oscillating field. Light's oscillating electromagnetic field varies from low-frequency radio waves to high-frequency gamma rays, and theoretically on to unnamed frequencies in both directions. Between these two extremes we have x rays (used for imaging bones), ultraviolet waves (notorious for the damage they cause to skin), visible light (the type of light our eyes can detect), infrared radiation (the light used in night-vision equipment), and microwaves (the very same that cook our convenience foods). The fact that these different types of light interact differently with each unique material is the basis for various important analytical techniques.

Earlier we noted how AA spectroscopy can be used to identify elements, and we will see in chapter 18 how infrared radiation can be used to identify some molecules. In chapter 19, we will investigate how molecules can alter the course of light and how this interaction can be used to our advantage in light microscopy.

We will discuss the interaction of electric fields that produce images where the light never shines: through scanning electron microscopy. In chapter 20, we will explore some of the more exotic light-utilizing techniques such as laser ablation, and in chapter 21, we will illuminate light-producing chemical reactions such as the luminol reaction that occurs in the presence of blood.

Each of these chapters demonstrates that light can be a very powerful forensic tool, so let's have a look.

DEMONSTRATION 18
BEHIND PRISM BARS

Of all the Inventions none there is Surpasses
the Noble Florentine's Dioptrick Glasses
For what a better, fitter guift Could bee
in this World's Aged Luciosity.
To help our Blindnesse so as to devize
a paire of new & Artificial eyes

Henry Powers, ca. 1660

Take the prism suggested for purchase in "Crime Lab and Crime Solutions" and bring it out into the sun. Hold it by the ends so the sunlight goes through a clear side. If you rotate it slowly, you will eventually find an orientation that breaks the sunlight up into the different colors of the rainbow: red, orange, yellow, green, blue, indigo, and violet.

The effect is, no doubt, quite beautiful, but is there any difference in the light besides color? Yes, and the difference proves to be very important when light is used as an analytical tool: the different colors of light have different frequencies, which means they have different energies.

Now is the time to get out the different-colored see-through plastic disks or squares that were suggested for purchase in "Crime Lab and Crime Solutions." Find an outdoor spot where you can lay out some newspaper so that the sheets will be exposed to the sun for an afternoon. Weigh the newspaper down at the corners to protect the sheets from gusts of wind. Place the see-through shapes onto the unprinted parts of the paper. Take a marker or a pencil and indicate on the newspaper where each shape has been placed and what its color is. You can write down the name of the shape, too, if you would like. Let the assembly sit in the sun for three to four hours so that the newspaper pages can bleach.

After its time in the sun has elapsed, bring the newspaper into the shade. In the shade, your eyes will adjust to the lower light level and allow you to see contrast better. You should see that the newspaper has bleached by comparing it with a newspaper that hasn't been out in the sun. You should also see that the area under the plastic pieces was protected, but that some colors protected better than others. We found the best protection was provided by the blue filters, while yellow provided the newspaper with the least protection against the photo-bleaching process. The analysis of color will also play an important part in "A Case of Canine Karma."

CHAPTER 18

Enough Rope: Infrared Spectroscopy for Fiber and More

Small crimes always precede great crimes. . . .
Crime, like virtue, has its degrees. . . .

Jean Baptiste Racine, ca. 1670

A Case of Canine Karma

Isabel Ringing picked up the phone. "Yurbakup Police Department. Detective Ringing speaking."

She was greeted by the amused voice of her friend and former colleague, Detective Bud Inski. "What's up Detective Ringing? I'm in town, so I wondered if you were free for lunch."

"Sorry, too busy right now," Isabel answered. "I've got some paperwork to finish."

"Anything interesting?"

"Yes. In a sad sort of way. A month ago a sanitation worker detected an animal carcass in a trash container over on Headingfore Court. He didn't notice it until the bin was emptying into the compactor, so he couldn't retrieve the carcass, but he informed his supervisor. Two weeks later, the same sanitation worker found a small dog carcass in the same bin before it was dumped, so he left it, and the supervisor called the house and informed the residents that Animal Control had to be called for animal carcass removal. The residents denied any knowledge of the carcasses.

"The supervisor thought it was unusual to find two carcasses in the bin from the same residence, so he called me. I got to the last carcass before Animal Control had a chance to dispose of it and found what looked like ligature marks. I asked the Animal Control vet, Dr. Fleason Tick, to look at it. He said the marks were consistent with strangulation. I collected some blue cotton fiber from the dog and sent it to the lab. I asked Animal Control to let me know of any further animal-related activity at the house, and two weeks ago an officer from Animal Control called and told me a neighbor had complained about a dog carcass in the backyard of the same house."

Detective Inski interrupted. "Are things so slow you've got to do doggie whodunits?"

Detective Ringing shrugged. "It's against the law to purposefully injure animals. And it's been my experience that a lot of violent offenders abuse animals before they graduate to human assault. I tend to take it seriously."

"So what happened?"

"I went to the address with Animal Control. When we got there, a young man answered the door, dressed in a stained T-shirt and blue jeans with tears at the knees and the side. I introduced myself, and explained about the neighbor's complaint. I told him I was accompanying Animal Control, who was there to collect the carcass. He let us in and took us to the backyard through a cluttered living room with sagging drapes, a tattered couch, and a worn rug. He pointed out the carcass and said he didn't know where the dog came from or how the dog died. When we got the remains to Animal Control, I examined the dog and saw a similar ligature mark and similar fiber. I collected the fiber and submitted the sample to the lab. When the results came back, I was able to return to the house with a warrant and place the young man under investigative detention for aggravated animal abuse."

"On what grounds?" Detective Inski snorted. "I didn't hear you describe anything in that house that could have been used to tie up a dog, let alone tie up this case."

The Chemistry of the Case

Infrared spectroscopy (IR spectroscopy) is a powerful yet relatively inexpensive instrumental analytical technique found in virtually every analytical lab. The principle of operation is as fundamental as eyesight: infrared light interacts differently with different materials, and these differences can be detected and used to identify or characterize samples of forensic interest. Materials that can be analyzed by IR spectroscopy range from fiber to glass to blood to breath, and, in most circumstances, when the analysis is done, the evidence is still intact. This last advantage—that infrared spectroscopy is a nondestructive technique—is an important one. Showing a jury a lab report is never as impressive as showing two fibers side by side. And if a particular analytical method is destructive, then the test cannot be rerun. So in the repertoire of the forensic chemist, infrared spectroscopy will likely always have a place.

Spectroscopy exploits the interactions of light with matter to determine the nature of an analyte—the way our eyes do. Our eyes are useless in the absence of a light source. But given a visible light source, our marvelous minds can analyze, instantaneously, from the amount of light reflected and the amount of light absorbed, the nature of the object being observed. Our optic nerves sense visible light because that is the type of light that is given off by our sun and is the dominant light in our human lives. But there are other types of light, such as infrared, which other animals can, in fact, detect. A type of snake known as a pit viper has sense organs for infrared light because it needs to sense prey in the absence of visible light, and infrared light is the type of electromagnetic radiation emitted by a warm body.

In the introduction to part III, we said that the spectrum of light stretching from gamma rays to radio waves is characterized by frequency. And, as we would intuitively surmise, frequency is related to energy. Gamma rays are high-frequency electromagnetic radiation and they are also high-energy radiation. Nothing is to be gained from standing in a field of high-energy gamma radiation, except, perhaps, to cook your own liver. On the other end of the spectrum, no harm is realized from standing in a field of radio waves; we do this every day that we stand on planet Earth. Visible light is light in a frequency range midway between gamma rays and radio waves. Infrared light is a slightly lower frequency and, consequently, lower energy than visible light. Infrared spectroscopy is particularly useful because infrared light can be used to analyze organic materials, which are very common analytes forensically.

As previously presented, organic materials are covalently bonded molecules composed of hydrogen and concatenated carbon with other elements such as oxygen, nitrogen, or sulfur sometimes thrown into the mix. And, as we mentioned, many natural products, and certainly all living or previously living materials, are made up of organic molecules. But organic materials are even more pervasive than that. Organic materials are used in medicines, fillers, fibers, dyes, solvents, lubricants, foods, paints, plastics, and more. Infrared spectroscopy uses infrared light the way our eyes use visible light: the instrument focuses light in the infrared range on the material of interest and measures how much IR light is absorbed and how much is either reflected or passes through.

Earlier we introduced the notion of atoms absorbing light in atomic absorption (AA) spectroscopy. Our model for the interaction was that electrons are located in specific orbitals around the nucleus, and transitions between orbitals are *quantized*; that is, the movement from one orbital to another requires a specific amount of light energy and no other. The light interacting with the atoms in AA spectroscopy is in the visible region, like the light emitted in the flame test in demonstration 3.

Now we are dealing with infrared light, which also interacts with materials, but via a different mechanism. Infrared radiation carries less energy than visible light. Our eyes do not see it, but our senses can perceive the infrared radiating warmth from a stovetop heating element, even if it is not visibly glowing. Infrared light is not energetic enough to cause electrons in atoms to move to new orbitals, but it is energetic enough to make molecules move faster. The movement caused by infrared light is vibrational motion.

In chapter 14, we said that all atomic-sized particles are in a state of constant motion, either flying about the room or rotating or vibrating or doing all three at once. We also said that when a molecule absorbs energy, it can start vibrating faster. Light is a form of energy, so absorbing light can also cause a molecule to vibrate faster, if it is the right frequency of light. Because the frequency of a molecule's vibrations depend on the mass of the vibrating nuclei and how strongly they are bonded together, characteristic groups, such as the OH group on ethanol, can display signature vibrations. Detection of these features in an IR spectrum can help in the identification of materials. In fact, the region of the IR spectrum in which these features are most pronounced is referred to as the fingerprint region.

To visualize why infrared light might cause a molecule to change vibrational motion, let us recall our discussion of molecular dipoles. If the molecule has a permanent dipole; that is, if there is an uneven distribution of electron density in a particular bond, then the bond has a more positive end and a more negative end. Light coming along with its changing electric field would tug alternately on one end of the bond and then the other. The utility of IR spectroscopy for an analytical tool derives from the fact that the frequency of IR light that interacts with a particular vibration is specific to that vibration.

Consider a child on a swing. On a swing set at a playground, each child may be swinging at a different frequency, established by factors such as the mass of the child and the amount of energy the child is expending. For parents to push their children higher, they have to match their energy input to the frequency already established by the child and the parent has to push forward when the child is swinging forward. If the parent were out of synchronization with the child, the result would be an inefficient input of energy, if not a spill. But if the parent can match the frequency of the swing, the child can absorb energy from the parent and be boosted to a higher level.

In IR spectroscopy, the frequencies of IR light absorbed by the sample are detected, recorded, and correlated to the type of bond that absorbed the energy. Figure 18.1 is a sketch of the infrared spectrum of ethanol, a forensic analyte of frequent interest that can be detected by IR spectroscopy.

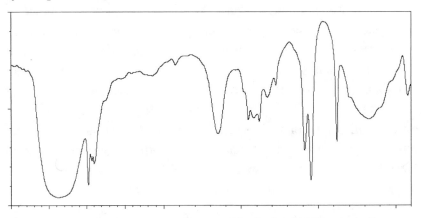

Figure 18.1. An infrared spectrum of ethanol. Although the specific units on the scales have been omitted because their discussion is beyond the scope of this book, we can say that the horizontal scale tracks the frequency of the light impinging on the sample. The vertical scale tracks the amount of light that makes it through the sample without being absorbed. Some frequencies of light are absorbed more than others, as indicated by the dips in the vertical scale at those frequencies. The pattern of absorbed frequencies can be used to identify the molecule.

In an effort to focus our discussion on essential features, we have omitted units on the spectrum and say only that the scale along the bottom tracks the various frequencies of the infrared light to which the sample is exposed. The scale on the side tracks how much of a particular frequency of light passes through the sample. A dip in the amount of light passing through indicates that some light has been absorbed.

From figure 18.1 we can see that some of the frequencies are absorbed by the ethanol molecule and some are not. For those frequencies that are absorbed, all ethanol molecules absorb just exactly these frequencies. So the IR spectrum provides a "fingerprint" for ethanol.

For an unknown analyte, IR spectroscopy can move us a good way toward identifying that material. Each vibrational mode can be influenced by the vibrations of the bonds near it (just as the frequency of the child on the swing set is somewhat coupled to the frequency of other children on the same swing set), so the IR spectrum can tell us something about the arrangement of bonds in the molecule, too.

On a good day.

We live in a messy world, and forensic chemists are called upon to deal with some of the biggest messes. In many circumstances of interest to forensic chemistry the material in question is not pure or cannot be removed from its surroundings without destroying it, such as dye on fiber or colorant in glass. In these cases, the spectrum of the entire sample must be obtained without separation. And without separation, the exact molecular makeup of the material cannot be obtained. But if two samples are to be matched, then many times it is the entire picture that is compared—sample and matrix—so separation wouldn't be an advantage. In fact, separation might be a disadvantage because, as we said, the frequency of vibrations may be influenced by the environment in which the material finds itself. The big picture may carry information that would be lost in separation.

For instance, an IR analysis of a sample of tape might be able to identify the glue used, the fibers in the tape body, and the type of plastic backing. But there might be millions of yards of tape from the same manufacturer that match this description. The weathering of the glue or backing, however, might be unique to two sections of the same piece of tape because of their shared history.

Although it would seem that mass-manufactured dyes would be of little value for identification, fashion demands unique and ever-changing combinations; thus small batches are the rule rather than the exception, and dye combinations can be used to identify or match samples. The manner of dye application adds another layer of individualization. And weathering will be unique to each garment, so fading and discoloration can also help to distinguish a specific material. The exact mixture of a manufactured material that uses a variable feed stock—for instance, products made from recycled materials—can sometimes show a unique spectrum that may be matched between samples.

Another example of intact-sample analysis can be found in investigations of glass. Glass has an inorganic material as a base: silicon dioxide. The IR spectrum of a glass is not composed of the relatively neat, narrow features of an ethanol-like spectrum, but rather broad, amorphous bands that change with the specifics of manufacture and colorant. As a quantitative or diagnostic measure, IR spectroscopy of glass is relatively unrevealing. But as a comparison tool, it is highly valuable. Two pieces of glass from the same batch should have virtually identical IR profiles. The fact that glass does not have to be broken up to be analyzed by infrared spectroscopy highlights one of the main strengths of spectroscopy: it does not always have to be a destructive technique. A GC mass spec analyzes a material by blasting it into fragments and then lining up the fragments to discern a pattern. In infrared spectroscopy, the material can often be analyzed while still whole, breaking up the light into its frequencies instead.

An interesting aside on instrumentation must be made at this point. Infrared spectroscopy has existed as an analytical method for many years, but with the advent of readily available and reliable computer and laser technology, an improved form of data acquisition called *Fourier transform analysis* has been introduced. Fourier transform infrared spectroscopy, FTIR, can take many scans of the same sample in a short period of time and give a statistically more accurate analysis. In traditional infrared spectroscopy, the infrared light is separated into select frequencies by mechanically changing the angle of gratings or prisms before or after the light is sent through the sample. In Fourier transform instruments, an entire spectrum of IR light is sent through the sample at once and then sorted out into its individual frequencies by computer analysis. The precision and reproducibility gained allows infrared spectroscopy to routinely identify artificial fibers, paints, inks, and dyes and to discern between samples that are physically very similar but chemically different. The ability of FTIR to collect scans via computer opens up another possibility: peaks in the spectrum due to contaminants can sometimes be identified and subtracted electronically from the sample.

Other frequencies of light, such as ultraviolet light, visible light, and even microwave light can be used for analysis, but infrared spectroscopy is by far the most versatile and the most common. It was also all that Detective Ringing needed to tie up "A Case of Canine Karma." Detective Ringing found blue fiber on the first dog, and the state crime lab used infrared spectroscopy to analyze it. By using IR spectroscopy, they were able to confirm that the material was cotton, and they were able to profile the fiber dyes without destroying the fiber. When Detective Ringing found the second sample of blue fiber, the lab showed that the dyes suffered similar fading from a shared history and therefore shared a common origin—just the connection Detective Ringing needed to clear up the canine crime.

Case Closed

"It was the fiber that did him in," explained Detective Isabelle Ringing.

"How did the fiber on the dogs give enough probable cause for a warrant?" asked Detective Bud Inski impatiently.

"The lab said it was blue jean material," replied Detective Isabel Ringing. "And the judge gave me a warrant to search the house for a pair of blue jeans."

"That doesn't make sense! Of course you found blue jeans. You're going to find blue jeans in every house in the country!"

"I was looking for a specific pair . . ."

"How could you identify a pair of jeans that were used to strangle a dog? For that matter, how the heck do you strangle a dog with blue jeans?"

"I didn't say they were strangled by blue jeans. I said I found blue fiber, but I didn't say where I found it."

Detective Inski sighed with impatience. "Okay! I give up! Where did you find it?"

"In their teeth. The warrant was for the pair of blue jeans with tears in the side. When we found the jeans, we tested them, and the IR spectrum was consistent with the fiber in the dogs' teeth. The perp denied all knowledge of the dogs, but the fibers told a different story. Before these dogs went down, they took a bite out of crime."

DEMONSTRATION 19 EXAMINING THE EVIDENCE

The shepherd always tries to persuade the sheep that their interests and his own are the same.

Henri Marie Beyle, ca. 1830

Setting the Scope

Place a sheet of newspaper flat on a tabletop. Find two books about 3 inches (7 centimeters) thick and place them on the newspaper, about 2 inches (5 centimeters) apart. Take one of the large-diameter magnifying glasses suggested for purchase in "Crime Lab and Crime Solutions" and lay it across the books so that the lens is suspended over the newspaper in the gap between the books. Shine the light from a flashlight on the newspaper under the magnifying glass.

Now hold a second magnifying glass about 3 inches above the first. The writing should be greatly magnified compared to how it appeared through the single glass. Move the second magnifying glass up and down to change the magnification. Note that if you hold it too close to your eyes, it loses its magnifying power.

Diffraction Infraction

Warning: Never look into a laser of any kind. The beam is capable of doing serious damage to your eyes. The reflections of a laser beam are quite intense relative to a regular light source, so guard against looking at reflections as well. As a safety precaution, you should wear sunglasses when performing this demonstration.

Find a large clear or transparent bowl or glass. You should be able to see through it when looking from the side. Fill it with water to within an inch (2 to 3 centimeters) of the top and add a very small amount of milky white dishwashing liquid or milk. Both of these materials are made up of very fine particles suspended in water, a situation called a *suspension*, appropriately enough. Put on the sunglasses and take up the laser pointer suggested for purchase in "Crime Lab and Crime Solutions." Turn on the pointer and hold it at a low, grazing angle to the surface of the water. Holding the pointer still, look through the water container from the side at right angles to the laser beam. You should be able to see the beam of laser light as it moves through the solution.

Compare the line of the laser beam in the water to the line of the laser beam that comes from the pointer. The *refraction*, bending, of the laser light due to water is apparent. This refraction is what makes poles sticking out of water appear to be broken at the surface and what makes spearfishing difficult: you have to aim at where the fish *should* be, not where it appears to be.

Now move the laser pointer and see what effect that has on the angle between the entering beam path and the beam path in the water, the *angle of refraction*.

Light through a Loop Hole

Find a food item that is packaged in a cylindrical container with a thin metal bottom and a clear plastic lid. In the United States, there are potato chip cans and coffee cans that fit these specifications quite nicely. Empty the contents. This container will serve as the basis for your pinhole viewer.

Take a nail and make a small hole in the metal bottom of the container, as close to the center as possible. Make the smallest-sized hole that you can; a large hole reduces the effect. Place the clear plastic lid on the container.

Arrange a small birthday candle so that it is standing upright. You can do this by lighting the candle, allowing some of the wax to fall onto a ceramic plate, and placing the candle in this small pool of melted wax. Make sure it remains standing. (Be careful—you want a single flame; you don't want to start a fire!) Darken the room and, holding the bottom of the container one foot away from the lit candle, look at the image of the candle that appears on the plastic lid. It may take a moment to train your eyes to focus on the lid as opposed to the candle itself. Do not look straight through the container because you will see the flame directly. You may want to look at the lid from an angle.

When you have achieved the correct orientation, you will see the image of the flame upside down on the lid. If you let the candle flicker a bit, it may be easier to orientate the image.

The above trilogy of demonstrations is designed to show the peculiar properties of light. First, light can be modeled as traveling in rays, which result in the inverted image in the pinhole viewer. The rays come off the flame in all directions, but only those angled down from the tip of the flame and angled up from the base of the flame make it through the pinhole. Light can also be modeled as waves, which result in the light's ability to turn corners as demonstrated by its refraction at interfaces. These two properties taken together create a powerful forensic tool: the magnifying lens. And, as we will see below in "The Case of Courting Trouble," this classic instrument will always have its place in the investigator's arsenal.

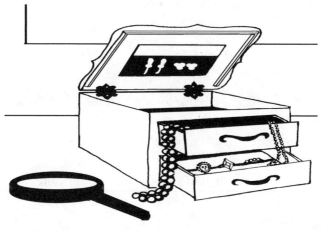

CHAPTER 19

UNDER THE MICROSCOPE: MICROSCOPY

. . . we come closer to the truth the more often we concentrate our investigations on one and the same thing at different moments.

Antonie van Leeuwenhoek, early microscopist, 1707

In a closed society where everybody's guilty, the only crime is getting caught. In a world of thieves, the only final sin is stupidity.

Hunter S. Thompson, ca. 1970

THE CASE OF COURTING TROUBLE

T he dispatch officer spoke into her headset. "911. What is your emergency?"

Candy Hart spoke between sobs. "I've been robbed!"

"What is your address . . . "

Within ten minutes, a uniformed officer, Rea Zun, was at Ms. Hart's apartment taking down her information. A young man stood comforting Ms. Hart.

The young woman introduced him, "This is my fiancé, Leanon Mee."

Mr. Mee stood with a protective arm around Ms. Hart.

Officer Zun got out her notebook. "Have you touched anything?"

Ms. Hart looked around despairingly. "Yes, of course. I checked to see what had been stolen." She pointed toward the hallway just off the small living room of the apartment. "They took my jewelry!"

Officer Zun made a note. "How did they get in?"

Ms. Hart gestured toward a sliding glass door that led out onto the courtyard of the apartment complex. Officer Zun noted the bent metal where a tool had been forced into the aluminum slide before the door was lifted from its frame and pushed in.

"May I see where the jewelry is missing?"

Ms. Hart led Officer Zun to an open, empty jewelry box on a bureau in the bedroom.

"Is this how you found it?"

"Yes," sobbed Ms. Hart.

"Was it shut when you last saw it?"

"Yes. I shut it every morning before I go to work."

"You were insured, weren't you?" asked Officer Zun.

"Yes," Ms. Hart argued, ignoring the the voice of Rea Zun. "But the jewelry had sentimental value, too."

Officer Zun looked carefully around the area to see if any trace from the perp was apparent, though the owner had already compromised the scene in her concern for her property. Officer Zun noted a small velvety ring box under the thrown-back lid of the jewelry case and used her pencil to push the velvet box from under the open lid. "What is this?"

Ms. Hart gasped and grabbed the little fuzzy box, opening it quickly. "Our brand-new wedding set! They didn't get our platinum wedding set!"

Officer Zun removed a small utility tool from her pocket and opened out a magnifying lens. She examined the wedding set Ms. Hart held open.

"Are you sure this is platinum?" asked Officer Zun.

Ms. Hart clasped the box to her chest, "What do you mean! Of course it is platinum!"

"What are you, a police officer or a jeweler?" interrupted her fiancé. "Are you going to ogle our wedding set all day or go out and find the person who stole the rest?!"

"May I take the wedding set for evidence, please?" said Officer Zun. "I will write you out a receipt."

Back at the station, Rea Zun contacted the detective heading up the investigation on a string of apartment burglaries, Robin Stores.

"I think," she said. "I may have a lead for you."

The Chemistry of the Case

At first, microscopy may not seem to fall under the purview of chemistry, but take a closer look: properties of materials that result in magnification are attributable to the molecular structure of the magnifying medium. Microscopy, from magnifying glasses to electron microscopes, is fundamental to forensic investigations and operates on principles founded on chemical structure.

Magnifying lenses magnify because molecules interact with light. We've already noted how the interactions of infrared light with molecules could be used to identify bonds within the molecule. If IR (infrared) light is of just the right frequency, it can be absorbed by certain molecular bonds, like children on a swing set absorbing energy from pushes at the right frequency. But even when there is not a match of just the right frequency, there can still be an interaction. The demonstration at the beginning of this chapter shows how the path of a beam of light can be bent by passing from one type of material to another.

Light can bend on passing from one medium to another because the speed of light is constant *in a vacuum*, but in a medium such as water or oil, light can slow down. If a beam of light hits a new medium at an angle, not only will the light slow down but it will also change direction.

An analogy can be found in driving. If a car is traveling at a good clip on an asphalt surface and the surface suddenly turns to gravel, the car will slow down because it is getting less traction. If the car is going at a good clip on an asphalt road and hits a strip of gravel at an angle, then the first wheel that hits the gravel will slow down while the other three keep going. The predictable result is that the car will go into a spin. When a beam of light hits a new medium at an angle, it will change direction, too.

This bending of light by a change of mediums is called *refraction*. Refraction is also responsible for the splitting of light by a prism: different frequencies of light—that is, different colors—interact differently with the vibrating molecules of the prism. Blue, it turns out, bends more than green, which bends more than yellow, which bends more than orange, which bends more than red—just as different cars will experience different spins when they hit loose gravel. Refraction also accounts for the behavior of light in lenses. In fact, the *refractive index* of a pure sample can be used to identify the material.

But the refractive index is rarely used forensically because forensic samples tend to be pretty messy. Physical separation might be possible, but the materials, once separated, are not the original sample. Preservation of the primary sample is always preferable forensically. But destruction is not necessary when examining samples under a magnifying lens. The sample stays the same while lenses bend light reflected from it or passed through it.

There are several varieties of lenses, but the two main types are convex and concave lenses, as shown in figure 19.1. Lenses work as they do because prisms bend light (figure 19.1a). The concave lens can be envisioned as two prisms balanced one atop the other, tip to tip (figure 19.1b). Light bends outward from a concave lens as though from two prisms. A convex lens can be envisioned as two prisms stacked base to base. Light bends inward in this arrangement, converging at a point (figure 19.1c).[1] The opposite is true, too. Light from the point of convergence would spread out if it passed back through another convex lens. The final result, a magnified image, is the principle behind a magnifying glass (figure 19.1d). Although a discussion of optics is beyond the scope of this book, we must point out that a parameter called the *focal length* is important, too. As can be seen from the sketches in figure 19.1, the effects only occur at a certain distance from the lens, a distance that depends on the thickness and the curvature of the lens. Some of these properties of lenses were illustrated by the demonstration at the beginning of this chapter.

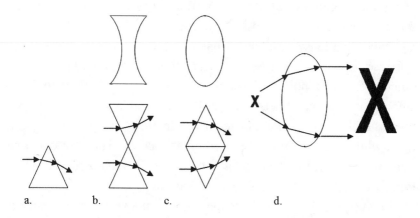

Figure 19.1. A prism separates light by causing it to bend (a). A concave lens can be envisioned as two prisms balanced one atop the other, tip to tip (b). A convex lens can be envisioned as two prisms stacked base to base (c). Magnification is achieved by reversing the path through a convex lens (d).

But while simple magnifying lenses are very helpful for enhancing normal-sized objects, extra magnifying power is often needed in forensic applications, and microscopes can be employed for this purpose. Light microscopes use lenses to magnify objects up to a thousand times. By using light microscopes, forensic investigators have been able to match the torn edges of tapes, tool marks on doorjambs and windows, and firing-pin and rifling marks on bullets. The device most often used for this type of analysis is a *comparison microscope*, which allows the analyst to look at two objects at the same time and to optically align the objects being compared, such as the two edges of a cut rope.

Another type of microscope, a *polarized light microscope*, has also found use in forensic applications, and this microscope's special properties are again based on the lenses. Many molecules have nice, even, symmetric electrical fields associated with their electrons and protons, but many do not. Light encountering an asymmetric molecular field may experience a twist, which is more readily observed when the molecules are in relatively fixed and ordered positions, such as in a crystalline solid. Usually this twist would not be noticed because normal light has oscillating waves going in all directions. But if one orientation of light is selected, then it would be possible to detect a twist.

Polarizing lenses are lenses that select a narrow range of orientations for light. By selecting one orientation of light and blocking the others, lenses of polarized sunglasses reduce glare—they limit the amount of light that enters the eye. If you are able to secure a pair of these sunglasses, try holding them out in front of you and rotating them while you are looking at a computer screen. They cut out some light all the time, but in some orientations, they should cut out all the light, which will make the screen appear black.

In a polarized-light microscope, light with a very narrow range of orientations is allowed to pass though a sample such as a mineral or a crystal. Minerals lend themselves to this type of analysis because the components of the solid are held in relatively ordered, rigid positions. Any twist the minerals apply to the light has less chance of being canceled by a random opposite twist.

Polarized-light microscopy has been used to identify minerals, fiber, and a mineral fiber: asbestos. Asbestos is a type of mineral that is fibrous enough that it can be used to make fireproof cloth. Not only can asbestos be detected by polarized-light microscopy, distinctions can be made between the several types of asbestos.

If you find the subject of optics intriguing, an introductory physics book would probably be a good place to go for more information. But before we leave the subject of lenses, we might mention one more forensic application. The eyeball also has a lens, and the purpose of this lens is to focus the light onto the optic nerves on the retina. Sometimes this lens needs a little extra help, which can be provided by artificial lenses called glasses. To achieve the maximum correction, lenses have to be individually crafted to match the specific needs of each person. In some criminal investigations, suspects have been identified by the prescriptions of their corrective lenses.

We leave lenses now because there are times when more magnification is needed than light lenses can provide. In these cases, the scanning electron microscope, or SEM, is the imaging tool of choice. The principle of operation for the SEM is similar to that of light microscopy except that electrons are used to probe surfaces instead of light.

In a scanning electron microscope, the electrons are emitted from a heated filament and accelerated toward the surface to be analyzed by a region of positive voltage called a *cathode*. Many of the electrons are going so fast that by the time they get to the cathode they go zipping right past and hit the sample. When these electrons hit the surface, they knock off other electrons. These secondary electrons can be used to produce a three-dimensional image of the surface. Some light may also be emitted when the electrons hit and this light can be used with the electrons to achieve magnifications of up to two million times.

But this type of magnification is rarely needed in forensic applications. So why bother with SEM? Because the use of electrons as the "illumination" leads to the second big benefit of SEM: nondestructive surface elemental analysis. SEM can be used to determine the elements at the surface of gunshot residue, bullet markings, jewelry, paint, fiber, paper, hair, plant material, insects, and more. At one time, nonconductive materials had to be coated with a thin layer of gold or carbon to make them conductive before they could be analyzed, but improvements in methodology now allow for most samples to be analyzed intact.

The nondestructive aspect of light microscopy and SEM is significant because it allows evidence to be presented in an unaltered state and allows samples to be retested. For instance, if a piece of metal is found, it might look like a bullet fragment—or a filling for a tooth. SEM elemental analysis would allow you to differentiate between the two without destroying the sample. If the elemental analysis is consistent with a bullet fragment, you could examine it for microscopic marks caused by the gun from which it was fired. If the elemental analysis is consistent with a filling, you could look around for the tooth it fit into.

There are times, however, when even less magnification is sufficient. In "The Case of Courting Trouble," all Officer Rea Zun needed was a magnifying glass to tell her that Ms. Candy Hart might want to take a closer look at her jewelry—and her relationship.

Case Closed

Officer Rea Zun described the scene of the robbery to detective Robin Stores. She showed him the velvet boxed wedding set that she had taken into evidence.

"I agree," said Detective Stores. "Using a tool to lift the sliding door from its track in a courtyard apartment sounds like the same MO as the other burglaries in the neighborhood. Might be the same perp. But why would you think this wedding set would give me a lead?"

Officer Zun offered her magnifying lens. "If you look closely, you can see the surface coating is starting to crack. This isn't platinum, but white gold, and several years old at that."

Detective Stores shrugged. "So the boyfriend is cheap. Makes the guy a jerk, but as far as I know, that's not a crime."

"But insurance fraud is," said Officer Zun. "That ring box wasn't hidden when the jewelry case lid was shut, which is how a real thief would have found it. Only someone who knew that the contents of the ring box were relatively worthless would have taken everything else but left the rings. I think you need to do a background check on Mr. Mee."

"Hmm," said Detective Stores. "That does have a ring of truth."

DEMONSTRATION 20
POINT OF LAW

Personally, I wouldn't hang a mad dog on the basis of eyewitness testimony.

Anne Wingate,
Scene of the Crime,
1992

*W*arning: Never look into a laser of any kind. The beam is capable of doing serious damage to your eyes. The reflections of a laser beam are quite intense relative to a regular light source, so guard against looking at reflections as well. As a safety precaution, you should wear sunglasses when performing this demonstration.*

The following demonstrations are intended to display some of the unique qualities of laser light.

Using the same setup as was used for the refraction experiment in the last chapter, point your laser obliquely at the surface of the glass bowl, and again observe the refraction. But this time also observe what happens when the laser beam travels all the way through the suspension and strikes the glass surface on the other side of the bowl.

At the first inside surface of the glass that the beam strikes, notice that the beam continues out of the container at a bent angle. This bending is due to refraction. Also notice that part of the beam reflects back into the solution. When it strikes another surface, the refraction/reflection process continues until the beam becomes completely depleted.

The special focus of laser light can also be demonstrated by shining the laser pointer on a wall in a darkened room and noting how the size of the spot changes relatively little as you bring the pointer closer or move it farther away. Now try the same experiment with a flashlight. You should see the flashlight spot spread out considerably more with increased distance from the wall.

Now point your laser pointer at a spot on the wall and observe the appearance of the wall spot closely. If your laser pointer has a decorative cover to lend a shape to the light (some have hearts, flowers, smiley faces, etc.), then take the cover off. Once you have a simple laser spot on the wall, turn off the laser pointer and cover the end from which the light emanates with a smooth piece of aluminum foil. With a needle, make the smallest hole you can in the foil, right where the point of light would exit. The hole also needs to be round: the smaller and rounder the better.

Darken the room as much as possible and turn on the laser pointer with the foil still in place. The laser spot ought to be coming through the pinhole. You should be able to see several thin rings of light around the central bright spot of light. These rings occur because the laser light is very nearly one frequency, and the light waves that exit the hole overlap positively only at certain intervals. The arrangement is rather tricky, so you may have to try several times. Once you have seen the effect, try it with a flashlight. You will note that the demonstration does not work with normal light.

The nearly single frequency of laser light can also be demonstrated with a prism. Try shining the laser light through a prism as you did with sunlight. You will not see the laser light break up into any other colors.

These two properties of laser light—tight focus and single color—mean that laser light can be made quite intense. In fact, intense enough to blast apart "The Case of the Subtle Smear."

CHAPTER 20

SEXY SCIENCE: LASER ABLATION

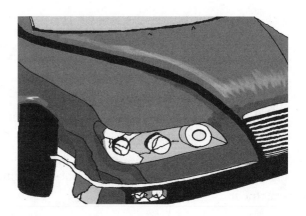

The coffin of Mary, Queen of Scots was opened in 1830. They found two ax marks on her body, one on the nape of her neck and a second stroke that removed her head. The queen was executed before a crowd of people, and there were numerous eyewitness accounts. Here is the mystery. Every witness claimed they saw her head fall with a single stroke of the ax. Isn't that strange. The first blow was erased from their memory as fast as the ax fell. The witnesses were all in a state of shock.

Jody Shields, *The Fig Eater*, ca. 2000

THE CASE OF THE SUBTLE SMEAR

Detective Izzy Able reached for a slice of pizza as he continued the story he was sharing with his friend Arty Fax, a museum publicity director.

"We found a microscopic paint smear on the victim's watch that was consistent with automobile paint," Detective Able concluded. "Because this was a hit-and-run that resulted in death, we requested and received FBI assistance."

"What were they able to do with a microscopic paint chip?" questioned Arty.

"They analyzed it via laser ablation."

"I've heard of research using that technique at the local art museum, but I don't know how it works."

"They used a laser to vaporize a miniscule spot on the paint, a layer at a time, without having to remove it from the metal link on the watch band."

"What did they find?"

"They were able to tell us that the top layer contained red pigment and the bottom layer was black."

"So did that help?"

"It did, especially since we have a witness who said she had heard brakes screeching and looked out to see a black Ford pickup swerving away."

"So much for eyewitnesses. How could you trust anything else she said?"

"Why not?"

"Well, she was wrong about the color of the truck, wasn't she?"

Detective Able shrugged. "It depends on how you look at it . . ."

The Chemistry of the Case

When you hold your hand too close to a lit lightbulb, it can start to feel uncomfortably warm, despite the fact that the light from the lightbulb is going in every direction. If all that light were focused on your hand, you would feel far more discomfort. If a magnifying glass focuses the light from the sun onto a leaf, it can quickly set the leaf smoking. Lasers can concentrate light even more than that.

The word *laser* is actually an acronym for "light amplification by stimulated emission of radiation." The source of the light that is amplified is similar to the source of the light from the flames that we examined in chapter 3. Atoms or molecules in excited states can relax to their ground states by giving off excess energy as light. Normally this light is pretty tame. You can read by it or warm yourself by it and not worry about it lifting off a layer of skin. So what is different about lasers?

The first difference is that laser light is given off in such a narrow band of frequencies that, for practical purposes, it can be considered one frequency, or *monochromatic*. The second difference is that laser light is *coherent*; that is, the light waves are marching along in lock-step, in phase with each other. They reinforce rather than distract from each other. This reinforcement, in addition to having all of the light at virtually one frequency, makes that frequency very intense indeed. The third difference is that laser light is unidirectional. Normal light is diffuse: it spreads out from its source in all directions. But laser light does not behave this way. So the question becomes, How does the laser achieve these advantages?

The first advantage of laser light—that it comes in a very narrow range of frequencies—is not such a big trick. We saw in our flame test that individual elements have their own particular light. The second advantage—that the light is coherent—comes from having all the light-emitting reactions occur at once, which is a bit more of a trick. To get a big cascade of photons (as we called the light energy packet in chapter 3 and the introduction to part III), you have to have a lot of electrons in a higher-than-normal energy level, ready to lose energy all at once when stimulated. This state of affairs is called a *population inversion*. A population inversion can be achieved in some materials (but by no means all materials) by hitting the material with a sudden pulse of energy, called *pumping*, either from electricity or from another light source. Then, once the population inversion has been achieved, the entire population can be stimulated to return to the ground state by a single stray photon. This stimulation is represented by the *s* in laser: light amplification by *s*timulated emission of radia-tion. A domino analogy might work well: the lowest energy, the ground state, for a domino would be lying facedown on the table. If a set of dominoes are balanced on end, this would be the "pump" cre-ating a population inversion. If our dominoes (or photons) are aligned so that the first one falling down stimulates another, then this would be the laser "dump" that creates the burst of coherent radiation.

The coherence of laser radiation is enhanced with mirrors. The lasing material is contained in a tube with mirrors at either end, so that when a burst of radiation occurs, it bounces back and forth between the two mirrors. The length of the laser is such that only waves of the right frequency will form standing waves. When we discussed standing waves in chapter 3, we compared standing waves to the pattern of waves formed on the surface of a cup of coffee during an airplane flight. Standing waves are waves that make the trip back and forth between the mirrors without encountering out-of-phase interference. When the light is finally released, virtually only one frequency of light is released. These mirrors also account for the uniform directionality of the light. One of the mirrors is only partially reflective, so when the light exits, it exits through that mirror and in that direction.

The description we've given here for lasers is vastly simplified. Lasers are very complicated systems. (The first working laser was demonstrated in 1960, so the technology is relatively new.) Our description is also a general description of lasers, and different types of lasers vary on quite a few points. For instance, you may be looking at your laser pointer about now and wondering where the little mirrors are. In truth, the laser pointer is actually a semiconductor laser, which operates with a significantly different design. Its light, while truly laser light, is not nearly as powerful as that of the lasers used in laser ablation—the technique mentioned in "The Case of the Subtle Smear."

Ablation means removal, and laser ablation uses the amplified, coherent directional light of a laser, focused into a very small area, to remove very small amounts of material. The resulting vapor is usually fed into a mass spectrometer for analysis. A special high-power microscope is used to manipulate the material being analyzed so that specific sites can be sampled by the laser. The laser can also produce a depth profile of the material by sampling successive layers. In "The

Case of the Subtle Smear," the portion of the watchband with the paint smear was placed under the laser probe, and the laser sampling started at the top and worked down to the watchband.

A mass spectrometer is a logical choice for analyzing the vaporized material removed by the laser because the masses can be compared, via computer, with a library of known compounds, such as car paints. As you may recall from chapter 6, this spectrometer breaks up materials into charged fragments and uses a magnetic field to sort the fragments by the mass-to-charge ratio.

Laser ablation falls into the category of techniques analytical chemists refer to as "sexy" techniques. These are generally more expensive, more targeted, and more exotic techniques than those normally maintained in a smaller forensic lab, but they are available in some larger municipalities, or in state labs, or are available under special circumstances from the FBI or from commercial forensic labs.

Another method that falls into the "sexy" category is neutron activation analysis (NAA). Neutron activation may not sound like it involves light (the light it involves is a part of the spectrum not normally thought of as light), but it deserves mention in part III because it is a light-dependent technique. In NAA, the substance to be analyzed is bombarded with neutrons that put the nuclei into excited states. Gamma rays are emitted as the nuclei relax to their ground states. These gamma rays can be used to identify the element involved. Most of the elements on the periodic table can be analyzed by this method, and many elements can be identified at concentrations as low as one part per billion (see chapter 7). Materials that may be traced through this precise elemental analysis are explosives, inks, and paints. It was the latter—and laser ablation—that painted the picture in "The Case of the Subtle Smear."

Case Closed

Arty Fax regarded his friend, Detective Izzy Able, with annoyance. "How could the witness be right? She said the truck she saw was black, but the laser analysis of the paint smear on the watchband showed a red layer on top and a black layer underneath."

"They analyzed the paint smear on the watchband," said his friend, "without removing it from the watchband."

Arty still looked confused.

"Well," said Detective Able, "if I were to smear this pizza on a napkin . . ."

He completed his thought by picking up a slice of pizza and rubbing it facedown on a napkin.

"And if I submitted the sample intact . . ."

He picked up the napkin with the pizza.

"The crust layer would be encountered by the laser first—then the sauce—and *then* the cheese, right?"

A look of comprehension passed across Arty's eyes. "So the paint that was the top layer on the car was the bottom layer on the smear."

"That's it," said Detective Able. "And the observant eyewitness was able to give us a license plate number, too."

"Wow," said Arty. "Some of your cases have a lot of layers to them."

"Yes," said Detective Able, "but forensic chemistry can get to the bottom."

DEMONSTRATION 21
ILLUMINATING
DETAILS

*. . . Death. It comes
equally to us all, and
makes us all equal
when it comes.*

John Donne,
ca. 1600

For this demonstration, you will need your alternative light source: your black light. And please be sure to wear your eye and hand protection.

Get the small bottle of tonic water (making certain it says "contains quinine" on the label), the dry laundry bleach with brighteners, the spinach, and the isopropyl alcohol (rubbing alcohol) suggested for purchase in "Crime Lab and Crime Solutions." Crush about four leaves of spinach and soak them in about a quarter cup (60 milliliters) of rubbing alcohol. If you cannot find spinach, then other dark green leafy vegetables should work (we used turnip greens, a regional delicacy). The alcohol will extract chlorophyll from the leaves as they are crushed. After a minute or so of crushing, pour off the extract into a clear cup. The liquid should have a green color indicating the presence of chlorophyll. Because the alcohol evaporates easily, you may want to put plastic wrap over the top of the container.

Pour about a tablespoon (15 milliliters) of the bleach into another see-through cup and then fill the cup about one-third full with tap water. Mix this solution so that the brighteners dissolve.

Turn on the black light and observe the light coming from the solutions. The tonic water glows with a soft blue emission. The brighteners in the bleach also cause that solution to glow soft blue, though the character of the two luminescent glows is different. You will have to hold the light source closer to the spinach extract, but when you do, you will see a beautiful orange glow that is especially pleasing. Dimming the room light and holding the UV lamp several feet away may enhance the effects. The soft glow emitted by the brighteners is the reason brighteners are added to bleach. The UV light from the sun can make the cloths treated with brighteners actually appear brighter.

In these solutions, the initial source of the energy is our alternative light source. The black light provides energy to the quinine, the brightener molecules, and the spinach. Quinine, brighteners, and spinach are very efficient at returning most of the added energy back to the outside world as light, but this light is shifted in frequency by being absorbed and reemitted. The light that comes from molecules that are placed in an excited state by an input of energy is called *fluorescence* because it lasts only as long as the external light source is on. *Phosphorescence* is light that comes from molecules and dies away slowly after the external light source is turned off.

For the second part of this demonstration, you will need the luminol preparation suggested for purchase in "Crime Lab and Crime Solutions." These luminol kits may seem surprisingly available; however, since the advent of high-tech police TV drama shows, luminol has become almost a household word. With shades of Shakespeare, we are led to believe that blood can never be completely washed away, and where it once existed, luminol will find it. The reality, however, is a bit different.

The following demonstration is designed to allow the reader to judge the range of usefulness of luminol, the exactness of the techniques that must be employed for a successful test, and the appearance of interferences. There are several materials that can produce a false positive.

Put on your safety glasses. Retrieve your butcher's paper from packaged red meat for your blood sample. Put a couple of drops of blood on two white paper plates. With your exam gloves on, put a few drops of copper sulfate solution on a third paper plate, and on a fourth paper plate put a few drops of liquid household bleach. Crush an iron tablet and make a dry paste by adding a few drops of water. Smear the paste on a fifth plate. Label each paper plate as to its contents. Allow these samples to dry, perhaps overnight.

After your samples have dried, wash one of the paper plates that has the now-dried blood until there is only a suggestion of a stain on the plate. Using the spray bottle suggested for purchase in "Crime Lab and Crime Solutions," practice misting a surface with plain water. Once you're satisfied that you have a technique for applying a light spray, prepare your luminol. Be sure to wear exam gloves and eye protection because the luminol solution is caustic.

Fresh luminol solution works better, so prepare only a portion of your luminol and save the rest for later. Follow the procedure that accompanies the packaged luminol. When you are ready, darken the room and lightly mist the five samples.

The dried blood should give a visible blue glow. The copper sample should give a very bright glow, and the bleach should also glow. The iron tablet should give a flash of blue glow that quickly fades. The plate that had the blood washed off, however, may or may not show any indication of blood. Your results will depend on the quality of the luminol used and the vigor of your cleansing.

The light that comes from luminol is called *chemiluminescence* because it is luminescence created by a chemical reaction. The luminol test for blood works because the light-producing reaction is catalyzed by the blood. As evidenced by the flash of blue from the iron tablet in the demonstration, the iron in blood contributes to the response. However, as we can see from the false positive created by copper sulfate and bleach, luminol on its own does not prove the presence—or the absence—of blood. Corroborating evidence is required.

Corroborating evidence, however, is not needed in "The Case of the Hirsute Homeless." Luminol merely ensured that the trail could be followed—to the bloody end.

CHAPTER 21

THE GLARING TRUTH: CHEMILUMINESCENCE AND FLUORESCENCE

Golden lads and girls all must,
As chimney-sweepers, come to dust

Shakespeare, ca. 1600

THE CASE OF THE HIRSUTE HOMELESS

The detective and the technician surveyed the scene before them. The alley was a staging site for trash cans and dumpsters and an impromptu lavatory for vagrants and drunks. But on this particular evening, some trash cans looked newly knocked over and there was an incongruent odor emanating from behind one in particular: the smell of a human body in the early stages of decay.

The detective, R. E. Grets, motioned the technician, Kana Wurms, toward the alley. Officer Wurms shrugged in resignation, and donned a particle mask, face shield, and latex gloves. She picked up her satchel of supplies and stepped forward carefully.

The body was that of a young man, but his jeans and T-shirt were torn and stained. He had about a week's growth of beard and dried residue of food stuck in the stubble. His throat had been sliced open, and there was a good deal of blood both on the victim and on the asphalt. His jeans pockets had been pulled out, rifled by bloodied hands. Officer Wurms began to examine the body for trace evidence while Detective Grets walked the scene.

"Cheeze, what a mess," complained Officer Wurms. "What people do to themselves."

Detective Grets paused in his pacing. "What do you mean 'What people do to themselves'? I don't think this guy was a suicide, do you? It's hard enough to slice your own throat, but rifling your own pockets in the process doesn't make sense."

Officer Wurms sighed. "I mean the states people get into. Instead of paying for a room so he could get off the street and be safe, this guy must have spent his money on dope or booze, and look where it got him."

Detective Grets regarded the corpse thoughtfully and then resumed his perusal of the area. After a moment, he stopped and called back to Officer Wurms. "Did you bring luminol?"

Officer Wurms looked at him in surprise. "No, but back in the trunk I've got the stuff to mix it up." She nodded at the copious blood splatter that had pooled around the body. "Do you think we need it?"

Detective Grets pointed at small, bloody prints leading away from the body and down the alley. "I'm going to follow these as far as I can. We're going to have to ID this guy. Maybe the dog prints will tell us something . . ."

Through the layers of protective face gear, Detective Grets could see the skepticism in Officer Wurms's eyes.

By illuminating the dimming footprints in the darkening alley with luminol, Detective Grets located a small clipped miniature poodle huddling behind a dumpster, caught by a rope leash on a drainpipe, but without a collar or tags.

"Hey, there, little buddy," Detective Grets spoke gently to the shivering dog. "Looks like you're homeless, too." He walked with the dog back to where the evidence technician knelt.

"He must have snatched the dog thinking he could sell it," surmised Officer Wurms.

The detective secured the dog in the back of the cruiser with the window cracked open while he and the technician completed their work at the scene. After the body had been removed, Detective Grets and Officer Wurms stopped by a twenty-four-hour emergency veterinary clinic to see if the dog had an ID implant, which it did. They obtained the name of the owner, who lived nearby at an upscale downtown address.

The woman who answered the door looked curiously at Detective Grets and Officer Wurms, but her confusion turned to delight when she saw the dog that they were holding.

"Oh, thank goodness! You found him! Was he on his medication?"

"How would we know if your dog—" Officer Wurms started, but stopped when she felt a warning pressure on her arm from Detective Grets.

The Chemistry of the Case

The chemistry of this case obviously has to do with luminol and the light that it gives off in the presence of blood. But before we get to that, let us briefly point out another type of light that was involved in "The Case of the Hirsute Homeless." The microchip ID implant that allowed our heroes to identify the owner of the dog is operated by radio waves, another form of light. The microchip can be made as tiny as a grain of rice because it needs no power supply. It does, however, have a microscale antenna. The microchip reader puts out a radio frequency sufficient to excite a current in the antenna. This current enables the miniscule circuitry to output its own signal, which contains a multidigit identification code. Likewise, the luminol reaction does not need a supply of energy to glow. The light from the luminol reaction is an example of *chemiluminescence*, light produced by a chemical reaction.

The explanation of chemiluminescence hinges on two concepts from our chapters on basic principles: the formation of molecular orbitals from atomic orbitals and the production of light from electrons that find themselves in higher-than-normal orbitals.

We said that molecular orbitals are formed when orbitals of colliding entities coalesce to form one large orbital that encompasses all the atoms in the molecule. We compared the process to the convergence of soap bubbles that meet and merge. We noted there are many atomic orbitals around atoms, but we did not mention that there are many molecular orbitals around molecules. Like atoms, molecules have a *ground state*, or an arrangement in which all the electrons are in orbitals that result in the lowest possible energy. Molecules also have higher-energy orbitals that electrons can occupy if the electrons are somehow moved up in energy.

These orbitals are regions of space where the electron waves are self-reinforcing and stable. An analogy for the orbitals of an atom or a molecule might be the orbits of various satellites around the Earth. These satellites are in stable orbits; that is, they are not in any danger of crashing into the Earth, but they are not all at the same distance from the planet's surface. Some are relatively close, such as communications satellites and weather satellites, but some are very far away, like the moon. With the right input of energy, an electron might be bumped to a higher orbital. Similarly there are occasional reports that the International Space Station is being moved to a higher orbit. In an atom or a molecule, an electron moved to a higher orbital by an input of energy will eventually fall back to its original orbital, and when it does, it may give off light. We cited this behavior earlier as causing the colored flames of various materials.

But when luminol is used, there is no flame, and this is because the luminol molecule does not need to have its electrons boosted to a higher orbital. When the luminol molecule undergoes a certain redox reaction, the electrons find themselves in molecular orbitals already above the ground state. Over time, they relax to the ground state and, as they do, they emit the soft blue light that you witnessed in the demonstration. The luminol prepackaged mix reacts, once it is in solution, to produce a molecule called 3-aminophthalate (abbreviated 3-APA) and nitrogen gas. The molecule 3-APA is initially formed in an excited electronic state that relaxes to give off light.

So far, however, there has been no mention of blood. That is because blood is not necessary for the luminol reaction, and neither is copper or bleach. But these ingredients enhance the production of light because they *catalyze* the luminol reaction.

As explained earlier, catalysts are materials that increase the rate of a chemical reaction without being consumed in the reaction. Luminol will react to form 3-APA without a catalyst, but the presence of a catalyst makes the reaction faster and the glow of light more intense. It turns out that the iron in blood is a good catalyst for the luminol reaction.

As was shown in the demonstration preceding this chapter, luminol will detect trace amounts of blood, sometimes even if the surface has been cleaned. The cleaning agent will wash away much of the blood, but because of the physical equilibrium between the dissolved blood and the undissolved blood, a small amount will remain. Bleach can do a better job than just soap because bleach chemically decomposes the blood; however, because of chemical equilibrium, some blood will remain. This small amount may not be detectable: even if there were some small reaction, the glow could be masked by the glow from the luminol reacting with bleach, as was shown in the demonstration. Evidence of heavy cleaning with bleach might raise some questions, but this would not give probable cause to search further.

Though much information can be gained from using luminol to find trace blood evidence, there are some drawbacks to using luminol, too. First of all, as pointed out in the demonstration, there are other substances that can catalyze the luminol reaction. In addition, any trace blood found by luminol has to be evaluated for its evidentiary value in context because all areas where people live are bound to have trace blood. Cuts happen in bathrooms and kitchens, broken blisters are treated in the living room, and many times spittle and urine contain detectible amounts of blood. Luminol has to be used with care if other tests are going to be performed on the same material. As we will see, blue seems to be a popular color for presumptive tests for body fluids, and luminol could mask results of another type of test. The luminol mixture contains a base and could be fairly corrosive, so luminol could potentially destroy evidence of other types of bodily fluids. Because luminol is in liquid form, it could cause trouble just by washing away or smearing bloody stains. It could also simply dilute a sample, making it harder to analyze by other techniques, such as DNA analysis.

There are alternatives to luminol, one of which is a chemical called fluorescein. The activity of fluorescein, however, relies on fluorescence rather than chemiluminescence, which means the electrons have to be boosted up to a higher orbital by an external light source before they will glow. The type of fluorescence that is useful forensically absorbs ultraviolet (UV) light or visible light of one frequency and emits visible light of another frequency. When fluorescein is used to detect blood, an *alternative light source* is used to provide the UV light. In our demonstrations, we use a black light to show on a minor scale how such a light source might operate, but the actual equipment used by law enforcement is much more specialized and costly.

Alternative light sources are useful because many organic, naturally occurring molecules can be made to fluoresce, as we saw with the spinach in the opening demonstration. In fact, we are now ready to move onto our discussion of trace evidence of bodily origin, which will be the focus of part IV. But before we go, let's close "The Case of the Hirsute Homeless."

Case Closed

Detective R. E. Grets gave Officer Kana Wurms a warning glance and cleared his throat. He addressed the woman in the open door as he handed her the dog.

"Ma'am, did you file a police report?"

"Of course! My son's been missing for a week."

"Your son . . . ?" began Officer Wurms, but Detective Grets stopped her again with a look.

"Can you describe your son?" Detective Grets asked the woman as she stood caressing the dog.

A look of concern passed over the woman's face. "Well, he's young, twenty-four years old and a good-looking boy. He just graduated—engineering—but then he got ill . . . youthful onset schizophrenia, they said. The medications help, though. Is he all right? He's such a . . . good boy . . ."

The dog in her arms whimpered.

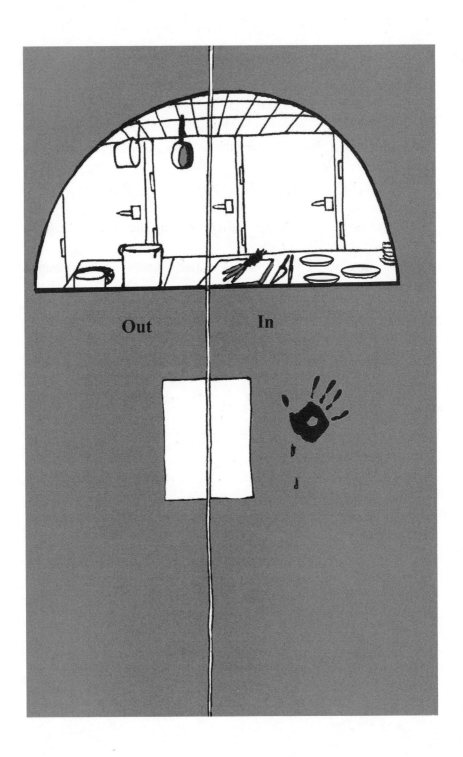

Out   In

PART IV

CORPUS DELICTI

We may brave human laws, but we cannot resist natural ones.

Jules Verne, *20,000 Leagues Under the Sea*, ca. 1870

*C*orpus delicti is a notoriously misunderstood term. Having no corpus delicti is often interpreted as not having an actual dead body to prove murder, but in fact corpus delicti means body of *evidence*, and with a sufficient body of facts, it has been possible to get a murder conviction without producing a physical body. Here, however, not able to resist the pun, we use *corpus delicti* as a title for part IV, our discussion of bodily evidence.

In part III, we introduced Locard's exchange principle, the idea that every contact leaves a trace. We explored some of the basics of light and methods that use light to locate and analyze trace evidence. In part III, we focused on nonbiological trace evidence so that we could concentrate on biological trace evidence in part IV. We did, however, conclude part III with the role of luminol in finding blood because this topic bridges both part III (light) and part IV (biological evidence). We have saved this important topic for the end because many times biological evidence is the best evidence—it can be linked with such high certainty to one specific individual—and also because biological evidence can be the most complex and difficult to handle. Moreover, we needed all the information in the previous chapters to prepare for this subject. Even so, to initiate our discussion of biological evidence, we need a briefing on biochemistry.

The body is composed mainly of macromolecules, that is, molecules that are hundreds, thousands, and even millions of times more massive than hydrogen. The body's need for macromolecules might be understood by considering the biological roles of the four main types of macromolecules: *lipids*, *polysaccharides*, *proteins*, and *nucleic acids*.

Lipids come in two main varieties: fatty acids and steroids. The common notion of a fat contrasts with the common notion of a steroid—one is associated with big bodybuilders and the other with just big bodies—but they are grouped together because they have the shared property of being soluble in oily liquids. The fatty acids are long chains of carbons terminated by an organic acid group, COOH. In their various configurations, these fats store energy (in all those troublesome fat cells) and also serve to protect and insulate internal organs. They form the insulation on nerve fibers and are the basic component of the cell membrane.

The other three macromolecules—polysaccharides, proteins, and nucleic acids—are polymers: long chains of repeating molecular structures. Most people think of carbohydrates in negative terms, as something to be avoided in excess, but carbohydrates are an essential component of our physical makeup. Originally carbohydrates were thought to be carbon surrounded by water (hence carbo-*hydrate*). But we now know that the basic unit of a carbohydrate is a monosaccharide, which is a ring-shaped carbon–oxygen–hydrogen molecule, as shown in figure IV.1. Sugars—glucose, fructose, and lactose—are monosaccharides, and the familiar *sucrose* is a disaccharide: two saccharides linked together. In demonstration 10, you hydrolyzed sucrose into glucose and fructose. When more than two saccharides are linked together, the result is a polysaccharide. Long-chain polysaccharides form the essential materials of *starch*, *cellulose*, and *glycogen*. Glycogen is a food-storage polymer in animals, starch is a food-storage polymer in plants, and cellulose is the structural material that enables plants to grow upward without skeletons.

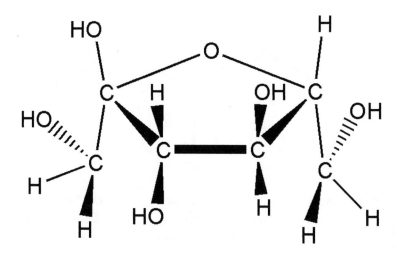

Figure IV.1. Fructose, a monosaccharide

Proteins are polymers of basic units called amino acids. Amino acids are small organic molecules that have both a nitrogen group and an organic acid group. A generic amino acid is shown in figure IV.2. The organic acid group is the carbon with the oxygen double-bonded and an OH group attached by a single bond. The nitrogen group is called the *amino* group (hence *amino acid*). The "R" to the side is a symbol meant to stand in for various other groups that can be added at this position and in this way make up a variety of amino acids. There are twenty different amino acids that are found naturally in the human body. The sequence in which these amino acids are strung together into a protein determines the protein's behavior and function. Just as plastic toy building blocks can be assembled into everything from spaceships to dinosaurs, amino acid building blocks can be formed into protein structures ranging from fingernails and hair to skin and cartilage, and many of the players in cell function. These structures occasionally or continually need to be replaced, a feat that is accomplished with another polymer.

The polymer we are referring to this time, however, is a bit unique in that it is built from three different types of fundamental

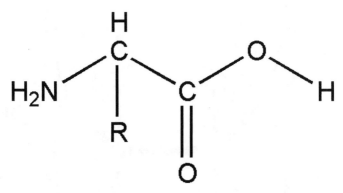

Figure IV.2. A generic amino acid. The appended "R" can be any one of twenty different carbon-, hydrogen-, sulfur-, and/or oxygen-containing groups. This R group determines the utility of the amino acid.

units: a nitrogen-containing base, a sugar, and a phosphate group. The linkage is between the phosphate group and the sugar, with the nitrogen-containing base sticking out to the side. Linked together, as we will see, they form an intricate scaffolding that twists and turns into the compact material called deoxyribonucleic acid: DNA.

If you did the experiment suggested in the introduction to part III—searching your environs to see what trace evidence you could find—you most likely came across some or all of the above biological materials, whether you knew it or not. For instance, you probably found fingerprints, and as it turns out, nearly all the bodily macromolecules show up in these fingerprints, too. For this reason, we will begin part IV with fingerprint technology. After our discussion of fingerprints, we will move on to the analysis of body fluids, such as saliva, and then we will round out our discussion with the grand dame of biological evidence: DNA.

That wraps up our briefing. Let's go out into the field.

DEMONSTRATION 22
POINTING THE FINGER

The Moving Finger writes; and, having writ,

Moves on: nor all your Piety nor Wit

Shall lure it back to cancel half a Line,

Nor all your Tears wash out a Word of it

Omar Khayyam, *Rubaiyat*, ca. 1100

Fingerprints are formed on virtually everything that is touched—paper, metal, wood, plastic, skin, food, fiber—the list is endless. The material of the actual fingerprint, the residue from the fingers that makes the print, can also be composed of nearly anything: oil, dirt, ink, food, soot, or whatever was last touched by the fingers. Because of all the possible combinations of surfaces and fingerprint material, fingerprint technicians have to have as many techniques as possible in their repertoire. In this demonstration, we will see only a few of these techniques, but even these few are fairly impressive. You will be using your own fingerprints, so at times you will need to remove your exam gloves. As a precaution, you'll put your gloves back on when you are done leaving fingerprints. And, because this demonstration requires you to work with superglue and other reagents, you'll need safety glasses.

Superglue fuming is a standard fingerprint preservation technique because it can yield a clean, clear, long-lasting fingerprint. To demonstrate this method, you will need two small plastic containers with snap-on lids. These containers must have enough area on the bottom to hold something the size of a soda bottle cap or a small foil dish shaped into a boat, as well as the item you will be developing for fingerprints. We have found that cylindrical plastic containers that are about 6 inches (15 centimeters) in diameter and perhaps 8 inches (20 centimeters) tall are good for this demonstration. A smaller tub such as that used for butter or a reusable disposable food storage container will do just fine. One of these will function as the fuming chamber and the other will be our rehydrating chamber.

Obtain some liquid superglue, not the gel kind. Make sure that *cyanoacrylate* is listed as the active ingredient. You will need several small glass items to put fingerprints on. The glass can be any color but not frosted or white because this would make visualization of the print difficult. The fingerprints fixed with superglue will be permanent, and although a developed print can be scraped off, it might be best to use glass items that can be sacrificed. If you can secure some glass microscope slides, these would work well.

Take two items for fingerprinting and wash them thoroughly. The purpose of this step is to make sure that any prints that develop come from the demonstration, so be careful how you pick them up. If you have clean tweezers or small tongs, you can use them to pick up the cleaned items.

Wash your hands thoroughly and then immediately yet carefully pick up one of the objects, noting where you touched the item. You want to pick up the item firmly to avoid smudging the fingerprint. Place it onto a countertop and carefully let it go. Again avoid smudging any of the prints. Use the tweezers or tongs to place the object into the fuming chamber.

Touch your forehead, nose, or neck with your hands and fingers in order to get natural body oil back onto your hands after having washed them. Pick up the other fingerprint item, place it carefully on a countertop, and use the tweezers or tongs to place it into the fuming chamber. If your chamber is not large enough for both items, they can be developed one at a time.

Place the small bottle cap or foil boat into the chamber and drop about six drops of superglue into the boat or cap. Snap on the lid to the chamber and allow the system to rest undisturbed for at least three hours. During this time, the superglue will evaporate and have a chance to react with material in the fingerprint.

Remove the objects with the tweezers or tongs, trying to avoid the areas where you expect to see fingerprints. Then make your observations.

We found a very clear difference between the washed-hand fingerprints and the regular fingerprints. We were unable to observe any prints on the item that had been picked up by the freshly washed hand. However, the item picked up by a regular hand had very nicely detailed fingerprints. This result demonstrates the role of normal body oils in the transfer of fingerprints onto objects.

Now take two other objects and wash them thoroughly. Allow them to dry. Take these two objects and place fingerprints onto their surfaces in known positions. You want easy-to-see fingerprints on these items, so don't wash your hands.

Heat and air dehydrate the fingerprint. Use a hair dryer to heat up the items for several minutes. Treat each object and the fingerprint area equally so that we can compare them at a later time.

Place water in a small bottle cap or foil boat into the rehydrating chamber. Use tweezers or tongs to place one of the hair dryer–treated items into the fuming chamber and place the other object into the rehydrating chamber. Replenish the fuming chamber boat with superglue and snap on the lids of both chambers. Wait at least three hours for the fingerprints to develop in the fuming chamber and for prints to rehydrate in the rehydrating chamber.

After the allotted time, remove the object from the fuming chamber with tweezers or tongs. Transfer the rehydrated object from the rehydration chamber into the fuming chamber. Replenish the superglue boat in the fuming chamber and snap on the lid. Wait at least three hours to develop the prints and then remove the object with either the tweezers or tongs and observe.

We observed a significant difference between the degraded and rehydrated fingerprints. The heat-degraded prints were not nearly as full or intense as the rehydrated prints. It is not hard to imagine circumstances in which a fingerprint might be exposed to sunlight for a period of time or otherwise dehydrated. When this happens, the prints can be very difficult to enhance. Once rehydrated, however, they may be recouped.

For this next demonstration, you will need two fuming chambers set up as described above, but you will leave the superglue out of one of the chambers. You will also need two small pieces of copy paper (such as used in a photocopier) and a small white plastic screw-on cap such as found on soft-drink bottles. Wash the cap with soap and water and dry it thoroughly.

Make sure that your fingers have a normal amount of body oil on them by touching your forehead, and then place a print on the top of the cap and on the two pieces of paper.

Use tweezers or tongs to set one piece of paper into one of the fuming chambers and the other piece of paper and bottle cap in the other chamber.

In the chamber with the piece of paper only, fill the boat or cap full of tincture of iodine (suggested for purchase in "Crime Labs and Crime Solutions"). Place the paper so that it stands upright and carefully snap on the lid. Place the usual amount of superglue into the boat of the other chamber, containing the piece of paper and the bottle cap, and snap on that lid. Set this chamber aside for three hours or so.

After about a half hour, carefully lift the lid on the tincture of iodine chamber and assess the progress of the fingerprint development. Iodine development is faster than that of superglue, and overdevelopment can occur. When the paper has taken on the light purple tinge associated with iodine, remove the paper and observe it in a fairly bright light. There should be a developed image of the fingerprint on the paper.

Once superglue fuming is finished for the other two items, remove them from the chamber and observe them in bright light. Because the superglue fingerprint image is grayish white, it is difficult to observe the prints on the paper and on the white cap. If, however, you have purchased fluorescent fingerprint powder, then take a camel-hair brush and very lightly dust both items with this powder. Before you apply the powder, you could try dipping in the brush and then tapping the brush lightly down onto the interior of the lid to the powder jar. This should leave enough powder on the brush for a light dusting. If more is needed, then stroke the brush across the lid interior. Switch on the alternate light source and dim the room lights. Observe how the bright green fluorescence of the powder highlights the fingerprint. Under the glow of the black light, the fluorescent powder really makes the image stand out.

Fingerprints and their acquisition are of major importance in law enforcement and also in "The Case of the Elusive Acetone."

CHAPTER 22

THE PRINCE OF FORENSICS: FINGERPRINT TECHNOLOGY

> *INK, n. A villainous compound of tannogallate of iron, gum-arabic and water, chiefly used to facilitate the infection of idiocy and promote intellectual crime.*
>
> Ambrose Bierce, *Devil's Dictionary*, ca. 1911

THE CASE OF THE ELUSIVE ACETONE

Detective JeWanna Dance and Detective Hank Eyring conversed as they climbed the stairs of the Bearing Arms apartment complex.

Detective Dance explained, "As I was saying, checkwashing is the crime of stealing checks from mailboxes, using a solvent to remove the ink or alter the amount, and then cashing them. It has been rampant in this area. We were lucky to get this tip. Keep your eye out for any solvents. Acetone from a hardware store is the best, but fingernail polish remover or ethanol will work, too."

Detective Dance knocked on the door of number 101. A clean-shaven young man opened the door and regarded them curiously. Detectives Dance and Eyring showed their badges.

"Are you Mr. Thor Losor?" asked Detective Dance.

"Yeh," answered the man, frowning.

"Is this your apartment?"

"Uh . . . yeh . . ."

"May we come in?" asked Detective Eyring.

Mr. Losor shrugged and opened the door. The detectives stepped into a small living area with a smaller kitchen area off to the left and a sofa and coffee table to the right. The furniture was worn but spotless with the exception of residue from Asian takeout on the coffee table, along with a book, scraps of paper, several pens, a cell phone, a TV remote, and a checkbook. On the far side of the room, directly across from the front door, were two open doors leading into two bedrooms.

Detective Eyring cleared his throat and reached into his jacket pocket. "Mr. Losor, we have a warrant to search these premises for checkwashing paraphernalia, including solvents, adsorbents, handling utensils, and checks, blank or otherwise, not belonging to the residents." He handed Losor the warrant, but Losor did not open it.

"Checkwashing? Never heard of it. Knock yourself out—" He stopped when he saw Detective Dance pulling on a latex glove and carefully lifting the checkbook by the corner and exposing a signed check underneath it.

Detective Dance straightened. "Do you have a roommate?"

"Yeh. It's my apartment, but the rent's a ripoff, so I let this chick—Anita Drink—stay here. That's her stuff on the table."

Detective Dance nodded and reached for her radio. She called a uniformed officer to come and take charge of Mr. Losor.

When the officer had Thor Losor under watch by his cruiser, Detective Dance took Detective Eyring aside and explained, "The embossed name on the signed check is Les Luc, not Thor Losor or Anita Drink."

Detective Hank Eyring brightened. "Great! We got them!"

"I don't think so," said Detective Dance. "Checkwashing is almost impossible to prove unless you can catch the perps with the ink on their hands. This is a common living area. He can say it's hers—but she can say it's his. If it went to court, there would be reasonable doubt for either suspect."

"But the check—"

"I'm betting the perp is a pro and knows how to handle a check without leaving fingerprints. There might not be anything on the check to link it to either roommate."

"Then our hands are tied?"

Detective Dance looked up once more at the apartment, then stopped. "Wait a minute. I think I see the missing link."

The Chemistry of the Case

A fingerprint is a copy—impression, outline, relief, or print—of the *friction ridges* of the finger. Friction ridges are fine raised portions of flesh on the fingers that are used to get a grip, just as the hairy feet of a fly help it walk on walls. Friction ridges are found on fingers, hands, and feet, but those on fingers are most useful forensically because the fingers are almost always exposed and almost always touching things. It is very hard *not* to leave a fingerprint, but, likewise, it is hard to find a fingerprint that isn't at least somewhat smudged.

Fingerprints are one of the most familiar forms of evidence and have earned their reputation for being reliable. Fingerprint evidence will probably never go out of style because fingerprints can often be found when there is nothing else. Currently, everyone who is arrested is fingerprinted, but a DNA sample isn't usually taken unless a person is convicted of a felony. For this reason, fingerprint technology is being expanded and improved all the time.

We won't distract the reader with an explanation of ridges and whorls because we promised to stick to chemistry and because the information is very well presented in several other sources.[1] Here we will focus on the stuff of fingerprints—the grease and grime that actually make up the print—and the chemical means for its detection. If we have not yet convinced you that forensic chemistry is applied basic chemistry, then this chapter on the various methods for obtaining fingerprints should provide conclusive evidence.

In addition, we will confine our discussion to *latent* prints: fingerprints that have to be enhanced or developed to be visible enough to accurately map their distinguishing features. *Patent prints* are prints that are readily visible, such as the fingerprints found on clean glass or left on walls if the hands are very dirty or bloody, or prints formed as impressions in soft materials such as waxes. Patent prints can be photographed or lifted without the need for further treatment. Latent fingerprints, on the other hand, must be enhanced by techniques such as the ones in demonstration 22 and others we will be discussing here.

To understand the enhancement techniques, it is first necessary to understand the chemistry of the fingerprints themselves. There are glands associated with the friction ridges that secrete a mixture containing mostly water as well as inorganic salts and organic compounds such as amino acids. This material, along with the dust and dirt trapped by the water, is the prints that the ridges leave: the fingerprint. A fingerprint also normally contains oily and fatty secretions from other parts of the body. These are not produced by the fingers but are picked up from the extraordinary amount of body touching that our fingers do. Try being aware of the number of times during the day you touch your face or arms. Your fingers pick up fingerprint material each time you do.

Touch a glass windowpane or a glass slide and observe your fingerprints. Now wash and dry your hands and see if they still leave fingerprints on the glass. Try swabbing your fingers with rubbing alcohol and letting them air-dry. Check to see if your fingers in this condition leave fingerprints. Now touch your face and see how this changes the fingerprint. Recall demonstration 2, in which we contaminated some paper money with "drugs" in the form of ibuprofen and tried to physically clean the bills. We found that some amount of the drug remained on the bill even after visible residue was gone. At the time, we said this was because of the intaglio printing process that caused tiny grooves that trapped the drug. A similar thing happens with fingers. The tiny grooves trap moisture and other materials, and these materials are sufficient to cause latent prints.

When it comes to developing latent prints, the best treatment, of course, is no treatment, so if fingerprints can be made visual using an alternative light source, then they are photographed. Fingerprints are mostly water, but when the water evaporates a residue is left behind, similar to the water spots that can be left on glasses that air-dry. This residue can sometimes be visualized using creative lighting techniques.

When a fingerprint must be enhanced, the fingerprint technician (or the detective in smaller departments) must decide which enhancement techniques to try. The decision is based on a number of considerations. First, if the fingerprint was made with some material that must not be destroyed, such as blood that can be a source of DNA, then destructive techniques, such as cyanoacrylate fuming, should be avoided. Some techniques require a solvent to deliver the developer, and in these cases, the surface that the print is on can be an issue. For instance, methanol might be used as a solvent for a fingerprint-enhancing chemical, but if the fingerprint is on a painted surface, then methanol might attack the paint. The result would be a gooey mess instead of a print.

The makeup of the fingerprint—mostly water, mostly fat, or mostly amino acids—depends on the fingerprint's history and is one of the most important considerations in choosing a latent fingerprint-enhancement technique. If the print is fresh, then it will be composed of mostly water, so cyanoacrylate fuming, if feasible, might work best. The cyanoacrylate acts as a glue because it can polymerize and form long chains, and water is a catalyst for this polymerization. Cyanoacrylate enhances fingerprints because it polymerizes along the lines of moisture left by the fingerprint. Powders might also work well on prints that are mostly water because of water's ability to hold the powder through intermolecular attractions.

If the print is older, then the water and other volatile components may have evaporated, leaving behind fats and amino acids. If this is the case, then one of two techniques can be tried. The print can be rehydrated in a moist environment or a developer can be chosen that reacts with fat, such as iodine. At room temperature, pure iodine is a solid but has a substantial amount of iodine vapor in equilibrium with the solid. When a solid converts directly to a gas without going through a liquid phase, the process is called sublimation. (Solid carbon dioxide, dry ice, is a familiar sublimating material.) Iodine, because it sublimates, is useful for developing latent fingerprints. It arrives at the print in the gas phase and doesn't require an applicator that could smear the print. Iodine is also an oxidizing reagent that reacts with fats, turning the fatty material brown.

But fats can diffuse, especially on a porous surface, such as paper. If you touch a piece of paper with butter on your fingers, you can observe how fast the butter spreads on it. If the print is very old, the fats may have diffused away, leaving only amino acids behind. In this case, a chemical called *ninhydrin* would be the reagent of choice because ninhydrin reacts with amino acids to form a *chromophore*: a colored compound. The chromophore that ninhydrin forms with an amino acid is a reddish shade of purple.

If the print is mainly composed of inorganic salts, such as the sodium chloride in sweat, then silver nitrate may be the reagent of choice. The silver ion forms a precipitate with the chloride ion on the fingerprint, and then the ambient light promotes the reduction of the silver ion to silver metal. The coating of silver on the fingerprint is such a fine powder that it appears black.

In addition to these standard techniques, there are many more specialized techniques and reagents that have been developed. Materials available in the fingerprint technician's arsenal include powders and preparations for lifting latent prints from the sticky and nonsticky sides of adhesive tapes, dyes to enhance prints in blood, fluorescent dyes to enhance cyanoacrylate, and metallic powders that can be applied with a magnetic wand so that nothing but the powder ever touches the print. There is even a material called Sudan Black that reacts with perspiration so exclusively that it can be used to highlight latent prints made on greasy foodstuffs or oily surfaces. But for all the technology available, a successful analysis relies on the skill of the technician. In "The Case of the Elusive Acetone," the fingerprint technology was not the sticking point; knowing where to look for the fingerprint was.

Case Closed

Detective Hank Eyring regarded his partner, Detective JeWanna Dance, curiously. "What do you mean, 'the missing link'?"

"Whoever was doing the checkwashing did not want to leave fingerprints. What would you use to pick up evidence that you didn't want to contaminate with fingerprints?"

Detective Eyring shrugged. "Tongs? Forceps? Maybe tweezers . . ."

"How about chopsticks?" said Detective Dance. "Remember the Asian takeout on the coffee table? Let's collect those chopsticks. If they have acetone on one end and prints on the other, we may be able to finger the culprit."

DEMONSTRATION 23
A BLOODY SHAME

When the Inspector examined the dead girl's watch, he found a minute dark smear on the crystal. To preserve the stain, he pressed a moist square of filter paper against it, waited a moment, then transferred the paper to a sheet of glass painted with gum Arabic. When a sliver of the stain was immersed in a saucer of bezidene reagent, the opaque whitish liquid sluggishly turned blue, which indicated the presence of blood.

If he were lucky, further tests might identify the blood type. It had been only seven years since the professor at the Institute of Hygiene in Greifswald discovered that human blood could be distinguished from animal blood. However, not all magistrates would admit this as evidence in a murder trial.

Jody Shields, *The Fig Eater*, ca. 2000

Before you proceed with the demonstration, put on your safety glasses and a fresh pair of examination gloves. You will also need two small plastic cups, two flat wooden sticks or disposable chopsticks for stirring, cornstarch, hydrogen peroxide, and a small bottle of tincture of iodine. You will also need a sample of beef blood from fresh, raw meat.

Our first demonstration presents a possible presumptive test for saliva. Spit into one of the cups (or find another, more graceful way to transfer your saliva) and label the cup "Saliva." Place a similar amount of water into the other cup and label it "Water." Take one of the wooden sticks and dip it into cornstarch so just a small amount of the powder clings to the stick. The less powder the better. Mix this powder into one of the cups. Take the second stick and dip it into the cornstarch so that a similar amount sticks to it. Mix this into the other cup. Wait at least one half hour to give the enzymes in the saliva a chance to break down the starch.

Starch will form a dark blue/purple complex with iodine. Get the small bottle of tincture of iodine and place two or three drops of tincture into the plain water-cornstarch cup first. You should observe a very dark blue/purple color because the starch is still present in the water. Now place two or three drops of tincture of iodine into the saliva-cornstarch sample. This sample should initially show the yellow-brown color of unreacted iodine. Depending on the size of your starch sample, the saliva mixture may have some dark blue/purple color to it eventually, but there should be a decided difference between the saliva-containing cup and the control.

Saliva contains enzymes that begin the digestive process by initiating the breakdown of starch. In the "Saliva" cup, your saliva processed the starch so that when you applied the tincture, there was very little starch present to react with the iodine. Although not conclusive, such a test could indicate the presence of saliva in a sample.

Our second demonstration presents a presumptive test for blood. This method is a fast and inexpensive test and is used in the field.

Put some blood from a meat package onto a bit of cotton cloth or a paper towel as though it had gotten there by some nefarious means. Let it dry overnight. Once dried, place the small bit of cloth or paper in a plastic cup. Place a bit of the same cloth or paper without blood in a second cup as a control.

Pour in enough hydrogen peroxide to completely cover both cloth or paper samples. You should observe that the plain cloth and peroxide just sits there, but the bloodstained sample is bubbling and foaming away.

Under normal conditions, hydrogen peroxide decomposes into water and oxygen bubbles, but it does so slowly. If a catalyst of some sort is applied, the reaction speeds up and liberates a large amount of oxygen all at once. Iron in red blood cells catalyzes the decomposition of hydrogen peroxide, which is why you observed the bubbling and foaming. As such, this bubbling and foaming is a presumptive test for blood, albeit a destructive one.

Bodily fluids can be critical pieces of evidence. The collection of bodily fluids is a central concern in "The Case of the Contraband Confection."

CHAPTER 23

STICKY CASES: BODILY FLUID IDENTIFICATION

Man consists of bones, flesh, blood, saliva, cells and vanity.

Kurt Tucholsky, ca. 1920

THE CASE OF THE CONTRABAND CONFECTION

The officers watched the video recording that displayed a buxom woman in a tank top and a short black skirt. She swayed on six-inch high heels while talking to an eye-patched pirate who sported a fake black beard and moustache.

"Undercover?" Officer Trainee U. Nuygen asked cautiously.

"It was Halloween," answered Officer Tanya Hyde dryly.

The pirate leaned toward Officer Hyde as she reached up and ran a black-gloved hand over his moustache in apparent appreciation.

"I heard rumors that Blackbeard the Pirate was distributing 'black sugar' so I attempted a buy," Officer Hyde explained.

"The guy was dealing drugs?"

"Yes."

"Wow. I know it was Halloween, but why would a drug dealer wear a pirate costume?"

"For the same reason you might hide a key under a rock. It blends into the background for people who don't know what it is—but stands out like a sore thumb for people who are looking for it."

"How'd you get the video?"

"I have a concealed dash cam in my vehicle."

The camera showed Officer Hyde stripping off her gloves and reaching into a voluminous shoulder bag. She made an elaborate show of extracting bills from a wallet she found inside it. She swayed against the pirate, grabbing onto his disguise, but he managed to hold it to his face.

"Couldn't get a shot of his face?"

Officer Hyde shook her head.

"But you made the buy?"

Officer Hyde nodded toward the ongoing action on the tape. "Yes. You'll see the exchange here."

In a barely discernible motion, the pirate pressed something into Officer Hyde's hand, and they parted. The pirate walked down the street, and Officer Hyde staggered back toward the camera.

"Did you call in backup to have him picked up?"

"I would have—if I knew what the 'black sugar' was."

"Didn't he tell you?"

"Wouldn't call it anything but sugar."

"Didn't you have any test kits?"

"Didn't even try. They would have all showed black. The same black as the dye on the so-called sugar."

"Oh."

"When I got back I submitted the sample to the lab and told them about the dye."

"And it was . . . ?"

"Heroin."

"And the dealer disappeared without a trace?"

"Not exactly."

The Chemistry of the Case

Bodily fluids, including fingerprints, vomit, saliva, sweat, semen, vaginal fluids, and blood, have high evidentiary value. One reason is that bodily fluid evidence persists. Liquid bodily material transfers easily, and once transferred it dries and becomes a stain, attached to fabric or flesh. Also, the aging of bodily fluids can help to piece together the sequence of events. And many bodily fluids carry biological markers—they can be used to identify the individual from which they originated.

The basis for many presumptive tests for bodily fluids is the specific enzymes the particular fluid contains. Enzymes, the body's catalysts, tend to be very large, very complicated molecules that expedite one specific bodily reaction and no other. For instance, individuals who are lactose intolerant lack the ability to produce the enzyme they need, lactase, in sufficient quantities. This enzyme can be supplied artificially in over-the-counter pill form, and if taken before eating dairy products containing lactose, it greatly ameliorates the problem. Another example of an enzyme that can again be supplied over the counter is the enzyme for digesting "gassy" foods. Humans normally rely on colonies of bacteria known as intestinal fauna to help digest these foods. These bacteria, however, produce gas-phase products that many societies have deemed objectionable. An enzyme, alpha-galactosidase, can be taken before eating to aid in the digestion of problematic foods before the bacteria take over. In the presumptive test for semen, the target of the test is *acid phosphatase*, an enzyme secreted by the prostate gland.

But there are, of course, difficulties. Acid phosphatase can also be found in other body fluids, so further tests must be performed to determine if a specific material is semen. Acid phosphatase can also be altered in form by changing the pH of its environment, which would make it more difficult to detect. Another problem with bodily fluid evidence is that these fluids can deteriorate through the natural processes of rot and *denaturing*: the disruption of the attractions that hold biologically active molecules in the correct shape for activity.

To understand the denaturation process, consider a car. Correct three-dimensional configuration is critical to the functioning of many biological molecules, just as it is to an automobile. A denatured car might have its wheels on the hood, not in the correct position for its natural function, so it would not work very well. The same can be true for enzymes, but instead of nuts and bolts, enzymes are held in their shape by *intramolecular* attractions. Intramolecular attractions have the same origin as intermolecular attractions—hydrogen bonding and dipole-dipole attraction—but the *intra*molecular attractions are between sites within the same molecule instead of between molecules. The best action to forestall rot is to dry the materials, but drying a material can cause some molecules to denature, which can confound certain identifying tests.

Another problem is that in the act of testing for one material, you can destroy another. If you swab for saliva, you can wipe out a fingerprint. If you expose a fingerprint to cyanoacrylate fumes, you could destroy DNA. So good old-fashioned logical deduction is still required to decide which tests to do and when to do them.

Another difficulty with bodily fluid evidence is that fluids can mix. Once commingled, they become difficult or impossible to separate. If bodily fluids from the victim are mixed with bodily fluids from the perpetrator, they may not be distinguishable. Bodily fluids can also be dangerous to handle because of the potential for exposure to blood-borne pathogens. "The Case of the Contraband Confection" points to yet another difficulty with bodily fluid evidence. Many of the presumptive tests for bodily fluids result in *chromophores*; that is, organic materials that absorb selective frequencies of light and therefore appear colored. Earlier we saw that ninhydrin, the chemical used to detect amino acids in fingerprints, is a chromophore. In figure 23.1, we reproduce the structure of the product of the ninhydrin–amino acid reaction so that we can point out the feature responsible for the color: a *double bond*. Double bonds arise when two pairs of electrons, rather than just one pair, are shared between bonded atoms. The reason for the extra electrons is the same as for the single-bond formation discussed in chapter 4: electrons are shared so that each nucleus has its most stable configuration. The electrons in double bonds tend to be easier to excite, however, so lower-energy light, light in the visible region of the spectrum, is sometimes all that is required to move an electron in a double bond to a higher molecular orbital. Normal visible light is a collection of colors. We demonstrated light is a combination of colors when we used a prism to break up light into its colors. When a chromophore absorbs one particular frequency of light, this light is removed from the spectrum of light incident on the material. The leftover light is missing one of its colors, which cancels the effect of this color, and so the reflected light appears as a different net color. Presumptive tests that produce chromophores are quite useful because the human eye can be used as the detector. The problem is that the color of one chromophore can mask the color of another.

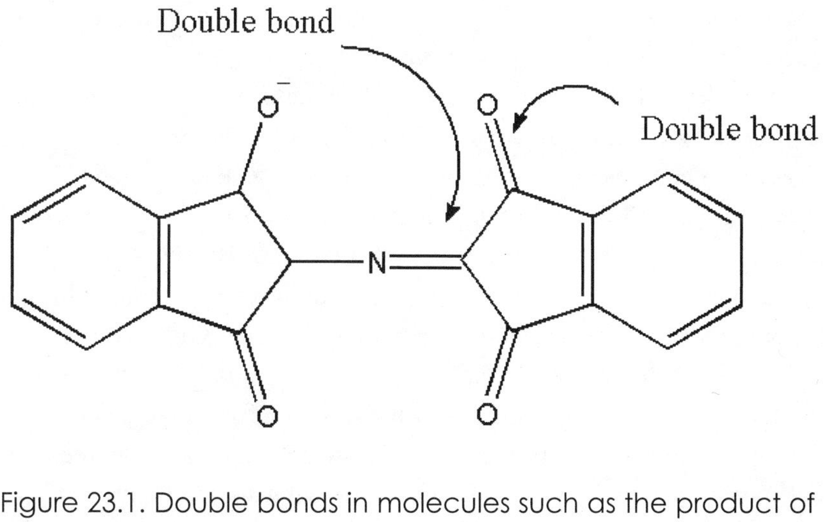

Figure 23.1. Double bonds in molecules such as the product of a ninhydrin–amino acid reaction shown here can absorb some components of visible light. As such, double bonds are responsible for the color of these compounds. The double bond structure was also present in the diagram of the colored indicator, bromothymol blue, given earlier.

Because of the complications of the chemical tests, physical examinations for biological evidence are usually performed first, and these physical examinations can be assisted by an alternative light source.

As we've demonstrated, several materials can be made to fluoresce. Organic materials in particular can be made to fluoresce if the right frequency of excitation light is provided—and if the fluorescence is not overshadowed by ambient light. Forensic alternative light sources are very expensive because they must provide very precise and isolated frequencies of light and they must be equipped with the viewing filters necessary to block the illuminating light while still allowing the fluorescent light to be observed. They are, however, worth the expense because they allow not only organic biological fluids to be observed but also fiber, hair, paint, glass, mineral residue, and gunpowder residue. Bite marks and bruises can also be emphasized with an alternative light source. Alternative light sources can also be used in forgery or checkwashing situations. Two inks that appear very similar in ordinary light might appear completely different under light from an alternative light source.

Another light technique utilizes light at an angle. *Oblique lighting*, as it is called, can be understood in terms of a less exotic concept: a shadow. When an object, even a very small object, casts a shadow, it looks bigger. Oblique lighting is used to make three-dimensional objects or materials stand out on a flat surface. By the same token, indentations, such as those from a pen, could be visible using oblique lighting even if the ink has been removed. By using oblique lighting, tool marks or tooth marks can be made more visible. Finding a tooth mark could be an indication to test for saliva before fingerprints.

Once a physical examination has helped to narrow down the type of body fluid evidence present, then chemical tests can be used. There are chromophoric tests for semen, vaginal secretions, saliva (as demonstrated at the opening of this chapter), and blood, though the test is really only necessary for small amounts of blood because blood is its own chromophore. Blood looks bloody.

The rust color of dried blood comes from the iron in hemoglobin.

Interestingly, bugs can have green- or blue-colored blood because they have copper in their blood, so even an inexperienced investigator wouldn't mistake bug juice for human. And you wouldn't think an experienced drug dealer would be fooled by an undercover police officer attempting to make a buy, but it happens, as in "The Case of the Contraband Confection."

Case Closed

"He was in a pirate costume, with an eye patch and a beard, he was wearing gloves, he didn't give a name, and the dope was dyed. How did you trace him?" asked Officer U. Nuygen.

"With this," said Tanya Hyde, holding up a labeled sample vial. Officer Nuygen squinted to see the contents.

"Hair? You got black hair from his moustache and beard? But it was fake! What good is fake hair?"

"The hair may have been fake," said Officer Hyde, "but the saliva on it wasn't."

She shook the bottle and smiled. "That'll teach him to give me lip."

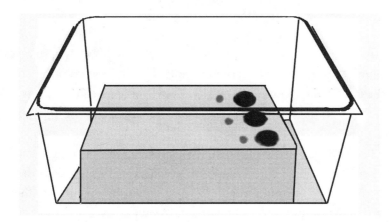

DEMONSTRATION 24
SORTING OUT THE FACTS

Blood, though it sleep a time, . . . never dies. The gods on murtherers fix revengeful eyes.

George Chapman, *The Widow's Tears*, ca. 1620

In this procedure, we will be demonstrating *electrophoresis*, a separation technique in which charged particles are pulled through a gel by their attraction to charged electrodes. Electrophoresis is the technique used to separate the DNA fragments in DNA profiling. Earlier we discussed and demonstrated some of the techniques that can be used to develop latent fingerprints and ways to detect and identify bodily fluids. During these demonstrations, the level of care necessary to obtain good results became apparent. This next demonstration requires every bit as much care and patience, if not more. It demonstrates two principles: not only how DNA separation might be carried out, but also the delicacy of the technique. Identification by DNA profile has been a wonderful boon to the justice system, but as with all science, it must be understood in terms of its limitations as well as its capabilities. A first step to this understanding is to realize the complexity of the method. In this demonstration, we will use electrophoresis to separate the colored molecules in food coloring, and we will achieve very satisfying results. But it should be kept in mind that we are observing only a few bands, and actual DNA profiling involves many more.

The first step (after putting on your safety glasses and gloves) is to prepare the buffered solution. A buffer is necessary to support the mild flow of electric current through the system and to ensure that the particles being separated stay charged. A *buffer* is a solution that is designed to withstand the addition of small amounts of acid or base without a significant change in pH. Buffers achieve this ability by being prepared with large amounts of weak acids and bases so that additional small amounts of acid and base won't make that much difference. By balancing the acid and base concentrations just so, the buffer can be designed to hold a preselected acidic or basic pH.

Before we attempt our electrophoresis, let's do a brief demonstration of the buffering capabilities of the buffer we will be using.

From the items suggested in the shopping list in "Crime Lab and Crime Solutions," select four small white plastic cups; household ammonia; distilled, clear vinegar; an eyedropper; and the aquarium pH adjustment kit. The kit should contain an acid solution for lowering the pH, a base for raising the pH, and the acid-base indicator we used in previous demonstrations.

Into two of the cups pour about an eighth of a cup of bottled or distilled water (30 milliliters) and label the two cups "Water" with a permanent marker. Place about half as much vinegar (1 tablespoon or 15 milliliters) into each of the other two cups and label them as "Buffer."

Add three drops of the indicator from the test kit to each of the four cups and swirl to mix the contents. The cups of water should be a pastel green while the cups of vinegar should be a rich pastel yellow. If the indicator is different from what we used, the colors may be different but the procedure will be the same.

Now take the eyedropper and add ammonia drop-wise to the

buffer cups until the buffer solutions both appear to be the same color as the water-indicator solution (green, in our case). Patience here is a virtue. You must swirl the contents of each cup after every drop is added to mix the solutions.

Once all four cups appear the same pastel green color, take one water cup and one buffer cup and mark them with a "B" for base. Set them aside. Take the other two cups and add one drop of the pH-lowering solution to each and swirl. The water cup should become yellow after one drop, whereas the buffer cup should remain somewhat green; in other words, it will be buffered against the effect of the pH-lowering solution.

Add another drop of pH-lowering solution to the buffer cup, swirl the contents, and note the color. Keep adding drops of pH-lowering solution until the buffer cup shows a yellow color. You should be able to add at least five or six drops to the buffer cup before its color changes noticeably.

Now take the other two cups marked "B" for base and add one drop of pH-raising solution to each of those cups and swirl. The water cup should turn to a pastel blue (or whatever color your indicator gives for base). The buffer cup, once again, should not change much in color. Continue to add drops of pH-raising solution, swirling the contents after each addition. You should be able to add four or five drops of pH-raising solution to the buffer cup before a significant color change occurs.

In the above demonstration, you have seen how a buffer can be used to keep the pH reasonably constant, even when a small amount of acid or base is added to the solution. It is important to keep the pH constant in electrophoresis because the objective is to separate compounds by mass, not charge. If the pH were allowed to change, then the molecules might gain or lose charge as they gained or lost the hydrogen ion, H^+.

Now let's proceed to electrophoresis.

To prepare the buffer for the electrophoresis, take two and a half cups (about 600 milliliters) of distilled water and add to it four capfuls (about 12 milliliters) of household ammonia and two capfuls (about 6 milliliters) of household vinegar. This combination makes the buffer solution slightly basic and provides ions to conduct the electricity. Set the buffer aside in a closed container.

In a small double boiler, take two-thirds of a cup (160 milliliters) of buffer solution and add one 1-ounce (30-gram) package of plain, unflavored gelatin. Warm the gelatin mixture over a medium-to-low heat until the gelatin has completely dissolved.

Next you will need the small plastic rectangular container suggested for purchase in "Crime Lab and Crime Solutions." (We used the disposable storage containers sold at supermarkets that are about 3 inches by 5 inches, about 7.5 by 13.0 centimeters.) Once the gelatin is completely dissolved, pour the solution into the container to a depth of a half inch to three-quarters of an inch (1 to 2 centimeters). Allow this gelatin to cool and set. Place the lid on it but don't seal it, and then place it in the refrigerator overnight to ensure firm gel formation.

While waiting for the gel to set, wire together five 9-volt batteries in series. To do this, you will need the kind of 9-volt battery holders that can be hooked together. We found snap-on caps in an electronics supply store that had wires that could be connected. If necessary, strip about three-quarters of an inch of insulation from the wires (about 2 centimeters) and join the wires red-to-black / red-to-black / red-to-black / red-to-black, leaving the red lead of the first one and the black lead of the last one unconnected. You can twist the wires together and then insulate with electrician's tape, or you can use alligator clips as you did for the lemon battery in demonstration 12. You should have a single red wire remaining on the first battery and a single black wire remaining on the last battery.

Get five 9-volt batteries and attach them to the five caps, making sure that the open ends at the first battery and fifth battery don't touch. If the first lead and the last lead touch, they will short and create a great deal of unwanted heat. Remove the gel block from the refrigerator and, while the gel is still in the container, use a small paring knife to cut off half an inch (about 2 centimeters) of gel from each end of the gel block. Make clean slices across the width of the container at the ends and then turn the container on its side. Use the knife to carefully pry the cut-off pieces out of their position at the end of the block. If the block has set properly, the end gel pieces should just slide out. Once you are finished, you will have about a 3-inch (7.5-centimeter) gel block in the center of the container with a half-inch (about 1- to 1.5-centimeter) trough at each end of the block.

Now obtain two 5-inch (12-centimeter) lengths of the aluminum wire suggested for purchase in "Crime Lab and Crime Solutions," one for each trough. Fashion each wire so that it can run the full length of the trough and then come out of the trough and over the lip of the container. Bend each wire over the lip so that it is held firmly in place.

Now take a small plastic cup and carefully add two drops of blue food coloring and two drops of red food coloring. You are going to put three samples in the middle of the container, running across the center, like horses at the gate, waiting for the race to begin. To set this up, first mix the four drops together thoroughly with the sharp tip of the paring knife. Making sure some food-coloring mixture has remained on the knife tip, insert it straight into the gel so that it is parallel to the short end of the container, about a third of the distance in and as close to the lengthwise center of the gel block as possible. Stir the food-coloring mixture with the knife again.

Again making sure that some of the mixture remains on the knife tip, insert it straight into the gel block at dead center. Mix the food coloring again with the knife and insert it a third time into the gel block so that it is a third of an inch up from the long side. You should now have three food-color samples inserted into the gel on a center line.

Carefully pour some of the remaining buffer solution into one of the troughs until the buffer solution level reaches a half to three-quarters inch (1 to 2 centimeters) above the full gel block surface. Take two alligator clip wires and attach one to each of the aluminum wires that are coming out of the container, making sure not to disturb the location of the wires in their troughs. Attach one alligator lead to the red wire at the first battery and attach the other alligator lead to the black wire at the fifth battery. Bubbling should slowly begin from each of the trough wires as the electric current establishes positive charge on one and negative charge on the other. The bubbles arise from electric current-induced chemistry: *electrochemistry*. Water will lose electrons at the positive wire and will form oxygen gas. Water will gain electrons at the negative pole, forming hydrogen gas. These are the bubbles that appear.

Run the electrophoresis for three and a half hours—checking on it while it is running—and then detach the batteries at the alligator leads and observe what has happened: the food colors that were once mixed are now separated.

The buffer solution will lend either a positive or a negative charge to molecules such as the food-coloring dyes. Under the influence of the voltage from the batteries, the dye molecules begin to move, attracted to the oppositely charged wire. As the dye molecules move through the gel toward the wire of opposite charge, the smaller molecules move faster than the larger molecules through the gel matrix. Given enough time, the larger molecules lag behind the smaller molecules, which separates the molecules according to size. In our sample of red and blue food colorings, we observed three distinct molecules. One was pink and moved the least, so it was probably the largest. We had dark red molecules that moved more rapidly and blue molecules that moved even more quickly. Where the blue and the dark red spots overlapped, we saw purple.

Strands of DNA or proteins behave similarly and can be separated based on their size by electrophoresis. Because everyone's DNA is different, everyone's DNA cleaves into a different distribution of fragments, which gives a unique electrophoresis pattern for every person. That is, of course, providing that the personal DNA can be isolated to begin with—which was the problem in "The Case of the Flowery Felon."

CHAPTER 24

UNLOCKING THE CELL: DEATH, DECAY, AND DNA

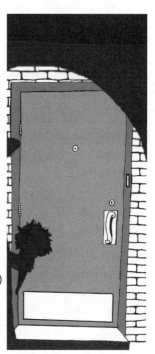

Rape is the only crime in which the victim becomes the accused.

Freda Adler, ca. 1990

THE CASE OF THE FLOWERY FELON

Detective Sergeant Lacy Littlecloud listened as Detective Cole Kase expressed his apprehensions about the reporter who was waiting in the outer office.

"There is a lot of public concern surrounding this case, so watch out for Barb Wire. She's sharp. Don't let her back you into a corner."

Sergeant Littlecloud assured her friend she would be careful and then took up her notebook and walked to the reception area where Ms. Wire waited.

Barb Wire went straight to the point. "Is this latest attack related to the four other attacks that occurred in this area in the last two years?"

Sergeant Littlecloud frowned. "We are looking at that possibility."

"You have made no arrests in any of these cases although they were described as sexual assaults. It's my understanding that all living things have DNA and DNA is exchanged with contact. Shouldn't there be DNA evidence associated with an assault?"

"Yes," agreed Detective Sergeant Littlecloud. "There is usually DNA evidence in cases of rape, but—"

"It's unfortunate," interrupted Ms. Wire. "But some people refuse to call it rape, given her profession—"

Sergeant Littlecloud's cell phone buzzed in the holster at her side. She held up a quieting hand, flipped open the phone, and listened intently for a moment. Her visage had darkened when she returned her attention to the reporter. "I'm sorry. You were saying?"

"I was saying," said Ms. Wire, "that some people believe a sexual act with a prostitute cannot be called rape."

Detective Sergeant Littlecloud stiffened. "I was just informed the victim died from her injuries—so whatever her profession, we can now call it murder."

*   *   *

Back in her office, Lacy Littlecloud combed through the notes provided by the lead detective, Cole Kase. Detective Kase sat across the desk and waited.

"So you're certain it was the same MO?" she asked.

"Matched up pretty well. Passion flowers and tissue paper scattered inside the door, just like the other scenes. He probably gains access that way. People don't suspect a guy carrying a bouquet of flowers—and people don't ID a guy with flowers, either. They look at the flowers, not the person carrying them."

Lacy Littlecloud tapped a pencil on the papers in front of her. "Can we trace the florist?"

"Nope," replied Detective Kase. "Chump was too cheap. The flowers looked like they came out of his backyard."

Littlecloud's restless pencil beat a tattoo. "DNA?"

Cole Kase sighed. "Sure. But it's no help. Given the lifestyle of his victims, the chances for a clean profile are pretty slim. Even if the lab can isolate sperm cells, there's nothing to say they came from the perp."

The tapping stopped. Littlecloud suddenly sat up straight.

"I think," she said, "I know where to find the sperm cells we need."

The Chemistry of the Case

There can be no doubt that identification by DNA is high-profile profiling. DNA has been used to crack cold cases, exonerate those wrongfully accused of capital crimes, solve murders on miniscule amounts of material, narrow the suspect list to one in a billion, and assemble a lineup of millions from a database. But what is DNA and how is it used to identify an individual? What are the prospects for the technique and what are the limitations? Is it a miracle, or are there mistakes? DNA technology is a new innovation and is subject to continuing debates—scientific, political, and ethical—concerning its application.

Chemically, DNA is yet another long-chain macromolecule and, like proteins, its repeating units aren't exactly the same. The backbone of the polymer is an alternating chain of a specific carbohydrate, *deoxyribose* (DNA stands for *deoxyribonucleic acid*), and a phospho-rous-oxygen group called a *phosphate*, as shown in figure 24.1. Attached to each sugar is one of four nitrogen-containing bases—thymine, adenine, cytosine, or guanine—again, shown in figure 24.1. The nitrogen bases provide the *code* of DNA, which works, roughly, as follows.

If we abbreviate the nitrogen bases as T, A, C, and G (for thymine, adenine, cytosine, or guanine), then the "code" of the DNA section shown in figure 24.1 is TACG. Other sections of DNA might carry codes such as AATCG or TTAACCGA, or similar sequences. These very specific sequences are used by the cell as instructions for assembling proteins. As we said in the introduction to part IV, proteins are assembled by the body to form fingernails, hair, cartilage, and enzymes, among other things. Certainly you would not want your body to assemble fingernail material when hair material is needed. A fingernail poking up out of a hair follicle would probably be painful,

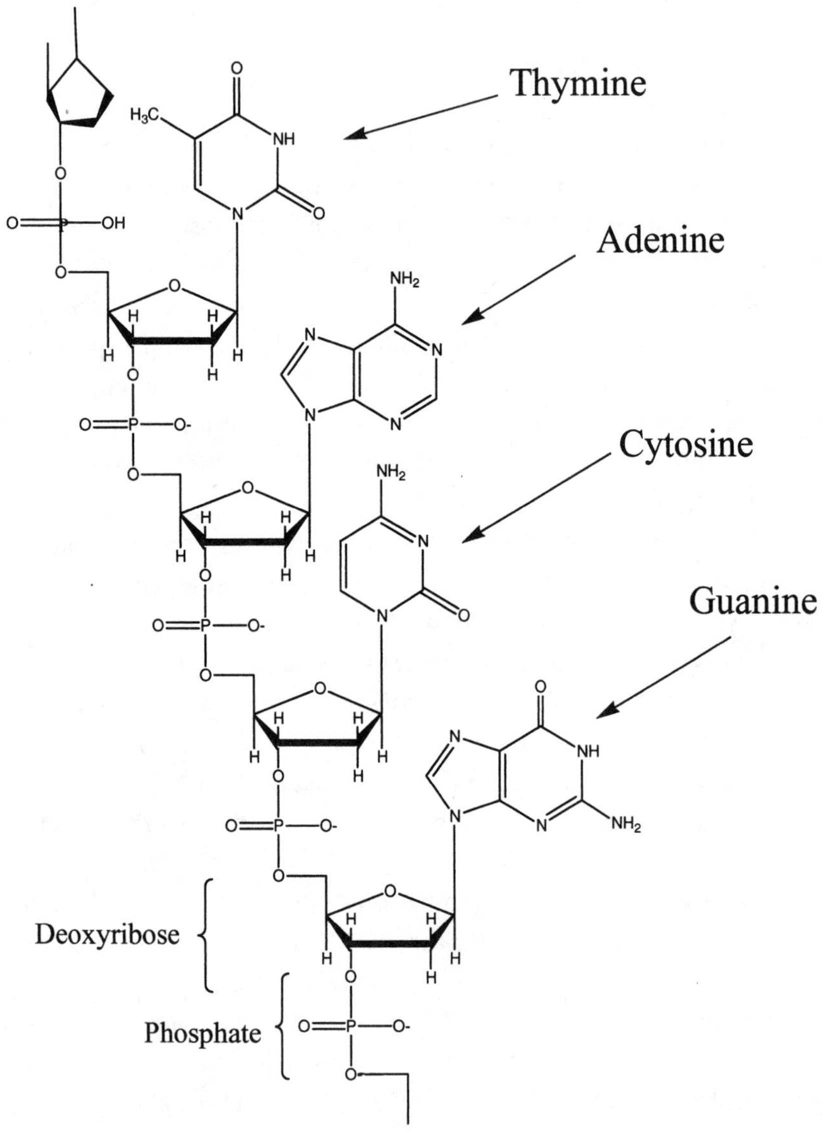

Figure 24.1. One small section of a DNA molecule showing the phosphate group, deoxyribose, and the four nitrogen-containing bases: thymine, adenine, cytosine, or guanine.

not to mention visually disturbing. So it is important that the right protein is assembled at the right time. The function of DNA is to provide the template for the protein synthesis.

When a particular protein is needed—when there is a deficit or an increased demand by the body—stress is put on an equilibrium that causes a section of DNA to unravel and eventually a protein to be assembled based on the exposed pattern. In this way, when the body needs more hair, the cells are stimulated to produce hair protein. When the body needs more digestive enzymes, the message is received and more are produced.

The aspect of DNA that makes it useful forensically is the same aspect of DNA that makes life interesting: DNA codes for hair protein, but not all hair protein is the same. Without going into all the details of genetics, let us briefly say that human bodies differ. The standard human body has ears, but not all ears are alike: some are attached at the lobe, some are free. Likewise, human DNA has some sequences that are constant, and it has some sequences that are variable. It is the variable sequences that determine the individual. By identifying and sorting out the variable sequences, individuals can be recognized by their DNA.

To understand how this is done, a few words need to be said about the fundamental building block of life: the cell. In evolved, complex cells, certain areas are segregated and enclosed for specific functions. The cell *nucleus* is one such structure. A major function of the cell nucleus is to house DNA, and each cell nucleus within the body that has DNA has an identical copy of DNA. To analyze the DNA of an individual, the first thing that must be done is to accumulate enough DNA to analyze. Just as it is impossible to see one flashlight from outer space—whereas entire cities lit up at night are clearly visible—it is impossible to analyze one strand of DNA. However, a large enough sample creates a visible mass. Luckily, other than rare exceptions such as red blood cells (white blood cells have blood's DNA), all cells contain DNA. So as long as some cells are collected, analysis is possible.

The other reason a large enough sample is necessary for a meaningful analysis is that the entire strand of DNA isn't analyzed, only very small fragments. The manner in which this is accomplished is rather ingenious. We have said that there are some constant features of human beings: hair, ears, legs, and so on. But there are some variable features, too: red hair, detached earlobes, long legs. To analyze DNA for individual features, researchers make use of enzymes that recognize constant features—features that should be present in all DNA of a particular species—to isolate these portions of DNA. These cut portions of DNA are separated according to length by electrophoresis, the technique illustrated in demonstration 24. Certain reliable fragments are selected by DNA probes, and their lengths are listed as the DNA profile. Because the length of the variable portions is such an individual matter, and because several of these variable portions are compared, if two profiles are identical, there is said to be a match, an identification. There are many variations and refinements of this approach this simplified discussion does not cover, but hopefully we have given you a glimpse of the process. In the United States, there are standardized methods that have a core of thirteen points of comparison that are used to identify individuals. These thirteen points are convenient for listing in databases, and several such databases have been developed.

There are other uses for DNA analysis. We have all noticed how family members look alike. Family resemblance shows up in DNA, too. DNA analysis can be used to show paternity. Plant family resemblance shows up in DNA. Marijuana DNA has been used to track the origin of drug shipments. So the technique is very powerful—but it is not foolproof.

DNA samples are subject to degradation because they are biological materials. In other words, they rot. To forestall this problem, samples collected at a crime scene must be dried and stored in paper bags. Another problem is that there may not be enough sample for DNA analysis. If this is the case, the sample size can sometimes be enhanced by a technique called PCR, *polymerase chain reaction*. PCR uses the same types of enzymes and amino acids that the body uses to copy the long strands of DNA, but it only makes copies of short segments. PCR also uses its own copies to make more copies, so the number of copies increases rapidly in the chain reaction. PCR is not itself a DNA analysis, but after PCR, there can be enough DNA to analyze through standard techniques.

If the sample has degraded to the point that DNA from the nucleus can no longer be retrieved, then there is one more approach that can be tried. The *mitochondria* are also separate cell structures and, interestingly enough, they have their own DNA. Though the details are beyond the scope of this book, there is a hypothesis that cells gained mitochondria when a one-celled organism absorbed another one-celled organism and instead of digesting it, entered into a symbiotic relationship with it. If true, the success of this cooperation lends credence to the notion that survival of the fittest is overshadowed by survival of the more symbiotic. Under any circumstances, however, the independent-minded mitochondria contain their own DNA. Because there are many mitochondria (as opposed to one nucleus), there is more mitochondrial DNA, so the sensitivity of the analysis is improved. Given this advantage, one might wonder why mitochondrial DNA is not always used. The reason is that mitochondrial DNA does not identify an individual uniquely because it does not include the father's contribution. In humans, sperm does little more than deliver DNA to the egg, so virtually all the mitochondria and mitochondrial DNA is inherited from the mother. But an analysis of mitochondrial DNA can show a relationship through the mother, if her DNA is available, which narrows things down considerably.

This use of mitochondrial DNA, however, brings up the privacy issues involved with DNA analysis. DNA can indicate relatives by the closeness of correlation, but some people don't want to know who they are related to and who is or is not related to them. There are still other ethical concerns. Databases currently contain DNA information from convicted offenders, but there is a movement toward including arrestees, too, which means that many innocent people could be included in databases that are searched for suspects.

There are also technical issues that are a concern in DNA analysis.

One major concern is contamination. If DNA is contaminated by saliva or other material from a second person, then contributions from both people will be in the DNA. DNA contamination can occur by a sneeze, or from skin flakes, or even through just breathing. Contamination can arise from airborne DNA (such as the germs that can cause colds or pollen from plants). Sterilization is not a guard against this contamination because sterilization just kills the contaminating organism, it doesn't destroy the DNA.

There are other weaknesses that must be acknowledged when deciding on the evidentiary value of a DNA analysis. A mutation can occur that renders a certain portion of the DNA unrecognizable to the cutting enzymes. Light bands called *stutter bands* can arise in the DNA analysis from slight variations in some of the DNA. It is not always possible to decide if shadowy bands in a DNA analysis are stutter bands, contamination, or valid bands from the DNA being analyzed. In addition, PCR copies small fragments faster than large fragments, which might make the small fragments appear more dominant than they really are. Because of these technical limitations, the statement that DNA could not be matched to a suspect does not necessarily exonerate the suspect. It could also mean the test was inconclusive.

These difficulties, however, are what separate forensic DNA analysis from clinical practices. Forensic DNA experts rarely deal with ideal samples, so they have become skilled in gleaning information from DNA mixtures. The effort required serves to remind us of the bigger picture. No one piece of evidence should ever stand on its own. Confirmatory evidence is necessary and proper before any decisions should be made regarding an individual's guilt or innocence. DNA evidence is very powerful evidence, but it remains just one piece of the picture.

The limitations caution strongly against overinterpretation of results. Mistakes have been made,[1] and there is a new culture of caution. In "The Case of the Flowery Felon," contamination threatened to prevent any resolution—that is, until Lacy Littlecloud saw through the fog.

Case Closed

Detective Sergeant Lacy Littlecloud was on her feet and heading out her office door. Detective Cole Kase pried himself out of his chair to follow.

"Where . . . ?"

"The evidence room."

"Why?"

"For evidence!"

"What?"

Littlecloud stopped and turned to Kase. "I think *you* should have been the reporter. Look, Barb Wire was right about a couple of things. Every living—or once living—thing has DNA. And DNA is almost always associated with sexual assault in the form of sperm. The problem here is finding an uncontaminated sample we can link to the perp—which I just realized has been at the scenes all along. Sperm called—"

"Pollen!" Detective Kase completed for her. "There are many people with a penchant for passion flowers—but only one that's our prep! When we've identified the plant by DNA, we'll know which scent to follow."

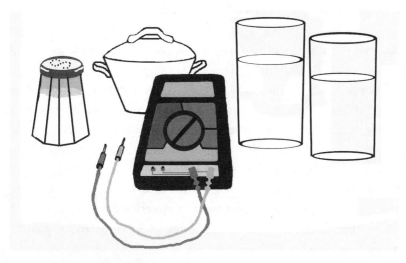

DEMONSTRATION 25
THE BIG JOLT

I like to inquire into everything. Hercule Poirot is a good dog. The good dog follows the scent, and if, regrettably, there is no scent to follow, he noses around—seeking always something that is not very nice.

Agatha Christie, *Peril at End House*, ca. 1930

One last time, put on your safety glasses and gloves. Prepare two solutions in plastic cups: one with sugar dissolved in distilled water and the other with table salt dissolved in distilled water. Take two alligator clips and attach one to each pole of a 6-volt or 9-volt battery. To the other end of the alligator clips, add a straightened paper clip. The paper clips are now our test leads.

Using the insulated part of the alligator clip as a handle, place both test leads into the saltwater. Make sure that the wires are in contact with the solution, but not with each other. You should observe bubbles forming at the leads. Remove the test leads, rinse them in distilled water, and place them into the sugar solution. There should be no bubbles in the sugar solution.

For electricity to flow through a solution, there must be some number of ions—charged chemical entities—to carry the current in the solution. Sugar in distilled water does not produce charged particles; therefore, current-induced reactions—electrochemical reactions—cannot occur at the leads. The salt solution, on the other hand, contains many charged chemical particles: ions. These ions transfer and carry charge through the solution and support the chemistry that caused the bubbles, that is, the electrolysis of water to form hydrogen gas (H_2) and oxygen gas (O_2).

$$2H_2O \rightarrow O_2 + 2H_2$$

What we are illustrating in this demonstration, however, is not electrochemistry, but the difference between the solutions. We have two essentially identical solutions behaving quite differently in response to the test probes, so we have created a *sensor*, a device that provides information concerning its chemical surroundings by responding in a predictable fashion to its chemical environment. Granted, our sensor is rather crude and limited in scope, but in the future, many of the labor- and time-intensive forensic tests of today will no doubt be replaced by fast, accurate, and discriminating sensors. We take a peek at this future for forensic chemistry in "The Case of the Clean Getaway."

CHAPTER 25

SNIFFING OUT THE TRUTH: THE FUTURE OF FORENSIC CHEMISTRY

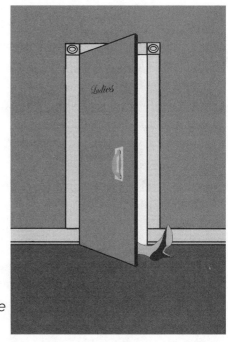

*Let us hope that
when we are
dead things will be
better arranged.*

Marcel Proust, ca. 1900

You know something, darling? I smell crime in the air.

Neil Simon, *Murder by Death*, 1976

THE CASE OF THE CLEAN GETAWAY

Officer Don Hillski escorted Inspector Rhett Trow to the door of the ladies' room, situated in a discrete corner of the mezzanine of the new, upscale Bridges Hotel. The hotel had been built a year before, in 2020, and it was easy to see why it was considered the most beautiful and exclusive hotel for miles around. This morning, however, its beauty was marred by the body of billionaire hotel heiress London Bridges sprawled across the restroom threshold, blocking the door.

Inspector Trow approached the scene slowly, as though he'd been there a hundred times before. Hillski noted that Trow seemed even more turtlelike than usual, his back rounded with age and his head seeming to disappear between his shoulders. Trow stooped over the body, hands shoved deep into his pockets, and frowned. After a moment, he lifted an inquiring eyebrow to Officer Hillski.

Officer Hillski opened his notebook. "The body was discovered at approximately 5:30 AM by Matt Erial, the housekeeping supervisor." He nodded to a man standing with a clipboard a few feet away. Mr. Erial was glancing anxiously at his watch.

Inspector Trow barked, "Hold him."

Officer Hillski frowned. "For what?"

"Witness."

Officer Hillski nodded and scribbled in his notebook: Matt Erial, witness.

Hillski continued his report. "There is a rather unusual wound on the body . . ."

"Gunshot," said Inspector Trow.

"Really?" said Hillski. "You don't see those much anymore. I'll radio in and see if satellite tracking can pick up a recently activated safety ring."

"We need to find the gun," said Trow.

"The gun won't fire without the safety ring, so it can't do any harm; when we find the person with the safety ring, we'll have the killer—"

"Unless," said Inspector Trow, "that person took the ring off."

Officer Hillski reddened slightly. "So what do you suggest—"

At that moment there was a commotion at the elevator. Evidence-recovery technician Lotta Klues wedged herself and two large satchels out of the elevator and began her trek down the mezzanine to where the two men stood. As she walked, her eyes scanned the floor, walls, and even the ceiling. She set down her bags on the carpet by the railing after convincing herself there was nothing there to be disturbed. She reached in one bag and pulled out booties, a lab coat, gloves, safety glasses, and a hairnet, all of which she quickly and expertly donned. She straightened and glared at the two men by the body until they stepped back several feet to give her passage. She reached into the second bag and pulled out a 10-centimeter-by-10-centimeter metal box that stood 3 centimeters high. She also removed a black plastic-wrapped cone, unsheathed it, and attached it to the box. She walked over to the bathroom, flipped a switch on the box, and set it down. Officer Hillski could now read the logo across the top of the box: The Hound™.

Lotta Klues adjusted some knobs and stared intently at a tiny screen on the top of the box.

"What's it read?" asked Inspector Trow.

Lotta Klues threw him an irritated glance, but she read off: "Urine, feces, gunpowder, blood, iguana—"

"Iguana?" asked Inspector Trow.

Officer Hillski offered politely, "London Bridges was beautiful but a little eccentric. She carried her pet iguana in her purse wherever she went."

Inspector Trow shrugged. "What else?"

"Shampoo, hairspray, perfume . . ."

"We have an exclusive beauty parlor, Leava's Salon, located in the lobby. Ms. Bridges liked to go there as a sort of getaway," a new voice interrupted. The police personnel looked up to regard Matt Erial, the housekeeping supervisor, who had moved closer to the scene. "Is this going to take long?"

Inspector Trow regarded the supervisor politely. "How did you happen to find the body?"

"I inspect all the rooms that are scheduled for cleaning, and last night's shift had the mezzanine on their list."

Inspector Trow nodded and turned back to Lotta Klues. "Anything else?"

"Her spoor—"

"Spoor?" interrupted Matt Erial.

"The combination of odors that is unique to a person—used for identification," intoned Lotta Klues. She turned back to Inspector Trow and continued. "Your spoor. Don Hillski's spoor. And his spoor." She nodded toward Matt Erial.

Matt Erial shrugged. "I found her." He looked at his watch again and moved off, shuffling through papers on his clipboard.

Inspector Trow asked, "Anything else?"

"Only low levels. Nothing significant within the last twelve hours."

Inspector Trow shook his head gravely. Officer Hillski moved beside him and spoke in a low voice. "Erial looks like he has business to take care of. I have his name and address. Can I let him go?"

"No," Trow said slowly. "I don't think so."

The Chemistry of the Case

In our futuristic "Case of the Clean Getaway," the metal box that Lotta Klues used to analyze the atmosphere at the crime scene might be described as a mechanical olfaction device, in other words, an artificial sniffer. In the future, no doubt, such an instrument will be standard issue for every evidence technician, and again, without doubt, it will be designed by a chemist. We, as humans, walk, live, and breathe in a sea of chemical markers that dogs, cats, and other animals are aware of, but that we are not. We tend to think of ourselves as disconnected, discrete units, but in truth, our existence is a continuum: we are joined to each other by the odors we emit. It is these odors—both environmental and body gases—that will be the basis for forensic instrumentation in the future.

Virtually all materials have some gas-phase product associated with them that can be interpreted as its odor. If this seems an extreme statement to make, consider the safety precaution we affixed to the use of latex gloves in "Crime Lab and Crime Solutions." Many people have an allergy to these gloves, though the rubbery material in latex appears fairly inert. Though it is true that latex is mostly immobile, there is enough free material to cause trouble. Or consider egg or peanut allergies. Sometimes it is sufficient to just have the material in proximity to cause a severe or even life-threatening reaction. Even rock or crystalline cocaine has vapor that can be detected by drug-sniffing dogs. So the clues are in the air, and in the future we will find them.

Even now, *sensors*—devices for detecting materials and physical phenomena—have a respectable place in crime detection. A breathalyzer is a sensor: the classic breathalyzer we described in chapter 10 is based on precipitate formation, and many current blood alcohol sensors use infrared spectroscopy. Still others use electrochemical reactions such as the sensor illustrated in demonstration 25.

Another well-known sensor used in law enforcement is the *polygraph*, or lie detector. The *poly* in polygraph indicates that several sensors are attached to the person being examined. These sensors usually measure the person's breathing rate, pulse, blood pressure, and perspiration. Although the value of the information gathered is often debated, the science behind the sensors is sound. The breathing rate, pulse, and blood pressure are measured by sensors that respond to pressure changes. The perspiration sensor measures changes in conductivity, which is similar to the detector in our earlier demonstration.

Other sensors include small, portable mass spectrometers developed for use in the field. When we began this enterprise, many chapters ago, we presented in our introduction a story about a police officer who used a portable alcohol sensor to foil a foul deed. These types of new handheld alcohol sensors do indeed exist and are currently being used by law enforcement.

But if we are going to discuss sensors and law enforcement, there is one sensor we would be negligent to omit: the nose of a well-trained police dog. Dogs have been known to detect evidence of cadavers underground or in car trunks years after an event. Dogs can be trained to sniff drugs in luggage, in lockers, and under hoods. Dogs can detect bombs, track people, and, perhaps at least somewhat literally, smell fear. Dogs not only have more sensitive receptors than we have currently developed, they are also able to make sense of combinations of scents. The scent signature of most materials is not one scent but many scents in a certain proportion. Dogs can be trained to alert only when the right mixture is present.

Living things constantly releases gas-phase chemicals to the air as waste, but they are also chemical signals. The combination of chemicals that make up an animal's scent contribute to its *spoor*, and it is the cumulative nature of spoor that makes artificial emulation of a dog's scenting ability so difficult.

Consider, for example, food. When we smell food, it is the combination of odors that allows us to make the identification. Italian and Asian cuisines both use oil and salt and have many other commonalities, but we can clearly distinguish lasagna from moo-shu pork by the combination of various scents. This composite odor, called the *chemical signature*, is what dogs are able to sort out. Computers hold some promise of emulating this ability someday, and it will be a good day for crime detection when they do. Dogs are wonderful, but they have some decided drawbacks, too.

For one thing, dogs are great at telling us something is there, but they cannot tell us how much is there. As may be recalled, the electrochemical response can be proportional to concentration, so our electrochemical sensors should not only be able to tell what is there but how much is there. In addition to not being able to talk, dogs tend to tire out. They can get distracted and they can get bored. Their noses, like our noses, can become saturated. Have you ever noticed that stale garbage or cat litter in need of changing becomes more apparent to your nose when you come into a house after having been outside? Our sensing mechanism, like that of a dog, becomes saturated after a given amount of time. An odor can also be kept from a dog by masking it with a stronger odor. A sensor, however, should be able to separate and register two different odors.

Dogs also have to be kept in training. For this reason, they may not be that different from instruments because instruments must be continually calibrated, checked, and certified. But instruments can be stored on a shelf until they are needed. Dogs can't be unplugged.

So there is little doubt that reliable, sensitive, intelligent sensors are the wave of the future. The ability to detect the gas-phase signature of materials is the ultimate nondestructive, nondisruptive technique. Materials could be analyzed without removing them from the scene. Intelligent sensors could instantly calculate concentrations and establish time lines: many materials deteriorate as they age and therefore their chemical signature changes with time. Sensors could be an extension of the police cruiser and even police personnel. Current efforts are being directed toward the development of handheld drug sensors, pollutant detectors, armament detectors, and even personnel detectors.

Of course, no change is ever made without consequences, so no doubt there will be lengthy debates, as there should be, concerning ethical implications and policy changes. Parents may appreciate not having to quiz their children because a sniffer even more sensitive than a parent's nose could tell all—but the children may not appreciate it. And although dogs are commonly used in law enforcement, other enhancements of the human senses currently are not allowed without a warrant. But in law enforcement, the "in plain view" credo of searches could possibly someday become "in plain smell," which could be much more inclusive.

But these concerns will be worked out, and new technology will continue to surface. Will the technology of the future snuff out crime? Unfortunately, probably not. Crime, and its cessation, is a matter of the chemistry of the mind. But then crime solving falls in this category, too. Crime solving is not a linear process but comes from inspiration, creativity, and the wonderful ability of the human mind to see the spaces between the clues as well as the clues. In fact, it was in the breach rather than the bridge that Inspector Rhett Throw saw the solution to "The Case of the Clean Getaway."

Case Closed

Inspector Rhett Trow and Officer Don Hillski walked over to where Matt Erial, the housekeeping supervisor, paced while holding his clipboard. "Excuse me," asked Inspector Trow, "could I please see that clipboard?"

Mr. Erial jumped and clutched the clipboard to his chest. "What?"

"Do what the inspector asks," came Officer Don Hillski's voice from behind him. "Give him the clipboard."

"Why?!"

"Because," said Inspector Trow, "we need to know what you were doing down here in the mezzanine when you discovered Ms. Bridges's body."

"What are you taking about? I was here to inspect the bathroom! When they clean a bathroom, I inspect!"

"No, son, I don't believe that's quite true. When we look at that schedule, I don't think we'll find the mezzanine bathroom on your list of rooms to check."

*   *   *

After Matt Erial was taken into custody, Officer Hillski asked the inspector, "How did you know that bathroom was not going to be on the list of rooms to check?"

"The Hound," explained Inspector Trow, "is a very sensitive odor sensor. It found lots of smells in that bathroom, but no significant bleach and no significant ammonia. They've invented a lot of things in my time, but they've never come up with better cleansers than ammonia and bleach. When you clean a bathroom, you're going to have one of those two smells."

"Some things change," said Inspector Trow, "but basic chemistry stays the same."

POSTMORTEM

*Television has brought murder back into the home—
where it belongs.*

Alfred Hitchcock, ca. 1950

Now that we have reached the end, we can honestly say that our highest hope for this book is that you enjoyed reading it as much as we did writing it. The mystery, the investigation, the thrill of solving the puzzle—and that was just the chemistry!

We admit that we have bragged a bit about the contributions of chemistry and chemists, but we believe our actions are justified. Our motivation was to share our enthusiasm and encourage an appreciation for our science. Chemistry is often called the central science because it is so central to everything that we do. From medicine to motors, from computers to crime, chemistry is part and parcel of our everyday lives. If we have accomplished just a little of our goal—if we have titillated your interest and motivated further investigation—well, then, we are guilty as charged.

We hope you enjoyed the vignettes, annoyed your friends and/or family by taking up space for your demonstrations, and learned a little about forensic chemistry along the way. We hope in these pages you were able to gain a sense— and experience some of the scents!—of the art of chemistry. We hope, above all, that you were entertained because that is what we feel chemistry is: excitement, intrigue—and solution.

We rest our case.

APPENDIX
THE PERIODIC TABLE OF THE ELEMENTS

1	2	3	4	5	6	7	8	9	10	11	12	13	14	15	16	17	18
1 H 1.008																	2 He 4.003
3 Li 6.941	4 Be 9.012											5 B 10.81	6 C 12.01	7 N 14.01	8 O 16.00	9 F 19.00	10 Ne 20.18
11 Na 23.00	12 Mg 24.31											13 Al 26.98	14 Si 28.09	15 P 30.97	16 S 32.07	17 Cl 35.45	18 Ar 39.95
19 K 39.10	20 Ca 40.08	21 Sc 44.96	22 Ti 47.88	23 V 50.94	24 Cr 52.00	25 Mn 54.94	26 Fe 55.84	27 Co 58.93	28 Ni 58.69	29 Cu 63.55	30 Zn 65.39	31 Ga 69.72	32 Ge 72.61	33 As 74.92	34 Se 78.96	35 Br 79.90	36 Kr 83.80
37 Rb 85.47	38 Sr 87.62	39 Y 88.91	40 Zr 91.22	41 Nb 92.91	42 Mo 95.94	43 Tc (98)	44 Ru 101.1	45 Rh 102.9	46 Pd 106.4	47 Ag 107.9	48 Cd 112.4	49 In 114.8	50 Sn 118.7	51 Sb 121.8	52 Te 127.6	53 I 126.9	54 Xe 131.3
55 Cs 132.9	56 Ba 137.3	57 La* 138.9	72 Hf 178.5	73 Ta 180.9	74 W 183.9	75 Re 186.2	76 Os 190.2	77 Ir 192.2	78 Pt 195.1	79 Au 197.0	80 Hg 200.6	81 Tl 204.4	82 Pb 207.2	83 Bi 209.0	84 Po (209)	85 At (210)	86 Rn (222)
87 Fr (223)	88 Ra 226.0	89 Ac† 227.0	90 Rf (261)	91 Db (262)	92 Sg (266)	93 Bh (264)	94 Hs (269)	95 Mt (268)	•	•	•						

58	59	60	61	62	63	64	65	66	67	68	69	70	71
*Ce	Pr	Nd	Pm	Sm	Eu	Gd	Tb	Dy	Ho	Er	Tm	Yb	Lu
140.1	140.9	144.2	(145)	150.4	152.0	157.3	158.9	162.5	164.9	167.3	168.9	173.0	175.0

90	91	92	93	94	95	96	97	98	99	100	101	102	103
†Th	Pa	U	Np	Pu	Am	Cm	Bk	Cf	Es	Fm	Md	No	Lr
232.0	231.0	238.0	237.0	(244)	(243)	(247)	(247)	(251)	(252)	(257)	(258)	(259)	(262)

On the periodic table, the elements are listed by atomic number. The shape of the periodic table is related to the energy levels occupied by the electrons around the nucleus. The average atomic mass, based on the natural abundance of the isotopes, is given below the symbol for the element. The masses for artificially created elements are given in parentheses. Forensic chemistry generally only deals with a limited number of these elements, but the entire table is presented here for completeness. The elements are represented on the table by their one- or two-letter symbols. Some of the elements discussed throughout the chapters are hydrogen (H), carbon (C), nitrogen (N), oxygen (O), chlorine (Cl), phosphorus (P), sulfur (S), aluminum (Al), sodium (Na), copper (Cu), iron (Fe), and zinc (Zn).

ENDNOTES

APOLOGIA

1. Please see the bibliography.
2. Suzanne Bell, *Forensic Chemistry* (Upper Saddle River, NJ: Pearson Prentice Hall, 2006), p. xv.

CHAPTER 1

1. Graig Anderson, "Presumptive and Confirmatory Drug Tests," *Journal of Chemical Education* 82, nos. 1809–10 (2005).
2. Robert A. Day, *How to Write and Publish a Scientific Paper*, 2nd ed. (Philadelphia: iSi Press, 1983).

CHAPTER 2

1. R. D. Guy, M. L. Fogel, and J. A. Berry, "Photosynthetic Fractionation of the Stable Isotopes of Oxygen and Carbon," *Plant Physiology* 101, no. 1 (January 1993): 37–47.

CHAPTER 5

1. Saul Alinsky was a criminologist who in the 1930s turned to the organization of underrepresented groups, such as the stockyard workers in Chicago.

CHAPTER 6

1. Rich Sleeman, Jim Carter, and Karl Ebejer, "Drugs on Money and Beyond: Tandem Mass Spectrometry in the Forensic Sciences," *Spectroscopy Europe* 17, no. 6 (2005): 10–13.

CHAPTER 8

1. Richard Saferstein, *Criminalistics: An Introduction to Forensic Science*, 7th ed. (Upper Saddle River, NJ: Prentice Hall, 2001), p. 109.

CHAPTER 13

1. Suzanne Bell, *Forensic Chemistry* (Upper Saddle River, NJ: Pearson Prentice Hall, 2006), p. 428.

CHAPTER 16

1. Richard Saferstein, *Criminalistics: An Introduction to Forensic Science*, 7th ed. (Upper Saddle River, NJ: Prentice Hall, 2001), p. 110.
2. Ibid.

CHAPTER 19

1. See http://www.howstuffworks.com for an excellent, understandable explanation of the properties of lenses.

CHAPTER 22

1. Anne Wingate, *Scene of the Crime: A Writer's Guide to Crime-Scene Investigations*, chaps. 4 and 5 (Cincinnati: Writer's Digest Books, 1992).

CHAPTER 24

1. Shen Fink, "Reasonable Doubt," *Discover* 27 (2005): 57–60.

BIBLIOGRAPHY

Bell, Suzanne. *Forensic Chemistry*. Upper Saddle River, NJ: Pearson Prentice Hall, 2006.

Bergman, Paul, and Sara J. Berman-Barrett. *The Criminal Law Handbook: Know Your Rights, Survive the System*. Berkeley, CA: Nolo Press, 1997.

Bintliff, Russell. *Police Procedural: A Writer's Guide to the Police and How They Work*. Cincinnati: Writer's Digest Books, 1993.

Crosby, Donald G. *Environmental Toxicology and Chemistry*. New York: Oxford University Press, 1997.

Di Maio, Dominick J., and Vincent J. M. Di Maio. *Forensic Pathology*. New York: Elsevier, 1989.

Dix, Jay. *Guide and Atlas for Death Investigation on CD-Rom*. London: CRC Press UK, 1990.

Evans, Colin. *Murder Two: The Second Casebook of Forensic Detection*. New York: Wiley, 2004.

Gerber, Samuel M., ed. *Chemistry and Crime: From Sherlock Holmes to Today's Courtroom*. Washington, DC: American Chemical Society, 1983.

Gerber, Samuel M., and Richard Saferstein, eds. *More Chemistry and Crime: From Marsh Arsenic Test to DNA Profiling*. Washington, DC: American Chemical Society, 1997.

Graedon, Joe, and Teresa Graedon. *Deadly Drug Interactions: The People's Pharmacy Guide*. New York: St. Martin's Griffin, 1997.

Johll, Matthew. *Investigating Chemistry: A Forensic Science Perspective*. New York: Freeman, 2007.

Page, David W. *Body Trauma: A Writer's Guide to Wounds and Injuries*. Cincinnati: Writer's Digest Books, 1996.

Saferstein, Richard. *Criminalistics: An Introduction to Forensic Science*. 7th ed. Upper Saddle River, NJ: Prentice Hall, 2001.

———, ed. *Forensic Science Handbook*, Volume 1. 2nd ed. Upper Saddle River, NJ: Prentice Hall, 2002.

Schmalleger, Frank. *Criminology Today: An Integrative Introduction*. 2nd ed. Upper Saddle River, NJ: Prentice Hall, 1999.

Stevens, Serita. *Forensic Nurse: The New Role of the Nurse in Law Enforcement*. New York: St. Martin's, 2004.

Thomas, Ronald R. *Detective Fiction and the Rise of Forensic Science.* Cambridge: Cambridge University Press, 1999.

Wade, Colleen, ed. *Handbook of Forensic Services.* Rev. ed. Quantico, VA: FBI Laboratory Publication, 2003.

White, Peter, ed. *Crime Scene to Court: The Essentials of Forensic Science.* Cambridge, UK: Royal Society of Chemistry, 1998.

Wilson, Keith D. *Cause of Death: A Writer's Guide to Death, Murder, and Forensic Medicine.* Cincinnati: Writer's Digest Books, 1992.

Wingate, Anne. *Scene of the Crime: A Writer's Guide to Crime-Scene Investigations.* Cincinnati: Writer's Digest Books, 1992.

INDEX